"SMILES"

A ROSE OF THE CUMBERLANDS

By ELIOT H. ROBINSON

AUTHOR OF
"Man Proposes," "The Maid of Mirabelle," etc.

A. L. BURT COMPANY
Publishers New York

Published by arrangement with The Page Company
Printed in U. S. A.

TO MY BOYS

THIS STORY OF A GIRL

WHO LOVED CHILDREN

IS AFFECTIONATELY DEDICATED

AN ACKNOWLEDGMENT

I WISH to acknowledge, most gratefully, the valuable assistance rendered to me, in the preparation of the chapters dealing with the medical and hospital incidents, by Robert W. Guiler, M.D.; by Alonzo J. Shadman, M.D., to whom I am indebted for my description of the unusual operation in Chapter XXI; and by Miss Elizabeth E. Sullivan, Superintendent of Nurses at the Boston Children's Hospital. And, above all, I desire to make acknowledgment of the debt of gratitude that I owe to Mr. Henry Wightman Packer for his helpful criticism throughout the writing of this story.

ELIOT HARLOW ROBINSON.

"SMILES"

CHAPTER I

DONALD MACDONALD, M.D.

THE man came to a stop, a look of humiliation and deep self-disgust on his bronzed face. With methodical care he leaned his rifle against the seamed trunk of a forest patriarch and drew the sleeve of his hunting shirt across his forehead, now glistening with beads of sweat; then, and not until then, did he relieve his injured feelings by giving voice to a short but soul-satisfying expletive.

At the sound of his deep voice the dog, which had, panting, dropped at his feet after a wild, purposeless dash through the underbrush, looked up with bright eyes whose expression conveyed both worship and a question, and, as the man bent and stroked his wiry coat, rustled the pine needles with his stubby tail.

The picture held no other animate creatures, and no other sound disturbed the silence of the woods.

By the hunter's serviceable nickeled timepiece the afternoon was not spent; but the sun was already swinging low over the western mountaintop, and its slanting rays, as they filtered through the leafy network overhead, had begun to take on the richer gold of early evening, and the thick forest foliage of oddly intermingled oak and pine, beech and poplar, was assuming deeper, more velvety tones. There was solemn beauty in the scene; but, for the moment, the man was out of tune with the vibrant color harmonies, and he frankly stated the reason in his next words, which were addressed to his unlovely canine companion, whose sagacity more than compensated for his appealing homeliness.

"Mike, we're lost!"

City born and bred though he was, the man took a not unjustifiable pride in the woodcraft which he had acquired during many vacations spent in the wilds; hence it was humiliating to have to admit that fact — even to his dog. To be sure, the fastnesses of the border Cumberlands were new to him; but his vanity was hurt by the realization that he had tramped for nearly an hour through serried ranks of ancient trees and crowding thickets of laurel and rhododendron — which seemed to take a personal delight in impeding the progress of a "furriner" — and over craggy rocks, only to find, at the end of that time, that he was entering one end of a short ravine from the other end of which he had started with the vague purpose of seeking the path by which he had climbed from the valley village.

Moreover, a subtle change was taking place in the air. Faint breezes, the sighing heralds of advancing evening, were now beginning to steal slowly out from the picturesque, seamed rocks of the ravine and from behind each gnarled or stately tree, with an unmistakable warning.

There was clearly but one logical course for him to pursue — head straight up the mountainside until he should arrive at some commanding clearing whence he could recover his lost bearings and establish some landmarks for a fresh start downward. With his square jaw set in a decisive manner, the man picked up his gun, threw back his heavy shoulders, and began to climb, driving his muscular body forcibly through the underbrush.

The decision and the action were both characteristic of Donald MacDonald, in whose Yankee veins ran the blood of a dour and purposeful Scottish clan. Aggressive determination showed in every lineament of his face, of which his nearest friend, Philip Bentley, had once said, "The Great Sculptor started to carve a masterpiece, choosing granite rather than marble as his medium, and was content to leave it rough hewn." Every feature was strong and rugged, which gave his countenance an expression masterful to the point of being almost surly when it was in repose; but it was a face which caused most men — and women over thirty — to turn for a second glance.

To-day, the effect of strength was further enhanced by a week's growth of blue-black beard. But his eyes, agate gray and flecked with the green of the "moss" variety, were the real touchstones of his character, and they belied the stern lines of his mouth and chin and spoke eloquently of a warm, kindly heart within the powerful body, a body which, to the city dweller, suggested the fullback on a football team. Indeed, such he had been in those days when great power counted more heavily than speed and agility. Not but that he possessed these attributes as well, in a degree unusual in one who tipped the scales at one hundred and ninety.

To some it seemed an inexplicable anomaly that a man of his type should have selected, as the work to which he had dedicated his life, the profession of medicine, and still more strange that he had become a specialist in the diseases of children. Yet such was the case, and many a mother, whose heartstrings were plucked by the lean fingers of Despair, had cause to bless the almost uncanny surgical skill which his highly-trained brain exercised through the medium of his big, spatulate, gentle fingers.

As "Mac" had, in the old days, smashed his way through the opposing line of blue-jerseyed giants on the football field, and as he now plowed through the laurel and rhododendron, so had he won his way to the forefront of the younger generation of his profession until, at the age of thirty-five, he had become recognized as one of the most able children's specialists in America. A "man's man," blunt of speech to the point of often offending at first the cultured women with whom his labors brought him into contact, he was worshipped in hundreds of homes as an angel of mercy in strange guise, and was the idol of hundreds of little folk to whom he had brought new health and happiness.

The toilsome upward climb brought its reward at length, and Donald's eye caught sight of a clearing, and unmistakable signs of near-by civilization, if a scattering mountain settlement of primitive dwellers in that feudal country which lies half in West Virginia, half in Kentucky, may be so designated.

No sooner had he stepped into the partially cleared land, and caught sight of a small, isolated cabin beyond, so toned by wind and weather that it seemed almost an integral part of its natural surroundings, than his own presence was detected, as the sharp and surly barking of an unseen dog evidenced. Mike made answer to the challenge, and instantly other, more distant, canine voices joined in the growing clamor.

As man and dog advanced across the clearing, not one, but half a dozen gaunt curs, summoned to the spot by a warning which meant the approach of a stranger, much as their clannish masters might have been in other years, mysteriously appeared from all sides and rushed forward, their lips drawn back from threatening teeth, their bristling throats rumbling ominously.

Donald sharply commanded the likewise bristling Mike to keep to heel, threw his rifle to hip and backed hastily toward the cabin. He had no wish to employ his weapon, and as retreat was the other alternative, for his companion's sake, if not his own, indeed, discretion seemed to be, by all odds, valor's better part.

A noisy and exciting moment brought him to the cabin's door, still face to the enemy. Fumbling behind him with his left hand, Donald found and lifted the latch. The door swung suddenly open under his weight, Mike scurried between his legs, and the combination resulted in his downfall, precipitate and sprawling.

Simultaneously came a startled exclamation in a treble voice, the clatter of a fallen kettle and then a quick cry of pain.

In an instant Donald had scrambled ungracefully to his feet and found himself face to face with a picture that he was destined never to forget.

Backed by a big stone fireplace, in which the embers were glowing ruddily, stood a young girl clad in a simple one-piece dress, which left neck, arms and legs bare. One dusty, but dainty, foot was held between her hands, while she balanced on the other. A tumbling mass of rich brown curls, shot with gleaming threads like tiny rays of captive sunshine, fell, unbound, over her shoulders, and partly veiled a childlike face, tanned to an Indian brown and now twisted with pain, but nevertheless so startlingly sweet and appealing that the man gasped in astonishment.

As it is with many who wear bluntness like a cloak, Donald possessed a deep-seated appreciation of the beautiful, without being capable of expressing it. But now he vaguely realized that here, where he would last have looked for it, he had blundered upon a child whom Mother Nature had designed lovingly and with painstaking care, perhaps in order to satisfy herself that, in the bustle of creation which nowadays left her little time for attention to fine detail, her hands had not wholly lost the cunning which was theirs when the world was young and women were few and fair.

Her face had the qualities of a sweet wild-flower, delicate of form yet hardy enough to stand up under the stress of a storm. A critic might have declared the sensitive mouth a shade too broad for the tapering lines which formed the firmly rounded chin; he might have said that the upper lip, against which its companion was now tightly pressed to check its trembling, was too short for classic beauty; but he would hardly have been able to find a flaw in the molding of the straight, slender nose or the broad forehead, or the cheeks which curved as symmetrically as the petals of a damask rose, or — if he were human — with the faint shadows at the corners of the lips which were not dimples, but fascinatingly suggested them. But, above all, it was the child's eyes, heavy with a sudden rush of unshed tears that merely added to their appealing charm, which left the strongest impression on the man. They were remarkable eyes, long of lash and of a deep blue with limpid purple shadows and golden highlights.

Her form, untrammelled by confining clothing and bending naturally, was slender and lithesome, but full of curves which told that the bud of childhood was just beginning to open into the blossom of early maturity — about fifteen or sixteen years old, Donald guessed her to be.

At her feet lay an overturned kettle the contents from which, a simple stew, was sending up a cloud of steam from the rough floor, and explained the reason for the misty eyes and tenderly nursed ankle.

The whole picture was graven on his mind in a single glance; but, the next instant the sunniest, most appealing of smiles broke through the girl's pain-drawn tears.

"Yo' . . . yo' looked so funny a-fallin' over thet thar dawg, an' a-rollin' on the floor," her words bubbled forth.

"I'm glad that you have something to laugh about, but dev . . . deucedly sorry that I made you burn yourself, child," answered Donald, awkwardly. "It must hurt like the . . . the mischief," he added, as he stepped forward to examine the injury with a quick return to his professional manner.

"Wall, hit *do* burn, kinder. But taint nothin'." She sniffed bravely, but a tear overflowed its reservoir and made a channel through a smudge on her cheek.

"Well, I happen to be a doctor — when I'm not on a vacation — so I can do a little toward repairing the damage I caused." He was already unfastening the small first-aid kit which experience had taught him never to go without.

"Taint nothin', sir, really. I'll jest put some lard on hit, an' . . ." began the girl, timidly backing away.

Donald did not stop to argue, but placed his strong hands on either side of her slender waist and lifted her lightly to the homemade table, while she gasped and again the wonderful smile, more shy this time, transformed her tear-stained face. In silence, and with flying, experienced fingers, the physician applied a soothing salve to the blotchy red, fast-swelling burn on the ankle, and deftly bandaged it.

"There," he said. "You won't know, in a few minutes, that anything has happened."

"Thank ye, sir," said the girl, as he lifted her again and allowed her to slip gently to the floor. "Yo' shore knows how ter do up a foot."

She hopped gingerly over to the fireplace, and began to clear up the wreck of supper, first calmly lifting the dog away from the steaming hot meat which his quivering nose was inquisitively approaching.

"Be careful. Mike might . . ."

"Oh, he won't bite *me*." She broke into his warning, and gave a playful tug at the coarse hair on the animal's neck. Somewhat to Donald's surprise, the dog wiggled ecstatically at the friendly advances and paid his lowly homage by licking her bare foot.

"Never mind that mess, I'll clean it up if you'll get me a shovel. And of course I mean to pay for it," said Donald hastily.

"In course yo' won't do no sech thing. We-all's got plenty uv pertaties, — I growed 'em myself, — this yere meat haint hurt a mite, an' water's cheap," she responded. "Yo' jest take a cheer, mister, an' yo' kin hev supper along with us as soon as grand-pap comes, which'll be right soon, I reckon. We-all don't see stranger folks much up yere, an' he'll be plumb glad thet ye drapped in." She tossed a morsel of meat to the expectant Mike; then added shyly, "An' so be I."

"Well, I certainly 'drapped,'" laughed Donald. "It looked as though all the dogs south of the Mason-Dixon line had gathered to give Mike and me a warm, if not cordial, welcome, so we didn't stop to knock before coming in."

"Lucky fer ye thet yo' struck a cabin whar the latch string air allus out," she answered, her silver laughter echoing his. "I hadn't a' ought ter hev been so skeered, but I warn't payin' no attention ter all the barkin', fer I jest allowed thet the dawgs hed treed a coon, er somep'n. Yo' see they haint exactly fond o' strangers, an' they be powerful fierce. I reckon they'd hev gobbled Mike right up."

Donald glanced affectionately at the wiry mass of bone and sinew which went to make the police dog every inch a warrior, and doubted it. The child had finished her task, and started the stew to heating again over the fire, and now she turned, swept back the mass of curls from her heated face with a graceful motion of her shapely arm, and stood regarding him with frank curiosity. Donald had no intention of remaining longer, or accepting the hospitable invitation, but there was a touch of romance in the adventure, and a strong appeal in the girl herself, which caused him to hesitate, and linger to ask a few questions about the neighborhood and her life. When he did regretfully pick up his cap and rifle, and call the dog, who turned protestingly from her-who-dispensed-savory pieces-of-meat, he found that he had suffered the fate of all who hesitate, for a glance through the window showed him that, although the glowing, iridescent reflection from the western sky still lingered in the mountain top, embroidering its edge with gold, it was fast fading, and already Night had spread her dusky mantle over the eastern slope. Already darkness had blotted out the lower reaches.

CHAPTER II

ENTER BIG JERRY

As Donald stopped, uncertain, there came the sound of measured, heavy footfalls on the beaten dirt path outside the cabin. The girl's face lighted up joyfully; she hopped to the door, flung it open, and a slightly stooping, but gigantic, form stepped in out of the darkness, caught her up in his huge arms and submitted with a quizzical smile while she pulled his face toward hers by tugging at his long beard, and kissed him.

Across the tumbled masses of her hair the newcomer's still piercing dark eyes, blinking a little under their shaggy brows as the fire leaped in the draft from the open door, caught sight of Donald as he stood back among the shadows. He straightened up suddenly, and his brows drew together in a suspicious scowl.

The city man knew enough of the primitive code of the mountain people to understand that the presence of a man, — especially a strange man, — alone in the house with a young woman, was fraught with unpleasant possibilities. But, before he could speak, the child-woman had launched into a vivacious, if ungrammatical, explanation and story of what had occurred. In substantiation she now raised her short skirt and lifted the bandaged foot, with utter freedom from embarrassment, and laughed deliciously until an answering smile crept slowly into the eyes of the old mountaineer.

With a simple courtesy, which seemed to hold something of innate majesty, he stepped forward, and extended a weatherbeaten hand, several sizes larger than Donald's, and boomed out in a deep voice that matched his physical proportions, "Yo're suttinly welcome, stranger. What happened warn't no fault o' yourn, and I'm plumb obleeged ter ye fer fixin' up my granddarter's hurt. Draw up a cheer fer the stranger, Smiles, he'll jine us in a bite er supper. The fare's simple, but I war raised on't, and 'pears ter me thet I top ye some."

"I should say that you did. You make me feel small, and it's not often any man does that . . . physically, I mean."

The two clasped hands, and Donald winced as his own powerful fingers cracked under the crushing pressure of those of the older man, who seemed to take a boyish delight in this display of his tremendous strength.

"What a colossus he is," thought Donald, as he gritted his teeth to keep back the involuntary exclamation of pain, for, although the massive shoulders and Jovian head of the mountaineer were stooped forward, he towered fully three inches above the six foot city athlete, and his iron-gray beard, rusted with tobacco juice about his mouth, swept over his chest almost to his waist.

"Thanks for the invitation," he said aloud, as he covertly nursed his right hand. "It's mighty kind of you, but I don't want to impose longer, and, besides, I'd better start back to Fayville before it gets dark altogether. If you'll just tell me the most direct way, . . ."

"Wall, I reckon the most *dee*rect way air ter go straight through the woods thar a piece, an' then jump off'n a four hundred foot cliff," the old man chuckled titanically. "But I likewise reckon taint pra'tical; leastwise, not onless yo' happen ter be one o' them new-fangled aviationeers I've hearn tell on. However, here ye be, an' here yo're goin' ter stay twill atter supper. Come, child. Sot on another plate fer the doctor man."

"Donald MacDonald's my name, sir."

"Peers like yo'r paw stuttered when he give yo' thet name," laughed the giant. "Mine's Jerry Webb — 'Big Jerry,' they mostwise calls me hyarerbouts." There was simple pride in the nickname evident in his voice.

"Of course, if you really want me to stay, I'd be glad enough to do it, Mr. Webb, although I don't like to cause any more trouble for Miss . . ."

"'Rose' air the given name of my leetle gal, but folks gener'ly calls her Smiles, fer short." The old man spoke with a noticeable tenderness toning his big voice.

"And there's no need of explaining the reason," answered Donald in a low aside so that the child, who was busy over the stewing kettle on its primitive crane, might not hear. "I never expect to see another to equal hers."

His host sent a sharp glance at him, then, softening, it travelled to the graceful form of the girl silhouetted against the ruddy glow of the open fire, whose reflection outlined her warm flesh with a tint of burnished copper.

"Yes," he responded simply. "Seems like, when thet leetle gal's sweet face lights up with a smile, hit's like a sunbeam a-breakin' through the leaves an' playin' on a waterpool in the quiet woods."

"Oh," interrupted Rose with a cry. "I done plumb ferget ter git the milk from Uncle Perly's, but 'twon't take more'n a minute. Kin I take Mike?" she added, pleadingly, as she buried her slim fingers in the rough hair on the dog's neck, while he stood sniffing acquaintance with the huge boots and homespun pantaloons of the giant.

"Sure; that is if you're not still afraid that the neighbors' dogs will make a meal of him," smiled Donald, and the object of the conversation, who seemed to sense its meaning, sprang eagerly erect and placed his forepaws on the girl's breast.

"No dawg haint a-goin' ter tetch him whilst he's with me," she responded with quiet assurance. "Come, Mickey."

"Which air a fact," supplemented her grandfather,

as girl and dog disappeared with a rush and a bark. "Dumb beasts an' children worships Smiles — an' hit haint scarse to be wondered at, fer she love 'em all. An' she's more rememberful than her grand-pappy. Yo' see, we don't gener'ly hev milk fer our coffee, 'ceptin' when company comes."

In some distress at this frank announcement, Donald said, "But I don't like to have you put yourselves out for me. I wouldn't have stayed if . . . "

"Now, don't let thet idee disturb ye a mite. We're glad ter hev ye with us, an' what fer air friends ef hit haint ter be an excuse fer a leetle extry celebration? Set down, set down thar."

Donald obeyed, and, while his host moved ponderously about, depositing the contents of a bundle which he had brought, studied his surroundings curiously. It was his first experience within a real "feud country" cabin, and he was interested to see how closely its appearance coincided with what his imagination had painted from reading fiction woven about them. To his quiet delight he found that it might almost have served as an illustration for such a book, as, one by one, he mentally checked off the salient features. There were the hand-hewn timbers of wall and unsheathed ceiling; the yawning rough stone fireplace with its wrought iron crane, and, above it, a rifle whose unusual length proclaimed its ownership; the strings of dried herbs and red pepper pods — few, to be sure, and dusty with age —

suspended from the rafters; and, in one corner, a crude ladder leading into the loft.

Only one thing was missing, the wall-beds or bunks, for the hand of civilization had pointed to one improvement, and doors, obviously not a part of the original simple structure, opened into a small addition, roughly partitioned into two sleeping rooms. They were of equal size, but there was no need of labels to proclaim their occupants, for one was so nearly filled with a bed which would have served for Golden Locks' biggest bear, that the rough clothing which was suspended from wooden pegs on the opposite wall hung against it, whereas the other contained, besides a narrow bed, a small chest of drawers with a cheap mirror above it, and a chair. The one window was draped with a daintily-flowered material, which Donald decided was calico, a cover of the same material lay across the chest, and on it — in the place of honor between an old comb and brush stood a small blue-and-white jar, whose cheaply glazed surface caught the flicker of the fire and winked at him as though it were aware of the absurdity of anything so trivial being held in such high esteem. More of the "calico," which really was an inexpensive but tasteful chintz, hung against the wall and served to hide from prying eyes the child's meagre wardrobe, and a bow of it was perkily tied to the back of the chair.

Donald smiled his amusement and caught an answering grin on Big Jerry's face. "She haint like we-all," he said. "Wants ter hev bright an' purty things erbout, an' . . ." he lowered his voice, "durned ef she didn't make me a *necktie* of thet thar stuff — seen one on a 'furriner' once." The visitor felt a warm satisfaction over the thought that his own costume didn't include such excess adornment.

"I put hit on . . . once, ter please her, but I reckon hit didn't make much of a showin' under *this*." He ran his fingers reflectively through his heavy beard for a moment; then, with his voice still a forte whisper, he added, "Say, stranger, I've got a leetle drap o' white liquor hid out in the woodshed whar Smiles kaint find hit, an' ef yo'd delight ter wet yo'r throat afore she comes back, why . . ."

The door flew open with a bang, and Rose and Mike tore in, panting and a-glitter with diamond drops of rain. Instantly the expression of simple guile on the old man's face changed so ludicrously to one of overdone innocence that it was all Donald could do to keep from laughing.

"Storm's a-comin'," cried the girl, gayly, while the dog rushed madly around the room, with his nose to the floor and barking hilariously, until his master seized him by the back and held him, squirming. A flash of distant lightning substantiated the announcement, and a few seconds later their ears caught the crescendo reverberations of thunder as it echoed down the valley.

Mike growled uneasily and crouched close to his master's legs, but Rose ran again to the door and stood, heedless of the rain which beat in upon her wind-whipped skirt, peering out with evident delight. A still more vivid, zigzag flash rent the serried masses of black storm-clouds which were rolling up over the mountain's top, edging the nearer one with fire, and she laughed merrily and clapped her hands like a child.

"Shet thet door, yo' young vixen," bellowed Big Jerry, plainly disturbed. The girl obeyed, and gave him a kiss, and the whining dog a reassuring pat, as she hurried back to finish setting the table — a simple matter, for there was no spotless damask, glittering silver and cut glass to deck the white-scoured top of the plain slab which formed a substantial table for many purposes.

In a moment she had announced, quite informally, that supper was served; but, just as the two men arose to take their places, there came a long "hulloo-oo" above the sound of wind and rain. Again Rose dashed to the door, with the cry, "Why, thet's Judd Amos; I knows his call."

Without reason or warning Donald experienced a quick tightening about his heart, the absurdity of which caused him to smile. What on earth was it to him if this mountain child's color heightened a shade at a familiar call in a masculine voice?

The next instant a tall youth, as lean and sinewy as an Indian, stumbled into the room, with his rough coat about his head, and water streaming from his drenched clothing and the barrel of a gun, which was every whit as modern and efficient as Donald's own.

"Gosh a'mighty," he said. "Thought I'd be drownded, shore. Hit's agoin' ter be a rip-snorter . . . worst storm er the summer, by the way hit's started." Then, as he dashed the rain from his eyes, and, for the first time caught sight of the visitor, he stopped short in none too pleased surprise, if the black look which went toward Donald from beneath his lowering brows meant anything.

"Make ye acquainted with Donald MacDonald, a doctor man from the city, Judd," boomed the giant's hearty voice. "Doc, shake hands with a neighbor uv ourn, Judd Amos."

As Donald stood up he managed to silence Mike's throaty growl with a warning shove with his foot. The men formally clasped hands, their eyes looking steadily into each other's from the same level, and this time, primed by his earlier experience, the city man exerted all of his strength, and felt a glow of childish satisfaction as the other winced.

"Set ye down, Judd. Draw a cheer up by the fire, yo're soaked," said Big Jerry. "Honey-rose," he added, addressing the girl in a wheedling tone, "Judd 'pears ter be powerful soaked an' cold. Kaint he . . . kaint we-all hev jest a drap o' white liquor?"

He stroked his beard and pushed aside his drooping mustache in anticipation, but to no avail, for her answer, uttered firmly and with no suggestion of a smile in her deep eyes this time, was, "'Deed yo' kaint: nary a drap. Yo' know, an' Juddy, *he* knows . . ." to Donald there seemed to be some special significance in her words, "thet thar haint a-goin' ter be nary a drap o' thet devil's brew in house o' mine. Why, I be plumb s'prised at ye, grandpap."

The tremendous old man rubbed his whiskers faster and hemmed apologetically. "In course I haint got none . . . in the cabin . . ." he glanced quickly at Donald, "an' I didn't mean nothin', Smiles. Come, swing yo'r cheer erround ter the table, Judd, we'll jest fergit the eeliments, an' enjoy a dry celebration in the doctor's honor . . . all 'cept Judd, he air plenty wet," he added, in a jocose attempt to turn his mistake into a jest. "Rose hurted her foot, an' doc, he done hit up fer her real nice."

More bashfully than before, the girl extended the injured member in its now mud-bedraggled bandage for the newcomer's inspection.

Donald had been watching the scene with quiet amusement over the child's assurance, and had noticed not only the look of sorrowful resignation on her grandfather's face, but the dull flush which mounted the swarthy cheeks of the younger man. Judd's mouth retained the straight line for some time, but a quick burst of light-hearted song on Smiles' lips, as she turned to dish up the savory stew, showed that the incident was forgotten by her as soon as it was ended.

"Better let me lift it down for you," said Donald,

as she swung the crane with its heavy iron kettle from the fire. "We don't want any more burns here to-night."

He jumped up and acted on the words without giving the matter a thought, but it seemed to him that the girl's pleased, "Thank ye, sir," was a bit embarrassed, and that the men regarded him with blank surprise. Not for a minute did it dawn upon him that his act had not been according to the code of the mountains.

They were all seated at last, but yet another surprise was in store for the visitor, for Rose folded her hands, bent her head until the curls veiled the glowing face, and began a simple blessing. Big Jerry sat bolt upright with his eyes screwed up ludicrously, and, although Judd bent his head the merest fraction, it was with obvious embarrassment, and his flashing optics kept sending suspicious glances at the "furriner" as though to discover if he were laughing at them all. In fact, nothing was further from Donald's mind. It had been long since he had partaken of a meal at which grace was said, but the simple, homely words touched a chord of memory and made it vibrate to a note which brought both pain and pleasure.

The host's stentorian "Amen" was the signal for attack, and for a time the business of satisfying the demands of healthy hunger was paramount to all things else. It was no feast of wit and wisdom, but of something, for the time being, more desirable, and the application of the other three gave Donald an opportunity to study covertly the unusual group of which he had so unexpectedly become a part.

Although he was essentially a man of action, his brusqueness of manner was, in part at least, a pose which had become unconscious, and, deep within his heart, in a chamber carefully locked from the gaze of his fellow men, dwelt Romance and Imagination — the spirit gifts of a mother, whose death, five years before, had brought him his first black grief. Had this visioning power been lacking in him he could never have accomplished the modern miracles which he had already wrought many times in constructive and restorative surgery. Now, the spirit of imagery in his soul was stirred by something in the romantic unreality of his surroundings — the rude, yet interesting room which served all family purposes save that of slumber; the mellow radiance from a crude lamp and the ever-changing light of the open fire; the long, wavering shadows within the cabin; and, without, the banshee wailing of the storm wind around the eaves, the occasional crash of thunder, the creaking of limbs and fitful dashes of rain. He found himself leaning back in his chair and mentally attempting to dissect and study not the bodies, but the personalities, of the three who were the representatives of a type, in manners and customs at least, new to him.

In his boyhood, and before the pressing demands of his profession had enslaved him, Donald had been an insatiate reader, and now he endeavored to recall to memory some of the stories which he had read about this strange people, whose dwelling place was within the limits of the busy, progressive East, yet who were surprisingly isolated from it by natural barriers, and still more so by traditions slow to perish. Pure of stock he knew them to be, for their unmixed blood had had its fountain source in the veins of some of America's best and earliest settlers; primitive in their ideals, strong in their simple purposes and passions, the products of, and perhaps even now factors in, blood feuds whose beginnings dated back generations. And, although he laughed at himself for his imaginings as he remembered that the twentieth century was ten years old, he found himself assigning both the men places in his memory picture.

Big Jerry, slow of speech, patriarchal in looks and bearing, powerful in body, became, to his mind's eye, the venerable chieftain of a mountain clan. Judd, with his aquiline face, which was undoubtedly handsome in a dark, brooding way, beneath its uncombed shock of black hair which swept low over his forehead, sinewy with the strength, quickness and much of the natural grace of a panther, was the typical outlaw of the hills.

CHAPTER III

AN INNOCENT SERPENT IN EDEN

DONALD turned his appraising gaze upon the child, and here the illusion yielded to another, quite different.

Even her primitive dress, her unbound hair, her crude forms of speech and soft, drawling intonation — such as the throaty, unvarying pronunciation of "the" as though it were "ther," and "a" like "er" — which sounded so deliciously odd to his New England ears, could not erase from his mind the impression that she did not belong in the picture. To be sure he had, during his tramps, already seen many a wild mountain flower so delicately sweet that it seemed out of place amid its stern environment. But Rose affected him differently, although the difference was subtle, indefinable.

In the company of the men he was conscious of the reserve which one of his type instinctively feels when first in the presence of people of another race or class. With her he was already wholly at his ease. Donald finally attributed this to the fact that she was, after all, merely a child — one of a class which is akin the world over, and which he understood better than any other.

As the simple meal progressed, Big Jerry began to ply the visitor with questions, and press him to talk on many subjects connected with the wide world of men; and, as Donald's natural reticence yielded to the naïve interrogations, he answered with a readiness which somewhat surprised even himself. The child ate little; but sat with her elbows on the table, her firmly rounded chin resting on her clasped hands, and drank in his words. Her luminous eyes were fixed on his face, and expressions of wonder and delight chased each other across her own countenance, like wavering light and shade on a placid pool.

Judd, too, remained silent, ill at ease, and his dark, morose eyes ever shifted from the face of the man to that of the girl. Once, while Donald and his host were engaged in an animated discussion, he awkwardly attempted to draw Rose into personal conversation; but he relapsed again into moody silence when he received a frank, though smiling, rebuff. Clearly the meal was not an enjoyable one for him.

All things of human invention come to an end, and at last Big Jerry lifted his towering frame from his chair to indicate that the supper was over. With obvious relief Judd crossed to the door and, opening it, announced that the storm had nearly passed. It was still raining, however.

"Ef yo' air goin' back ter the village, stranger, I'll be pleased ter sot ye on yo'r way," he announced as he drew on his coat, and to Donald's mind the sentence carried an unmistakable *double entente.*

Nevertheless he answered promptly, "Thanks, I'd be much obliged if you would. Perhaps Mr. Webb can spare me a lantern, too, since these paths are unfamiliar to . . ."

"Sho, yo haint a-goin' out er this house ter-night, friend," broke in the old man. "Leastwise, ef yo'r willin' ter put up with sech accommodations as the loft room offers ye. Thar haint no sense of yer takin' er five-mile walk through them drenched bushes, an' gittin' soaked yerself."

"In course yer goin' ter stay," echoed the girl, with childlike delight. "Besides, I wants ter hear lots more erbout the city an' city folks."

"But I have already imposed enough on your hospitality," protested Donald, hesitatingly, since the invitation held a strong appeal for him.

"Yo' haint imposed at all. Set yo'rself down. I shore appreciates yo'r company."

Judd scowled from the doorway, then flung back over his shoulder a short, "Wall, I reckon I'll be startin' home now," and, without further words, he went out, closing the door behind him with unnecessary violence. Donald said nothing, but he was frankly amused; for it was very apparent that the young mountaineer felt that he had a proprietary interest in Rose, and was undisguisedly jealous of the stranger who was held in such high favor.

Rose, however, lost no time thinking of her lover, — if lover she regarded him, — but flew about the final household duties, humming happily, and now and then breaking into unfinished snatches of song like a wild wood bird. Evidently the slight burn no longer troubled her and was already forgotten.

Her work finished, she joined the two men, who were smoking their pipes before the blazing fire, and seated herself crosslegged at her grandfather's feet. Mike got up leisurely from his post beneath his master's chair, stretched forward and back, yawned prodigiously, and then lay down with his shaggy head on the girl's bare legs. As Donald talked, Rose played with the dog, rolling him over and rubbing his underbody until his mouth opened in a grotesque animal imitation of her own wonderful smile, which constantly flashed to her lips like a ray of light, only to vanish as swiftly, and leave its slowly fading afterglow in her deep eyes.

"Dr. Mac," said the child timidly, during a moment of contented silence, her natural use of his intimate nickname, both startling and pleasing Donald, "yo-all allowed thet yo' doctored children mostly. I loves babies more'n anything else in the world, 'ceptin' only grandpap; they're so purty an' sweet an' helpless-like, thet I reckon the Lord loves 'em powerful, an' the' haint nothin' finer then takin' keer of 'em."

Donald nodded with pleasure, and the girl continued, dreamily:

"I allows thet, when God made people an' put the breath o' life inter them, he hadn't quite got outer his mind what he done on an earlier day, an' was jest improvin' on hit; fer hit sorter seems ter me thet big men an' women air like growin' trees, fashioned fer ter stand up agin ther eliments an' storms most times; but babies air like tiny leetle flowers — so weak an' tender thet we hev ter take mighty good keer of 'em. Don't yo' never feel, somehow, like yo' was tendin' a gyarden of purty flowers, an' a-drivin' away the grubs an' bugs what would make 'em wilt an' die?"

"To be sure I do, my child," he answered, wondering if she realized how apt was her simile, since most disease is, indeed, caused by "bugs an' grubs." "And many people, with imaginations like yours, have felt exactly the same. Did you ever read a poem called 'The Reaper'? No, I suppose not," he added, as the girl shook her curls, while a wistful look crept into her eyes.

"It was written by Longfellow, a very famous poet who used to live near my home city of Boston, and no man ever loved little children better than he did. I had to learn the verses years ago when I was a schoolboy, and I remember the first of them still: —

"'There is a Reaper, whose name is Death,
And, with his sickle keen,
He reaps the bearded grain at a breath,
And the flowers that grow between.'

"For — he has the Reaper say — the Lord has need of the pretty flowers to make his garden in Heaven more bright and fair."

"I never thought er thet," said the girl seriously, "but I reckon hit's so. Grandpap's bearded like the grain, but somehow he 'pears ter me more like er big pine tree, fer grain bends before ther wind, an' he haint never bent ter no storm."

"And I? Am I a tree, too," queried Donald with amusement.

She studied him judiciously and then answered with quiet assurance, "Yo're the oak. Hit don't bend, neither."

"And yourself?"

"Why," she laughed, "I'm jest a rose like my name. A rose jest growin' inter er bush."

"To be sure you are. Except that roses have thorns."

"I hev thorns, too," she said with conviction, and Donald doubted it — then.

"I should plumb love ter take keer of babies an' make 'em well an' strong like yo' do," she went on pensively.

"Perhaps you may, some day. You'll have babies of your own."

"Yes," was her simple reply, "I shall have babies ter love an' keer for, but I meant thet I wanted ter help all little children."

"A children's nurse, perhaps, like those who work with me," and he went on to tell her graphically of the wonderful things done at the Children's Hospital, upon the staff of which he was.

Rose listened, as enchanted as a child with a fairy story,—and indeed such it was, a modern fairy tale wherein medicine was a magic potion, and the merciful knife a magic wand. Told in simple language which she could understand, his story of the work in which his very life was bound up seemed to her like an epic, and, when he paused, she drew her breath with a sigh of keen delight, and cried, "Oh, granddaddy. Haint thet a wonderful thing fer ter do? I shorely wants ter be a trained nurse like thet when I grows up."

"Perhaps you will, some day, who knows?" said Donald thoughtlessly.

"An' what would this hyar old pine do without the rosebush blossomin' close beside him? What would the leetle wild mountain flowers hyarabouts do without thar Smiles ter take keer o' them?" asked the old man tenderly, but with a hidden undercurrent of distress.

"But ef I could larn ter take *better* keer o' them . . ." began the girl.

The old man moved uneasily, then said, "Wall, yo're only a leetle rosebud yerself now, an' hit's more'n time yo' closed up fer the night. Run erlong ter bed, hon."

Obedient, but a little rebellious, Rose got up slowly, kissed the strong, weather-scarred cheek of the old man and turned toward the door of her room.

"Good night, Smiles," called Donald. She hesitated a moment, then ran back to him with childish impetuosity, flung her slender arms about his neck and kissed him, too, whispering, "I loves ye, Dr. Mac, fer thet yo' loves little children."

The frank embrace embarrassed him a little, and he felt the thrill of an almost unknown glow in his heart. Many a time his patients — even those as old as Rose — had kissed him thus; but something in her act left a new impression. Judged by the standards of the mountain folks she was almost a woman, and he knew it.

Mike pattered to her door as it closed, scratched upon it with a low whine, and then lay down close against it.

There was a moment's silence in the room as the men, each busy with his own thoughts, puffed steadily. Then Big Jerry carefully knocked the ashes from his pipe and remarked, "Hit haint no fault er yourn, stranger; but I haint altergether pleased at ther thoughts yo'r comin' hes placed in my leetle gal's head. She won't easy ferget what yo' done told her, an' . . . an' I couldn't bear fer ter lose her."

"I'm sorry. I spoke without thinking that it might result in her becoming discontented," answered Don. "To-morrow I'll try to make her understand — what is a fact — that although her loving heart might be ever so eager, her ways and those of the city are so utterly different that she couldn't possibly hope to go there and become a nurse such as I described. You understand what I mean."

"Yes, an' I'd be powerful obleeged ter ye, friend," replied the old man with evident relief. "Hit's es yo' say. Rose air er mountain gal by bringin' up, ef not by birth, an' 'tis hyar thet she rightfully belongs now."

CHAPTER IV

"SMILES"

"'Not by birth?'" echoed Donald, in surprise. "But I thought that she was your granddaughter?"

"An' so she be — or perhaps my darter," hastily answered Jerry, realizing his error too late. "I reckon I shouldn't hev told ye," he added in distress.

"Don't let any such idea worry you, Mr. Webb. Where she came from is nothing to me, and, indeed, after to-morrow I shall probably never see her again. I've got to admit, though, that you have aroused my curiosity, and I'd like to hear the story that's behind her presence here, if you are willing to tell it."

The giant hesitated, then said slowly, "Wall, I kaint think of no reason why yo' shouldn't hyar hit. Hit happened this erway.

"Twar one mornin', thirteen summers ergone, an' I war ergunnin' down in ther woods er piece, not fur from ther Swift River. I rekerlect hit war er purty mornin', with ther dew still er-clingin' ter ther grass, an' sparklin' — like jewels, an' ther wood birds war singin' like they war special happy. I clumb erround er big rock, an' all of er sudden I seen — I seen er leetle mite of er gal, standin, thar, jest es still es still. She warn't more'n three year old, I jedged, an' she suttinly come from ther city, fer her leetle dress warn't like none I'd ever seen—hit hed sorter loose panterloons ter' hit, an', although her legs war bare — an' all scratched an' bleedin' — thar war tiny socks an' shoes on 'em. Thar war tears in her big blue eyes an' on her purty cheeks, but she warn't cryin' none, then. No, sir; she war jest erstandin' an' erlookin' up ter whar a robin war singin' in an oak tree, an' her leetle mouth war open fer all ther world like a rosebud. Wall, es I stood thar, erwatchin' like I'd seen er fairy, she smiles — yo' know thot smile of her'n, like a rainbow breakin' fer er minute through the rain, an' then fadin' erway slow?

"I calls ter her sorter soft-like, an' dang me ef she didn't come walkin' right up ter me, not a mite erfeered. She made a funny leetle bow, held out her chubby hand an' says, 'How do ye do, big man. Hev ye seen my papa an' mamma?'

"I tuck her on my knee, an' leetle by leetle — fer she couldn't talk much — she told me thet they come from a great, big city whar war 'lectric and steam cyars an' policemen, fer ter play in the woods, an' thet her pappa an' mamma hed gone out on the water in a boat ter ketch a fish fer baby's breakfast. Thar boat hed runned erway with her pappa an' mamma, she said, an' they war settin' in hit cryin'.

"I reckoned what hed happed ter them, fer thարer-bouts the Swift River air a most deceevin', treetcher-ous stream, what looks innocent, but hes a powerful swift current what don't show. City folks haint no business ter go campin' in woods thet they don't know nothin' erbout," he interpolated.

"Wall, I left the leetle gal ersettin' on the rock, an' runned es fast es ever I could down stream ter the rapids. Her folks warn't nowhar ter be seen, but I found part of thar canoeboat, smashed ter splinters, an' I guessed the rest." He paused, and smoked steadily for some time before continuing.

"In course the baby couldn't tell us much, 'ceptin' thet her name war Rose. She didn't remember the name of the city whar they come from, but she said thet erfore they come inter the woods, she slept all night on a train.

"We found ther campin' outfit of her paw an' maw, an' whar hit stood I built up a leetle mound with a sorter cross on hit, in thar memory.

"In course, I tried ter find out arterwards whar they come from, but hit warn't no sorter use. Thar war no address on anything in the tent or thar spare-close, and no one hed seen them in Fayville or thar-erbouts, so I reckoned thay come clar ercross the mountains from Kentuck. Mebbe, ef I hed hed more money, I mought hev found out erbout them; but us war powerful po'r them days. An'—mebbe, again, hit war wrong—but maw an' me couldn't holp thinkin' thet the leetle gal war sent us by the good Lord, fer we didn't hev no children, hevin' lost a leetle gal jest erbout es old es Smiles, ten years back."

"I don't think that you have any cause for reproaching yourself, Mr. Webb," broke in Donald, reassuringly. "It seems to me that you did all you could do, under the circumstances. Certainly the child was fortunate, for you have been very kind to the little waif."

"We war mostly kind ter ourselves," was Big Jerry's simple rejoinder. "She shorely hes been a ray of sunshine in this hyar cabin — 'specially since maw died three years ergone, since when Rose hes taken keer of hit, an' me. She air a leetle mite of a tyrant, et times, but I reckon I'm ther better fer hit.

"Wall, we brung her up like our own flesh an' blood, but altho' she called my woman 'Maw', she allus called me 'Grandpappy.' An' we didn't never try ter make her fergit her real paw an' maw, an' every birthday — leastwise we calls ther day she come ter us her birthday — she puts wild flowers on the mound I made. She's growed up like the other children hyar, and 'twar them what fust called her Smiles; but 'twarnt long erfore maw an' me sorter got inter the habit of doin' hit too, fer hit suits her right well."

The speaker became silent, his memory dwelling in scenes of the dimming past, while Donald's thoughts were busy with the story which he had just heard. The inherent difference between *her* personality and that of the average mountain girl was explained. The curtsy which she — a three-year-old baby —

had made Big Jerry, seemed to indicate that she had been a flower of city hothouse culture before being transplanted to the wilds, and there growing up, in outward semblance at least, in conformity with her environment. But, Donald felt, within the child lay an ineradicable strain of breeding, making her different from these others, an inherited fineness of soul of which her peculiar charm was evidence.

A little later his host arose, and said with native courtesy, "I reckon yo're tired enough ter want ter go ter bed, stranger, an' I'll show ye ter yo'r loft room."

The pair bade each other good-night, and Donald climbed the homemade ladder to his resting place beneath the roof, on which the rain was still keeping up a continuous patter. He felt that he was weary enough so that no rocking was needed to induce slumber, but it was nevertheless some time before he really fell asleep. And when he did it was with the mental picture of the child's smile, like a quickly vanishing sun-rift in the mist, before his closed eyes.

. . . .

Donald was awakened the next morning by the sound of laughing voices, and Mike's hilarious barking, outside his little window. Looking through it he beheld a delightful picture. On the dew-sprinkled grass of the little clearing about the cottage were merrily romping the dog, Rose and a small child. Beyond, lay the mountain's wooded descent, rich in variegated greens and seemingly rising like an island shore from a sea of pearly vapor, tinted with delicate mauve, rose and amber by the sun, which had itself not yet risen above the valley mist. Scrambling into his outer garments, the man ran down to join them in their game.

"Look out, er yo'll git yo're feet wetted, Mr. doctor man," cried Rose gayly, as she drew her own bare foot through the grass and held it forward shining with dew.

"Do you think a little thing like wet feet would stop me from getting into the game?" he answered. "And you called me a sturdy oak! Who is the little buttercup?" he added, looking at the child whose shock of bright golden curls made his nickname an apt one.

"She's Lou, Judd's leetle sister, an' her house air jest over thar beyond ourn. Yo' guessed rightly, she *air* one er my flower children, ain't ye, honey-sweet?" Rose dropped to her knees in the wet grass, and gathered the bashful child against her tenderly. The baby buried her face in her friend's neck without speaking, and in a moment Rose stood up, saying, "We-all thinks a heap er Lou, 'specially Judd."

"I've got a little niece at home just about Lou's âge. Her name is Muriel. Would you like to hear about her and her playthings? She's got a tiny pony and cart," he said, and soon the child was sitting in his lap, listening wide-eyed to the description of dolls who opened and shut their eyes, and wonderful mechanical toys which walked and turned somersaults, monkeys which climbed poles and other equally incredible things.

"He air a funny man, an' he tells funny stories," giggled the child, when Donald had exhausted his memory and imagination. "In course thar hain't no sech things."

"Indeed thar *air*, ef he says thar air," chided Rose with implicit faith in her friend.

"What, doll babies thet open an' shet thar eyes, an' say 'maw' an' 'paw' like weuns, Smiles?" asked the baby, unconvinced.

"Wait until I go back home, and I'll send you one that can do every one of those wonderful things," laughed Donald. "I mean to send Rose a present, too."

"Oh," cried the latter, "I shall be more'n obleeged ter ye."

"What would you like best," he asked.

She thought seriously a moment, then said, "I reckon I should like best a white dress an' cap, like the nurses wear."

Donald experienced a pang of regret, but responded lightly, "Very well, that shall be yours, and I'm also going to send you a little book of poems called 'The Child's Garden of Verses', written by another man who looked on babies as flowers, too."

At this moment the sound of quick footsteps caused them to look up. Judd Amos was coming around the side of the cottage, and the night had apparently not taken the black look from his countenance.

"Oh, Juddy," cried the baby, wriggling free of Donald's arms. "Thet man thar air er goin' ter send me er doll baby thet opens an' shets hits eyes, Juddy."

"We're obleeged ter ye; but I reckon thet I kin buy Lou all the presents she needs," said Judd gruffly. "Yo' maw wants ye ter come ter breakfast, sis," he added, and picked the baby up in his long arms, giving her an undoubtedly affectionate hug as he saw that the tears had sprung to her eyes.

"That's nonsense," snorted Donald angrily, as Judd disappeared with his burden. "I'll send the doll to you — along with the dress and book — and he can't stop *you* from giving it to her."

"I reckon he *kaint*," Rose responded with eyes flashing. "I kin make Judd Amos do jest whatsoever I tells him." And Donald thought that she probably spoke the truth.

"Haint we a-goin' ter hev no breakfast this mornin'?" came Big Jerry's deep voice, toned to assumed anger, as he appeared with an armful of wood, and, laughing merrily, Rose blew him a kiss and disappeared within-doors.

During the morning meal, which was quickly prepared, the girl talked continually of the delights of being a children's nurse, and as he observed the look of worry on the old man's face, Donald determined to put an end to the child's rosy, but impossible, dream as soon as possible. His duty was plain enough, even if he had not given his promise to Rose's grandfather; yet the more he saw of her the stronger grew the unbidden thought of what a wonderful woman she would make if she could be taken to the city and given the advantages of education.

His opportunity came when, breakfast over, Big Jerry started for the door, announcing that he would be back in a few moments.

"I'll wait for you to return before I go, and talk to the child as I agreed," said Donald, in an undertone. The old man nodded his understanding.

Hardly knowing how to commence, Donald turned to the girl and said hesitatingly, "Little Rose, I've got to go along in a few moments, but first I must tell you something which I'm afraid will cause you disappointment."

Smiles stepped close to him, with her large eyes filled with a surprised question.

"It is this. I wish, indeed, that you might grow up to be a nurse for little children, such as my story last night set you to dreaming of being, but, although I'm sure you would be a splendid one, it is impossible, you know, dear."

"Why haint hit possible?" she demanded.

"Well, you see, dear child, nurses of that sort have to study and know almost as much as doctors. They have to train — go to school in the hospital, that is — for three years."

"But I haint erfeered ter work. I *wants* ter study, an' larn," she cried eagerly.

"Yes, I know, but . . . well, it costs a lot of money in the first place; nurses don't get any pay while they're learning, and they have to deposit three hundred dollars before they can take the course, one hundred each year. Besides that, they have to have a good education to start with. Probably you don't know what is meant by a 'High School,' but a girl must have gone through one — studied steadily for twelve or thirteen years — or at least have an equivalent amount of education, before she can hope to enter the Children's Hospital."

"Wha . . . what do 'equivalent' mean?" she asked, with her lips beginning to tremble a little from disappointment.

"It means that you would have to know as much as though you had gone through a High School, and be able to pass an examination proving that you do."

Very slowly Rose turned back to recommence her work, and Donald sensed, rather than saw, that the tears were very near to the surface. Another roseate dream of childhood had been ruthlessly shattered, and he hated himself for having witlessly engendered it in her mind, since it could only be born to die unrealized.

When she spoke again, it was to say with a telltale quaver in her subdued voice, "I reckon thet us mountain folks kaint never do worthwhile things, fer all sech take er mighty lot er larnin'."

"There are two kinds of learning in this world, Rose, one of the mind, and the other of the heart. And without the benefits which come from the latter, the things of the former would be of little use. You may be sure that helping one's neighbors, as you are always helping yours; being happy yourself and making others contented and happier, and bringing smiles to the lips of friends by the example of your own sweet smile; are things very much worth while," said Donald, haltingly, but with sincerity. He placed his arm about her slender shoulder, with the half-hope that she would accept his comfort, and perhaps cry out the last of her disappointment with her head on his breast. Instead, she turned sharply away and went on with the work she had started, and the man followed her grandfather outside, realizing that hers, like most battles within the soul, must be fought out alone.

In a few moments, and while he was still talking to Big Jerry, Rose joined them on the stoop. A quick glance at her flowerlike face told Donald that her childish — but none the less real — grief was banished, for a smile of victory curved her lips.

"Ef ye haint a-goin' ter the city right away, doctor," said his host, "we would be downright pleased ter hev ye come up ergin. I've come ter like ye right well."

"Indeed I shall — come every day if I may, for you and little Rose seem like old friends of mine already. And, when I do go back next week, you may be sure that I shall not forget either of you, or your hospitality."

He picked up his rifle regretfully, whistled to Mike, who came bounding to him, but whose tail drooped ludicrously when he understood by canine instinct that the call meant separation from his new comrade, and with a final good-bye wave, struck off into the woods.

CHAPTER V

GIVING AND RECEIVING

THE call of the Jungle Folk, "Good hunting," was not fulfilled during Donald's day in the forest. Game there was aplenty, but he made clumsy work of following the fresh tracks in the wet wood mould, and missed the one wild creature that he saw, for he shot at it rather by instinct than design, and was not sorry that his bullet went wide. Indeed, love of the out-of-doors and the thrill of the chase, rather than the wish to slay, drew him into the woods for his brief respites from work and for recreation each summer. He seldom killed except for food; the convulsive pain-drawn death struggle, the cry of mortal agony, and the despairing look in the glazed eyes of dumb, stricken animals held no fascination for him. He saw too much of such things among human beings.

The day, truly, was a glory. The storm of the previous night had cleared and revivified the air, which, for many days, had been oppressively sultry; the irregular patches of sky, glimpsed through the branches, were a transparent blue; the springy ground was bright with wild blossoms and colorful berries, — dogwood and service berry, — adder's tongue, bleeding heart and ferns in rich profusion. His subconscious senses drank in the manifold beauties, but his active mind was otherwise engaged.

To-day the solitude, usually so appealing, so restful after fifty work-filled weeks amid the noisy turmoil of the city's life, lacked something of its customary charm and satisfaction. The man found himself with a real longing for the companionship of the simple old man and the intimate appeal of the child, whose acquaintance he had enjoyed for a few hours only. It was on them, rather than on his present occupation, that his thoughts were bent.

At last approaching night found him safely back in the valley village, where the keeper of the primitive boarding house expressed her solicitation over his prolonged absence, as she handed him several letters which had arrived the day previous. One epistle, from his associate physician, Dr. Bentley, carried a pressing plea that he return to Boston as soon as possible, and perform a difficult operation. The call was so urgent that Donald regretfully concluded that duty demanded his compliance.

He determined, however, not to leave without paying a final visit to his new friends, and, soon after sun-up the following morning, set forth for Big Jerry's cabin, carrying, as a present for Rose, a woven sweetgrass basket filled with such simple confections as the general store afforded. Nor had he forgotten a generous supply of pipe tobacco for her grandfather.

Donald plunged into the woods and headed for Swift River, whose broken, winding course he followed upward until he reached the rapids of rushing molten silver and the low, but dangerous, fall which marked the spot of the early tragedy in the child's life. As he stood there, cap in hand, the sound of a low treble voice in song fell on his ears, coming from a place not far distant.

Some one, alone under the cathedral arches of the forest, was softly chanting the words of the simple, familiar hymn, "Nearer, My God, to Thee," and, impelled by the unusualness of the thing at such an hour and in such a place, Donald moved quietly forward until the solitary singer was in view.

It was Rose. She was kneeling beside a low, rounded mound covered with fresh-gathered forest vines, and sprinkled with wild flowers.

The meaning of the picture flashed at once into the man's mind. This was the "birthday" of little Smiles — the anniversary of her advent to a new life — and this her yearly pilgrimage of love and filial homage to those barely remembered two who had given her being.

Donald waited in silence, leaning against a concealing tree trunk, until the child had ended her act of simple devotion by throwing an unaffected kiss from her finger tips, not towards the dead earth, but upwards to the spirit world above.

Then, as she arose and moved slowly away, her light step barely disturbing the grass, Donald followed and overtook her. The girl's greeting, although more subdued than on the morning before, was none the less delighted, and, with her hand snuggled warmly in his, they made their way to the cabin.

"I bids ye welcome, doctor," sang out Big Jerry, as he caught sight of them. "Hit shor' air a fine day fer ter spend in ther woods."

"And I cannot spend it there," answered Donald, ruefully. "I've been called back to the city to attend a little sick patient, and leave Fayville on the noon train."

"Wall, now, thet air too bad, an' hit's mighty kind er ye ter come way up hyar erfore yo' left," said the old man, while the girl's new disappointment, caused by the announcement, was evident enough without verbal expression.

"I brought you a package of tobacco, a little token of my appreciation for your kindness to me night before last, Mr. Webb; and Rose a 'birthday' gift, just a few sweets in a basket which I found at the store, and which struck me as pretty."

Jerry stumblingly expressed his gratitude for the present, and Rose unconsciously curtsied, much as she must have thirteen years before. Her lips and eyes smiled her shy thanks, but it appeared to Donald that mischievous amusement struggled with appreciation in her look.

"Something seems to be amusing you, little lady. Let me into the secret," said Donald.

Her silvery laughter broke from her lips, as she answered, "I'm shor' obleeged fer the compliment yo' paid thet basket. I made hit myself."

"*You* did? Why, it's wonderful, but it looks as though I'd been carrying coals to Newcastle. Newcastle is the name of a town in England where a great deal of coal comes from," he hastened to add, in explanation.

"Like kerryin' water ter the river. I makes them leetle baskets odd times, an' sells 'em ter the storekeeper in Fayville, but I never hev none fer myself, somehow, an' I haint never a-goin' ter part with this hyar one, leastwise ef I kin keep hit."

"Of course you may. It's my present to you just the same; but don't be afraid that it is meant to take the place of the other things I have promised you."

While he had been talking to the child, Big Jerry had picked up Donald's rifle, and now stood caressingly running his hand down the blue-black barrel, and over the polished black walnut stock.

Its owner watched him with inward amusement, yet fully understanding the woodman's love for a perfect weapon. As an ordinary man would lift a child's airgun, the giant tossed the rifle to a firing position, snuggled the butt against his shoulder, and leaned his gray-bearded cheek on it affectionately. Finally he lowered it regretfully to the ground, and remarked, with the suggestion of a sigh, "This hyar shor' air a mighty purty weepon, doctor. I reckon she'll drap a bullet purty nigh whar hit's aimed ter go."

"Try it," encouraged Don, catching a look of almost boyish delight cross the old man's face.

"Air she loaded? I haint right familiar with these hyar repeatin' guns, with thar leevers an' sich."

The other threw a cartridge into the breech, and handed the weapon over, with the remark, "She shoots a trifle high, compared with the average rifle, I've found — perhaps an inch at a hundred yard range."

"Thank ye, sir," replied Jerry, and added simply, "I reckon I'll jest chip the top off'n thet big rock erfore the oak tree, yonder." With the last word came the gun's flash, and to Donald's amazement he saw a tiny cloud of white dust rise from the peak of the boulder.

Rose was already running lightly towards the target accompanied by the excited Mike, and her twinkling legs held such fleetness that the trained athlete barely caught up with her as she finished the dash, and triumphantly laid her finger on a leaden mark across the stone.

"Good Lord," gasped Donald, as Big Jerry approached more sedately, "I thought that I could shoot some, but that . . . that beats anything I ever saw in the West, or on the stage. And with an unfamiliar gun, too."

"She shoots erbout ther same ter the left, too,"

commented the marksman judiciously. "But et thet she air a moghty fine rifle-gun, an' I shor' would be pleased ter own her, only I reckon yo' haint anxious ter sell."

"I'd as soon think of selling Mike, or any other of my good friends," promptly responded Donald, whereat a quick shadow of disappointment crossed the old man's countenance.

"I erpreciates the feelin' thet ye hev fer hit," he said as he handed it back. "Er gun air mighty nigh like blood kin ter a hunter."

"But we sometimes part even with certain of our kindred when the right man comes along whom we can trust to love, honor and cherish them," laughed the younger man. "And, since I feel that I would be insulting that gun to fire it again after the way *you* fired it, I'm going to honor it by giving it to you."

"Why . . . why, in course I'm mightily obleeged ter ye, doctor; but I jest couldn't think of acceptin' hit from ye," stammered Big Jerry, struggling between the dictates of honor and insatiate desire.

"Don't say another word, my good friend; she's yours and I have several others at home. Only please don't use it in any shooting feuds — if there are such things still in existence nowadays. Since my profession is to save human lives, I mustn't have a part in the taking of them even by proxy, you know." Don's eyes were laughing.

"Yo' hev no cause fer worriment erlong thet line,"

earnestly answered Jerry, as he patted the rifle, cradled in the crook of his arm like a child. "My fightin' day air over, praise ter Gawd. Thar war a time when I war sorter proud of ther notch thet's cut in the stock er my fust gun; but now . . . wall, I'd give a good deal ef 'twarn't thar. I figgers, nowerdays, thet hit haint the Lord's purpose thet humans should spill each other's blood, leastwise onless thar's somethin' bigger et stake then spite er revengement."

"Tell him erbout the shootin' matches at the County Fairs whar yo' used allus ter bear erway the prize, grandpap," interposed Smiles hurriedly, with the obvious design of changing the current of the old man's thoughts.

The latter seated himself on the rock, his face lighting with reminiscence, as he complied, with the words, "Wall, ef I does say hit, thar warn't many in Kentuck er West Virginny could handle a shootin' iron with Big Jerry in them days, an', come County Fair time, I mostwise allus kerried off the money prize an' the wreath give by ther queen. 'Twarn't fancy shootin', like they hes on the stage yo' war erspeakin of, p'raps, but hit took a stiddy hand an' a clar eye ter do the trick. Gener'lly the spo't ended with the pick er the rifle shooters a-trying ter cut down ten weighted strings et a hundred paces, an' more times then once I done hit in as many shots."

Then, as though somewhat ashamed at the boastfulness in his words, he added hastily, "But I take no credit fer thet Gawd give me the skill ter do hit, an' I might hev used hit ter better purpose then ofttimes I did, fer I was overproud er my skill.

"I shor' thanks ye fer this hyar rifle-gun, an', come Thanksgiving time, I hopes ter send ye a wild turkey bird killed by hit."

"If you do that I shall be more than repaid," responded Donald. "Well, good friends of mine, I must be on my way; but don't think that you have seen the last of me. I've found the ideal spot in which to spend a vacation, and next summer I'll be back here again, D. V."

"What's 'D. V.'?" asked the girl, curiously.

"It stands for *Deo Volente*—Latin words which mean, 'God willing.'"

"I hopes thet yo' *does* come back, an' we-all will be here ter welcome ye, D. V." said Rose; then added, shyly, "I hev a gift fer yo' ter take back home ter leetle Muriel, ef yo're willin'. Hit's in the cabin, an', ef yo'll wait, I'll run an' git hit fer ye."

"Of course I'll be glad to take it to her, my child, and I know that she'll be delighted both with it and the stories I shall tell her about Smiles. But wait, I will go with you, for there is one thing more I want to do before I leave, if you can find me a piece of string."

With a question in her wide-eyed glance, Rose led him back to the little mountain homestead and, as soon as they were inside, hurried to produce the desired article.

"Now then, hold up your arms," commanded Donald lightly.

Rose obeyed, and, slipping the string about her yielding waist, he drew it taut and tied a knot to mark the resultant measurement. Following the same procedure, he took the circumference of her chest, the length of her arm, and from her neck to a few inches above her slender ankle. Suddenly her puzzled expression gave place to one of understanding, and the starry smile broke over her countenance.

"You've *guessed*," cried Donald with feigned disappointment.

"Ef hit's a secret, I won't even whisper hit ter no one," the child responded gayly.

"Good. It *is* a secret, but not a dark one."

"I reckon thet hit's all white," she gurgled. "An' now I hev a secret fer *yo'* ter keep — leastwise till ye gits ter the city. Yo' promise, too?"

"I solemnly swear," said Don, and, breaking away, the girl ran into her own room and bashfully brought out a paper bundle through the top folds of which protruded the twisted reed handle of a basket, somewhat similar to the one of her own manufacture which he had given her. "This hyar basket's fer the little girl; but, inside hit's something fer yo' ter remember leetle Rose by. Also thar's a writin', askin' ye ter do something fer me an' ef yo' kin do hit I will shor' be mightily obleeged ter ye."

"I can't guess what on earth it is, but you may

be sure that I will do it if it can be done," he answered earnestly. "Good-by, Smiles. Even without your gift as a reminder I shouldn't have forgotten you, and I shall not think of the Cumberlands without seeing your dear little face."

Donald took both her small hands in his big ones, and, yielding to a sudden impulse, bent down and drew her towards him. For just an instant she held back slightly, and the color swiftly mantled her cheeks. Then, as he was on the point of releasing her, a little ashamed of his intention, she freed her hands and, flinging them about his neck, kissed him warmly again.

With the fresh, childlike pressure of her young lips on his, Donald went hurriedly out, and, after a last hearty handclasp from Big Jerry, turned towards the woods, an unaccustomed song in his heart.

CHAPTER VI

AN UNACCEPTED CHALLENGE

"I WANTS ter hev speech with ye, stranger."

The words, spoken in a harsh voice, fell gratingly on Donald's ears, and brought to an abrupt end the happy thoughts with which his mind was occupied. He stopped, forcing the growling Mike behind him, as Judd stepped out from the bushes, squarely across his path.

"I would be glad to stop and talk with you, Judd, but I'm due in Fayville before noon, and have already stayed too long at Big Jerry's."

"Yo' hev," was the prompt and surly reply.

"What the devil do you mean by that?" snapped Donald, with rising ire.

"What I says, goes," was the reply. "This hyar place air a powerful good one fer yo' ter keep erway from, stranger."

"Indeed? Well, you don't own it."

The younger man's color heightened, and his lean jaws clamped together.

"I warns ye fair," he said, after a brief pause.

"And I don't accept such a warning from any one," shot back Donald, momentarily growing more angry. "It's no business of yours, whether I go or stay."

"I makes hit my business," replied the other sullenly. "Big Jerry air growin' old an' foolish, I reckon; but I seen what I seen, an' thar haint no city man ergoin' ter come up hyar an' make trouble fer a gal uv our'n."

"Judd, it's you who are the fool. I don't admit your right to discuss this, or any matter, with me, but Rose is nothing to me but a very good friend. Besides, she's only a child."

"She's nigh onter old ernough ter wed," was the uncompromising answer. "An' ef she haint nothin' ter ye, the more shame on ye fer tryin' ter make her love ye, an' mayhaps break her heart."

"But I haven't tried to make her love me," broke in Donald impatiently.

"Then fer what did yo' put yer arms erbout her an' kiss her, like I seen ye through the winder awhile back, I wants ter know?" demanded the other, as he hastily frustrated Donald's attempt to step by him.

The man felt his own face flush hotly, and was angry over this visible display of feeling.

"I tell you she's only a child. I kissed her as I would any little girl of whom I was fond."

"Yo' love her, an' yo' haint the man ter say hit."

"Very well, then. Supposing I admit that I love her, what is it to you?" replied Donald, with a flash of heat.

"I loves her, too. I've loved her since she come ter these hyar mountains, a leetle baby; an' I don't calkerlate ter hev yo', er any city man, make a plaything uv her. Hit's man ter man, now. Air yo', er haint yo', agoin' ter leave hyar, an' keep erway?"

"As I told you before, it's none of your business," replied Don shortly.

"An' es I told ye before, hit air. Now I tells ye thet yo' haint a-comin' back."

"That . . . remains to be seen," Donald answered wrathfully as he stepped past Judd, this time unimpeded.

He had not gone more than a score of swinging strides, keeping the bristling dog close beside him, when he heard the staccato crack of a rifle, and simultaneously the high-pitched whine of a bullet past his head.

Once before, in the Maine woods, he had been an unwilling target, on that occasion for an overanxious deer hunter. Then he had sprung up, waving his arms and shouting a warning, but now instinct told him that the opposite procedure was the proper one, and he threw himself precipitately into the enveloping rhododendrons. As he did so, from the path above him came a derisive laugh which set his blood boiling.

It awakened in Donald all the blind, fighting spirit which, in gridiron days, had driven him with clinched teeth into the thick of the battering mêlée. He sprang into a crouching posture, face turned toward the taunting sound, every muscle taut, every nerve tingling, and with but one thought surging through his brain — the desire to charge back and attack Judd, barehanded.

Slowly the red demons of primitive passion vanished before the returning light of wisdom, born of maturity and the restraining power of civilization. He quickly realized that he had no right to make a fool of himself for the sake of such a cause, and in such a childish manner. His duty was paramount to the satisfaction of an atavistic impulse, and, placing a strong mental grasp upon his nerves, which cried for drastic action, Donald turned downward into the footpath again, and broke into a run.

Haste was doubly essential, for little time remained before the hour for the departure of his train, and, even in Virginia, it *might* leave according to schedule. As he crashed impetuously through a bush whose branches blocked the path, he heard again the laughter from above him and caught a new note therein — that of exultation.

Donald stifled an oath, while an additional reason for returning to the mountain burned its way into his heart.

. . . .

On the path above, Judd deliberately blew the fouling smoke from his rifle barrel, turned about, and, with a satisfied smile mingling with the expression of hate on his lips, climbed back towards Jerry's cabin.

In its doorway stood Rose. The happy flush still

lingered delicately on her cheeks, and her limpid eyes were full of a soft, dreamy light.

"What war yo' ershootin' at, Judd?" she cried, as the man came into view, carelessly swinging his long weapon.

"Et a pole-cat," was his brief reply, as he removed his broad straw hat and sank with the unconscious grace of a wild animal onto the stoop at her feet.

Neither broke the silence for several minutes, but the man scarcely took his burning gaze from the child's lovely face. At length she sighed ever so gently, and, seating herself beside him, dropped her firm chin into her cupped hands.

"Smiles," began Judd, with all the harshness gone from his voice, "I don't enjoy fer ter hear yo' sigh thet erway, er ter see ther fur-off look in yo'r purty eyes, 'cause I fears thet hit means thar's some one else then me in yo'r heart."

Instantly she sat up straight, and turned her eyes, full of surprise, upon him. "Why, Juddy!" she said.

"Ef hit's thet doctor man, I likes hit least uv all, Smiles," the man continued, speaking bitterly. "He haint come fur no good, leetle gal, an' I don't want fer yo' ter think on him."

"I reckon I thinks on whom I likes," she responded briefly.

"Don't go fer ter git angry with me, Rose gal. Hit aint thet I wants ter be selfish er onreasonable, but . . ." Judd stopped. Words of passionate love trembled on his lips, but were held there by a barrier of inherited reticence in matters of the heart. Iron reserve and laconic speech were essentially typical of his breed; but, at length, the eager utterances strained against the fetter of his will, and broke them.

"I kaint speak as I desires to, Smiles. I fears I kaint make ye understand what's in my heart; but I've keered mightily fer ye, dear, ever since yo' war a smilin' leetle baby gal, an' now . . . now yo'r most a woman grown, an' I love ye, want ye more come each new day an' each new night. Thar haint one ef them passes but thet I make excuse fer ter see ye, an' jest ther sight o' yo'r sweet face somehow kindles a light inside me that burns, 'thout scarcely dimmin', till I sees ye agin. Thet's ther reason I said what I done, a moment back.

"I jest kaint bear fer ter think uv yo' lovin' some one else then me. I . . . I keers so much thet I believes I'd rather see ye dead then thet, Rose gal."

Fairly trembling with the sweep of his unloosed emotion, the reserved, strong-willed man paused, and, as the girl stood up hastily, she was trembling, too.

"Why, Juddy," she cried softly, distress in her voice, "I didn't rightly understand thet yo' felt thet erway. I likes ye, in course, but I'm only a leetle gal, an' I haint keerin' fer any one . . . thet erway. I . . . I don't enjoy fer ter hyar yo' say sech words ter me now, Juddy."

"I reckon yo'r right, an' I shouldn't hev told ye

yet, Rose," answered the man, almost humbly. "I kin bide my time, but I wants ye ter know thet I feels es I does. I'm a-goin' ter keep right on lovin' ye more an' more, and, when yo'r older, I plans ter ask ye ter marry with me."

"I likes ye . . . indeed I likes ye, Judd, but . . . oh, please don't ever go fer ter do that. I kaint never marry ye, Judd."

The man stiffened, and his face grew black again. "I believes thet yo' air in love with thet doctor man, atter all," he shot out.

"I haint neither," cried the girl, angrily stamping her bare foot, "I does love him, but I haint *in* love with nobody, 'ceptin' grandpap."

"Yo' submitted ter his takin' ye in his arms an' kissin' ye," burst out the mountaineer.

"Judd Amos, yo'r a mean, spyin' sneak, an' I hates ye!" stormed Rose, while her eyes filled with angry tears.

"I didn't go fer ter spy on ye, Smiles," he protested, "I seen ye by chance. But, whether yo' love him er not, yo' might jest as well fergit him. He keered fer ye jest because yo' air er purty mountain flower, an' he haint never ercomin' back hyar ergin."

"He air, too," contradicted the girl rebelliously. "He air ercomin' back an' he's promised ter help me git edercation."

Judd laughed shortly.

"I warned him fair ter keep erway, an' p'inted my warnin' with a rifle ball."

Rose's eyes widened in horror.

"Yo' . . . yo' means yo' shot him, Judd?" she whispered, with both hands pressed to her breast.

"Shot him? No. I didn't aim fer ter hurt him, an' 'twarn't in nowise necessary. I jest put a bullet past his head an' he run like a skeered rabbit."

"Taint so. He never run from no one," she cried staunchly.

"Wall, hit shor' appeared like hit ter me," was the gloating answer.

Feminine instinct gave Rose an intuitive insight into the real reasons which underlay Donald's apparent flight; but pride sealed her lips, just as she was on the point of explaining triumphantly that the doctor had been called back home that day, and that it was the following summer when he would return.

"Juddy," she said gently, after a moment, "yo' hed no reason fer doin' what yo' done. Hit war mighty wrong, but I fergives ye. I wants ter still be friends with ye. I wants ye ter help me, Juddy."

The last words were breathed softly, and the naïve appeal in her voice brought the hostile man quickly back to submissive and worshipful fealty.

"Yo' know thet I'd do enything in the world fer ye, Smiles," he answered simply.

"I believes thet yo' *think* yo' would, Judd, but I wonders ef, deep in yo'r heart, yo' really keers ernough fer me ter . . . I kaint scarcely explain what I means. I reckon I air powerful ignerrant in speecherfyin'."

"I don't rightly know what yo' means, Smiles, but I give ye my promise ter do whatsoever yo' wants, ef hit takes my life," he declared earnestly, his former selfish desire to bend her will into compliance with his own for the moment yielding to his blind eagerness to prove his love.

Youthful and unsophisticated in worldly wiles as she was, the eternal feminine in Rose sensed her victory and power, and, still maintaining her half commanding, half tenderly appealing tone, she outlined her plan, for the accomplishment of which his aid was all essential.

Judd protested, pleaded and stormed — all to no avail. He felt himself like a man caught in a snare of his own weaving — a snare strengthened by fair, yet unbreakable, silken threads added by the child.

Finally, miserable at heart, he yielded, and departed with his hand tingling from the impulsive affectionate pressure of Smiles' fingers upon it. But, as the conscious thrill which it caused in his being lessened, his thoughts became immersed in gloom, through which no encouraging light made its way. He realized that he had lost the first battle for her heart, and the loss brought closer the dark spectre of ultimate defeat.

CHAPTER VII

"SMILES'" GIFT: AND THE "WRITING"

"Now, my boy, let us hear an account of your trip. Did you enjoy it, and find anything of especial interest in the mountains of the feud country?"

The doctor's father lighted his after-dinner cigar, and leaned back with the indolent satisfaction which a man ripe in useful years may feel when surrounded by his family. Since the death of his wife, he and his children had been more inseparably attached one to another than ever, and each drew a full measure of happiness from these all-too-infrequent reunions, when Donald could be with them. Even little Muriel was not left out of the group, for she had been granted the exceptional privilege of sitting up an extra hour, and listening to the wonderful hunting tales told by her beloved Uncle Don, upon whose lap she was now contentedly curled. Her mother and father sat near by.

"Yes, to both questions," responded Donald.

"Did you shoot any bears?" queried his little niece, expectantly.

"No bears this trip, although I almost scalded to death a bare-legged little girl," was the reply. And with Rose thus made the central figure of his recital at the very outset, Donald proceeded to tell of his experiences and new friendships; but consciously refrained from mentioning the unpleasant incident with which his trip ended, and Smiles' parting embrace.

His faithful reproduction of the soft mountain dialect brought frequent smiles from his listeners, and filled the child with delighted amusement.

"I just love Smiles," she cried, as he finished his story.

"Indeed, so does every one who knows her. *You* do, don't you, Mike?" added Donald, and the dog beat a tattoo on the rug with his stumpy tail.

"Witchery," laughed his father. "Even your clumsy description has strangely stirred my youthful blood, and 'I longs fer ter see this hyar wonderful child dryad of ther primeval forest.' If you ever go back there, you had better wear magic armor as protection against that illusive smile which seems to have cast a spell of enchantment over your civilized senses."

"Pshaw, you needn't be concerned about my feelings for her. She's no siren, but a very real little person. I'll admit that she's amazingly attractive; but she's merely a child."

"Children grow up," teased his sister.

"I'm aware of that natural phenomenon," answered Donald, somewhat curtly. "But . . . Great Scott, can't I describe a fifteen—no, sixteen-year-old little savage, without all you people imagining that I'm going to be such a fool as to fall in love with her?"

"Sometimes it isn't what one says, but the way he says it, that incriminates," put in his brother-in-law, adding his voice to the general baiting which had apparently disclosed a tender spot.

"Hang it all, I believe that I'll go back and ask Smiles to marry me, if only to put an end to your teasing," cried Don with a laugh not entirely natural. "At least I might perhaps succeed in frustrating *your* obvious designs, Ethel. Oh, I'm not blind!"

"I've almost concluded that you *are* — or hopeless," answered his sister. "However, I'm perfectly willing to admit that I would like to see you married to Marion Treville — she's my closest friend, and would certainly make you a perfect wife."

"Too perfect, by far. Can you imagine me hitched with that proud and classic beauty? I should go mad."

"But I want my pretty basket that little Smiles made for me," broke in Muriel, to whom the present remarks held no interest, and who emphasized her demand by seizing his cheeks.

"To be sure you do, and I want to see my present, too. I'll bring them right down."

Not at all ill pleased at this opportunity to escape from his family's jesting, which, for some indefinable reason, aroused his belligerency, Donald jumped up hastily and departed for the sanctuary of his bedroom, to get the bulky bundle with its mysterious enclosure. Minutes slipped by, and he failed to return to the group downstairs.

At last his absorption was broken into by the arrival of Muriel, whose entrance into the room, with the traces of tears on her cheeks, brought him back to the present with a remorseful start.

"You didn't come down, an' you *didn't* come down, Uncle Don, an' now mother says it's bedtime, an' I want Smiles' basket to take with me."

"Why, I'm terribly sorry that I've been so long, sweetheart-mine. I stopped to read the letter she wrote to me, and, I'm ashamed to say, forgot that you were waiting for me. But see, here's your present. Little Rose made it all herself for you. Isn't it pretty?"

With a cry of delight the child gathered the simple basket into her chubby arms and bent her head over it. "Oh, don't it smell sweet, Uncle Don. Does Smiles smell like that?"

"Perhaps not exactly," he replied, chuckling.

"Now please show me what she sent to you. Was it a basket, too?"

"No, not a basket. It's a very great secret; but, if you'll promise not to tell a soul, no matter how they tease, I'll show it to you."

"Cross my heart, an' hope to die," said the child earnestly, making across her pinafore the mystic sign, so potent to the childish mind.

Donald opened a drawer in the chiffonier and

took out a small and obviously cheap glazed blue-and-white vase. The child took it wonderingly and, removing the cover, sniffed audibly and deeply.

"My. *This* smells like Rose," she said with conviction.

"You're right, it does, indeed, because it *is* roses — dried wild rose petals which she gathered and preserved herself. I saw it in her little cabin, and know that it was her most precious possession, yet she gave it to 'Uncle Don' as a keepsake, so that he might remember her whenever he smells of it."

"Wasn't she just *too* sweet to do that. My, how I would like to see her, Uncle Don."

"Well, perhaps you may, some day."

The sentence echoed out of the past, carrying his recollection back to the night when he had heedlessly spoken the identical words to Smiles, and there entered his mind the sudden realization of what amazing potentialities for good or evil often lie hidden in the simplest utterances.

The sound of his sister's light tread in the hallway caused Donald to return his homely gift to its hiding place hurriedly, and little Muriel, with roguishly twinkling eyes, imitated his action as he laid his finger on his lips as a seal of secrecy.

"Well, you *two* kids," laughed Ethel, as she caught sight of the picture framed by the doorway.

"I'm glad that I haven't wholly forgotten how to be one," answered her brother, as he kissed first his little niece, and then the basket which she held up with the demand that it be paid similar homage, and bade them good-night.

Rejoining the diminished group in the living-room, Donald was preoccupiedly silent, until his father asked,

"Well, have you read your little friend's 'writing'? I confess to a mild curiosity as to what sort of a letter a girl like her would write, and what sort of a request she would be likely to make of you."

Don drew from his pocket the letter, painfully scrawled on cheap, and not overclean paper, and handed it over. Adjusting his eye-glasses the older man read aloud: —

"'Dear Dr. Mac,

Truly I want to be a nurse like you told me about some day.'

"Well," commented the reader, "at least she starts right off with the business in hand, without any palavering.

"'And I reckon that even a little mountain girl like me can be one if she wishes hard enough and works hard, too.'.

"Why," he interpolated again, "there doesn't seem to be any evidence of your weirdly wonderful spelling and grammar here."

"Go on," answered Donald, smiling slightly.

"'I reckon it will take me a long, long time to get education and earn all that money, but I can do it, Dr. Mac. I am sure I can do it. I told my grandfather all that I mean to do, and he won't try to stop me none. Of course he does not want for me to go away from him, but I explained that I *had* to, and of course that made it all right.

When you was telling us what those nurses done, something seemed like it went jump inside my heart, and straightways I know that the dear Lord meant for me to do it, too. I read a story once about a girl in france named Jone of Ark and I reckon I felt like she done when she see the angel.

I know I can do it, Dr. Mac, if you will help me a little bit like you promised. Most of all I figures I need a heap of book learning, and it is books I wants for you to get me. You know the books I need to have, Dr. Mac., and in this letter I am going to put $10.

It is an awful lot of money; but I reckon books cost a good deal, and you can bring me the change next summer, for I have not got no use for money here. Don't be afeared. It is my own money. It was in my father's pocket among the camp things granddaddy found, and there was some more. Grandfather, he kept it for me until I was a big girl and now I am keeping it for a rainy day, like the copy book says, although I don't think money would be much use to keep off the rain.

Their is a preacher man who lives on our mountain winters, when he can not travel about none, and I know I can get him to help me learn if I help his wife with her work, and I can read pretty well now and write pretty well when I have a spelling book to study the words out of, although I have to go sorter slow, for they do not allus spell words like they sound, and sometimes I cannot find them at all. I guess my book is not a very good one.

I reckon it will take me a long while to earn more than $300; but I am going to work awful hard, making baskets and other things, and I am going to get Judd Amos, our naybor, to sell them for me at the village store, for he goes down their trading every week, and he will do anything I ask him, like I told you.

This is a pretty long letter and it has taken me all the evening to right. I hope that you can read it. Well, I guess that is all now from your loveing little friend.

I most forgot to say please give my love to Mike.'

ROSE WEBB.

"Well, I've got to admit that I have seen many a letter, written by a grown-up, that fell a long ways short of that one in clarity of thought and in accomplishment of a definite object," said Mr. MacDonald, as he handed it back. "Do you suppose that her eagerness to become a nurse is just a passing childish whim, or has she really got sand enough to put her almost impossible plan through?"

"Clairvoyancy was not included either in the Harvard or Medical School curriculum," responded Donald, with a shrug.

"Meaning that the things of the future are in the laps of the gods. Of course, but I was merely asking for your personal opinion. I'm not jesting now; that letter really aroused my interest in the child."

"Well, then, I believe that Smiles really possesses the strength of purpose to go through with even so difficult a task as she has set for herself. Remember, she comes of city stock, and hasn't the blood of those unprogressive mountaineers in her veins."

"And you? Are you going to help her as she asks? What about your promise to Big Jerry?"

"I lived up to both the spirit and letter of that, when I tried to explain to the child the almost unsurmountable difficulties which lay between her and the accomplishment of her dream. Besides, I know that she has told the truth in her letter, and has somehow managed actually to win over the old man. I can't help feeling mighty sorry for him, if the foster birdling is really going to fly away from his nest after he has reared and loved her so tenderly, but, after all, it is only the history of the human race. Still, I can't blame him if he looks on me as a serpent who stole into his simple Eden, carrying the apple of discontent."

"There have been, of course, plenty of cases similar to this, where the adventurer's spirit was really big enough and the vision strong enough to carry him or her through to victory," mused Donald's father. "Such a one was the immortal Abe Lincoln, who came from just such surroundings. But the task is doubly hard for a young girl, and the experiment of thus breaking away from the ties and traditions of many years, and seeking a place in a wholly new, wholly dissimilar life, cannot but be fraught with dangers. There, in that simple environment she naturally appealed to you as not only an attractive child, but as a somewhat unusual personality. Tell me, lad, how will, or would, she measure up, if transplanted a few years hence into city life, where the standards of comparison are so utterly different; so much more exacting?"

"Frankly, I don't know," responded Donald. "Since I read her letter I have been asking myself that question, and the answer worries me, since I feel in a way responsible for having opened the gates before her untrained feet. Somehow I cannot disassociate little Rose from her present environment, and, although she certainly *has* an unusual charm for such a child, I must admit that, in part, at least, it was the result of — no, not that, but made more obvious by — her surroundings."

"Well, she has apparently decided to take the moulding of her life into her own hands and, without knowing the quotation, determined to be 'the master of her fate and captain of her soul.' However, a little more education can scarcely hurt her, and, if she succeeds in saving up some money, it will come in handy enough as a 'dot,' in case she marries your friend, Judd Amos, and raises a family of mountain brats."

Donald's reply was unnecessarily positive.

"I'll wager that she'll never do that." And with that the conversation, as far as it concerned Smiles, ended.

. . . .

During purloined hours in the next few days the eminently successful young physician might have been seen engaged in strange errands, which took him into such places as a dressmaker's establishment, and several stores which sold textbooks. It was also a noteworthy fact that the decidedly soiled and crumpled ten-dollar bill, with which he had been commissioned to purchase the means through which education might be acquired, was never taken from the special compartment in his bill folder.

Then the flood of fall practice engulfed him, and gradually the memory of little Smiles faded from his busy mind, although it never quite vanished, and from time to time fresh breezes from the distant Cumberlands fanned it to life like a glowing ember.

CHAPTER VIII

SOME OF SEVERAL EPISTLES

I

COMMONWEALTH AVENUE
BOSTON, MASSACHUSETTS.
September 15, 1912.

Dear little Smiles:

If you had been able to look inside of my heart when I opened your present and read your letter, you would have beheld as many different lights and shadows there as you can see in your own eyes when you look in the glass over your bureau.

The sight of that little jar, and the scent of the spiced rose-petals, brought you so near to me that I thought I could almost see you by just closing my eyes — which may seem to you a funny way of "seeing" a person. It made me very happy.

The letter, too, pleased me a great deal; but I must tell you that it also troubled me. That is when the shadow fell on my thoughts of you.

The reason? I will tell it to you, because I feel that I should, although please do not think that I want to croak like an old black crow in one of your pine trees.

If you have really set your whole heart upon becoming a nurse when you grow up, and your granddaddy has consented, it is not for me to say that you cannot do it. But I *do* know the path which you must travel. I know that it is much steeper, much more rocky and full of briary bushes than any one your feet have ever climbed on your mountain, and you will have to keep a very brave little heart inside you, if you hope to reach the summit. And then, if you succeed, instead of finding a fairy castle filled with all sorts of pleasant things, you will only discover another long and weary road which must be traveled until your tired little body, and heart, made heavy by the sufferings of little children, long for the quiet restfulness of your dear old mountain home.

Am I still trying to discourage you? I suppose that I am, for, you see, *I* can look back along that road which lies *before* you, and I can remember the rocks I had to climb over, and the bushes I had to struggle through, and yet I know that it was far easier for me than it will be for you.

You have read parables in the Bible. Well, I am preaching a modern parable. "Book learning" is a sword and buckler — or perhaps it would be better to say that it is a suit of strong hunting clothes and thick leather knee-boots, and I was pretty well clad like that when I started my trip, while you are dressed only in thin gingham, with your legs and feet bare — as I first saw you. Please shut your eyes, dear child, and try to see the parable picture I have drawn for you.

Have you done it? The picture is not as pretty as the one I painted the night I told about how fine it was to be a nurse, is it? But it is more nearly true to life.

Now, think hard before you make up your mind as to whether or not you really mean to go ahead, for — after all, little Smiles — each boy and girl has soon to decide, all alone, what he or she is going to do with that strange thing which we call life.

If your courage is really as strong as that of the wonderful Joan of Arc, I, too, believe that you can succeed and make your dream come true, and of course I will help you, gladly — in every way that I can.

Now I am all through preaching. It is out of my line, and I promise not to do it again. Within a few days you will, I hope, get a boxful of the books which I have sent you as you asked me. Most of them are just what you wanted — school books — but on my own hook I added one or two not strictly for study — like plums in a dry bread pudding. And, of course, there is something else in the box and *I* guess that *you* can guess what it is.

This, little Smiles, is the longest letter I ever wrote to anybody, I think. Don't you feel proud? It must end now, however; but not before I ask you to give my best regards to your kind granddaddy.

Don't let the cold winter that is coming, chill your warm affection for

Your sincere friend,
DONALD MACDONALD.

P. S. I told Mike what you wrote to him, and he wig-wagged a message of love back to you with his tail.

II

BIG JERRY'S CABIN
IN WEBB'S GAP, VIRGINIA.
Sep't. 20, 1912.

Dear Doctor Mac:

Oh, dear doctor, can you ever forgive me for waiting two whole days before I wrote you back to thank you with all my heart for the many wonderful things which came in that box? It was like a fairy's treasure chest. And most of all I am obliged for that letter you wrote me. It was the first letter I ever got from any one and I shall keep it as long as I live. I think, of all the things I got, I like that the best. Those others you could *buy*, but you had to *make* that yourself, and it seemed like I could almost hear you talking the words in your strong voice, like the sound of the falls in the Swift River.

When I looked inside that box I could not make up my mind what I liked best. The many books kind of scared me when I opened them and remembered I had got to know all that much; but the book of beautiful poetry I just love. I have read all of the poetrys and know some of them to speak already.

Then there is that nurse's dress. O how I love it, and how I wish for you to see me in it. I plans to put it on a little while everyday and pretend that I am a real nurse *like I am going to be.* I done it yesterday, and somehow when I shet my eyes and run my hands over its crackely stiff whiteness, it seemed to me that the room was full of sweet little babies for me to take keer of.

And now, doctor, I must tell you that I done what you said for me to do. I closed my eyes up tight like granddaddy does when I say prayers, and I saw little Smiles acliming that rough path, and walking along that rough road you wrote about, but by the side of that long road I kept aseeing beautiful little flowers what were fading and drooping and calling out in tiny voices like baby chickens for Rose to keer for them. So doctor, the picture did not scare me none.

The Lord give Joan of Arc (I know how to spell it now) a silver armor to protect her, and I reckon the white nurse's dress that you give me is my armor.

Now doctor I must tell you about little Lou and the wonderful doll you sent to her. She was so funny when I give it to her that I got a chreek in my side laughing. First thing, she held it up tight against her and when it went Ma-a-a- like a calf, she dropped it quick and run and hide under the bed. But pretty soon she crep out again and I showed her how to make it shut its eyes.

Then she jumped around and cried. 'O Smiles, hit *kaint* do them things but hit *does* do them.' Well, pretty soon, Judd Amos, her brother, come in and, when he saw it in Lou's arms, his face got as black as a storm cloud and he went for to take it away from her.

I just stepped in front of him, and said, 'Judd Amos, if you ever go for to take that doll baby away from her, or even *touch* it, I won't never speak to you again.'

He was powerful mad with me, but he seen that I meant like I said, so Lou can keep her doll. And what do you think she has named it? She has named it Mike. Even Judd had to laugh a little when she said that was the doll baby's name.

I am making baskets as fast as ever I can and Judd is going to take them to the store at Fayville for me. I went down with him and seen the store-keeper man myself last week, and he promised me to buy all that he can from me.

Granddaddy shoots with your rifle gun most every day. He can hit a string like he used to, but he would not shoot a apple off my head like a man did in the book that had about Joan of Arc in it, although I wanted him to.

I have ritten a piece of poetry like Mr. Eugene Fields did, and this is it

The cold may make my lips turn blue,
But it can't freeze my love for you.

Your happy and loving little friend

SMILES.

III

COMMONWEALTH AVENUE
BOSTON, MASSACHUSETTS.
October 24, 1912.

Proprietor of the General Store,
Fayville, —— County,
West Virginia.
Dear Sir:

I am informed that you are occasionally purchasing, through one Judd Amos, of Webb's Gap, sweetgrass baskets made by a little mountain girl of that settlement.

I am interested in her work, and herewith enclose a money order in the sum of ten dollars ($10.00) with which I will ask you to purchase at a rate reasonably in advance of the one you are now paying, all the baskets which she sends to you. You may express them to my address each month, and I will forward further funds upon request.

Please do not mention my name in connection with this transaction; but, if any questions are asked, merely say that you have obtained a city market for them.

Very truly yours,
(DR.) DONALD MACDONALD.

IV

WEBB'S GAP. VIR.
November 24, 1912.

Dear Dr. McDonald:

How many letters do you guess I have written to you so far this month? 24. Yes, I have written you a long letter every day, telling you all the things I did, and thought, but of course I did not mail them, for I knew that you would get tired of reading them.

But this one I am going to send, for grandfather has asked me to let you know that he has shot that wild turkey bird for your Thanksgiving — which is Thursday — and has sent it to you by express package from Fayville. I was with him when he did it.

Evenings come right early now and we went into the woods just before sun down. It was right beautiful, and I wished that you could have been with us. I will try and tell you what I saw like I do in my daily letters that my teacher says are practice themes. (I could not have spelled that to save my life a month ago.)

Well, except for the big pine trees which never seem to change, just like granddaddy, all the tall forest people and the half grown-up children-bushes, had put on bright new dresses in honor of Thanksgiving time. They were red, made of many colored patches like Bible Joseph's coat, — yellow green and brown, some as bright as God could paint the colors, some soft, like they had been washed and washed.

Granddaddy thought it was beautiful too — although he called it "purty." But he did not like the brown grass and fallen pine needles, and called the marsh near the river an ugly mudflat; but *I* thought it was beautiful, for that oozy mud was deep purple (the reverend told me the word), and the little pools of water were all gold. Those are the colors that kings dress in, yet that old mudflat wore them, too.

Well, finally, when it began to grow dusk, we found a wild turkey bird roosting on a tree limb and granddaddy said, 'Hush, I aims ter shoot hit right thru ther head.' When you get it look where the bullet went.

Now perhaps you would like to hear about what I have been doing. Well, I have been doing many things, but most of all I have been studying.

The minister, whose name is Reverand John Talmadge, came back to our mountain when it began to get cold, for he is in not very good health and can't go about much, although he sits out doors most of the time.

He is my very good friend, and I have found out a lot about him. One thing is that he went to college like you did, and he knows a great deal more than there is in all those books, even. So you see he can help me a good deal. He is even going to teach me some Latin, *D. V.* I think that God must have sent him to our mountain.

Every day I study the books you sent, first with him and then at home, and I am getting along so nice that last week, when the teacher in our little school was away, they let me be the teacher.

And who do you think was one of my pupils? It was Judd Amos. He has bought some books and is learning, too. I reckon he does not want a girl to be smarter than he is at book learning, which he says is nonsense for girls. But I know that it is not nonsense. Why, I can travel in far-off lands and see things that I did not even know *were*, by just reading books, and the reverend has lent me some to read.

Then I am still making my baskets, and what do you think? The storeman is buying all I can send him, and paying me more than he used to for them! He says that city folks like to buy them for they smell so sweet and like the woods. I am saving all my money and, with what I had, have nearly $75 already, and, by next summer, will have over $100. Isn't that wonderful? Granddaddy pays me 10 cents a week for keeping house for him, too. Isn't he good?

Don't you think I ought to be a very happy little girl? Well, I am, and I guess my face is getting all out of shape, I find so many things to smile about.

Your affectionate friend,

Rose.

P. S. Please give my love and a turkey drumstick to Mike.

V

Commonwealth Avenue
Boston, Massachusetts.
December 23, 1912.

Dear little Smiles:

Although I am very busy, for the Winter has given colds to many little folks here, I can not let Christmastide go by without writing a letter to you, little forest friend. It was very dear of you to send me that basket of holly, which I found waiting for me when I returned, tired out, last night.

Its dark green leaves and bright red berries looked up at me when I undid it, almost as though they were your personal messengers and were trying eagerly to say, "Smiles wishes you a Merry Christmas through us." The basket was indeed a work of art, but to me it seemed even more than that — a labor of love.

I could almost imagine you tramping through the snow-covered mountain woods and gathering the holiday berries, and the picture which my mind painted was so attractive that I heartily wished I might have been there, too.

I am delighted with the accounts of the progress you are making in your studies, and your all-too-infrequent letters themselves tell the story. I'm afraid that I shall not know you next summer. Write me just as often as you feel like doing so, dear, and if I do not always reply you may know that it is only because I am so very busy.

Now I have two pieces of news to tell you. I am sure that you will be very much pleased with one of them and I hope will be with both.

First, Muriel's mother had a wonderful present just a little ahead of Christmas day — not from Santa Claus, but from Old Father Stork. It is a fine baby boy, whose eyes are almost the color of yours, and his name is to be

"Donald MacDonald Thayer." I suppose I have now got to be extra good in order to set my namesake the right example.

Knowing how dear all little ones are to your heart, I am sure that you will be almost as pleased as we are over this happy event, and I can almost see your sweet face light up with its wonderful smile as you read this.

Second, I am engaged to be married some day, if I can ever find time. *Her* name is Marion Treville and she is very good and kind, and every one thinks she is very beautiful, too.

I hope that you have by this time received the little friendship box which I sent to you and your grandfather. The dress is a present from Muriel, who loves your basket more than any of her toys, and continually speaks of you as her "dear friend Smiles"; the hair ribbon is from Mike and the book from

Your sincere friend,
DONALD MACDONALD.

VI

WEBB'S GAP
January 7, 1913.

Dear Dr. MacDonald:

When I tell you that there has been a great deal of trouble here, you will understand why I have not written you long before this, to thank you for those lovely Christmas presents.

Grandfather was delighted with his tobacco, although he has not smoked it yet, and all my gifts made me very happy. The dress dear little Muriel sent me is so lovely that I don't believe I shall ever dare to wear it, especially as, when grandfather saw me in it, he looked so sorrowful as he said, 'Hit's powerful purty, but hit haint my Smiles no more,' that he almost made me cry. I wonder if I can really ever leave him? He needs me very much now.

Oh, I was so happy for all of you when I read about Muriel having a dear little baby brother. I sat right down and wrote a verse. The reverend helped me with some of the words, but still I'm afraid that it is not very good and I am afraid you will laugh at it. It is the best I can do now, and I guess I will send it to you in this letter.

Now I must tell you that your friend, my grandfather, has been very sick since Christmas. The doctor from Fayville has been to see him several times and he says the trouble is — I know that you will laugh at me now, but I can only write what it sounds like to me — 'Aunt Jina pecks her wrist.' He has pains in his heart and has to keep very still, which he does not like to do, so I am the nurse and, whenever I feed him, or give him the medicine that the doctor left, I put on my nurse's dress.

Of course I have not been able to go to the reverend's for my lessons, and I have not been able to study much, except when grandfather is asleep; but he — the reverend, I mean — comes to our house as often as he can, and we take turns in reading aloud to grandfather, sometimes from the book you sent me, but most times from the Holy Bible, which he likes best.

The reverend says that it is better than medicine to sooth a troubled heart, and I reckon it must be so, for it almost always puts grandfather to sleep, and the trouble is with his heart, like I told you.

Then, beside that, a little wild mountain flower was born to a neighbor of ours last week. We tried — oh, so hard — to make it live, but the cold was so bitter here that God took pity on it and took it back to his garden in Paradise.

At first I could not help crying, and I came home and tore up the verses that I wrote, but then I remembered what you told me about the Reaper, and I went back to the poor, sorrowful mother and told her. And I remembered what you said about making people smile by smiling myself, so I did that, too.

This is not a very happy letter, but grandfather is getting better every day, and summer will soon be here now. The new year seems to me like the top of a snow covered mountain. When we have climbed over it, it is not long before we can hurry down into the valley where the sun is warm and the flowers bloom.

Your affectionate friend,

ROSE WEBB.

P. S. I am very glad that you are going to be married.

(The Enclosure)

Deep the world with snow was covered,
Cold and barren was the earth,
Low the Christmas angels hovered
As a little babe had birth.

Just a tender little flower,
Dropped upon the world below
Out of God's eternal bower —
Pink as sunrise, white as snow.

But the little blossom stranger,
As its earthly life it starts,
Need fear neither cold nor danger,
For 'tis planted *in our hearts.*

VII

"THAYERHURST"
MANCHESTER-BY-THE-SEA.
August 15, 1913.

My dear little Smiles:

This is going to be a very short letter, and can you guess why? Early next month I am going to run away from my work and everything here, and hurry down to your mountain for two whole weeks of wonderful vacation. So the next time you hear from me the words will come from my lips instead of my pen.

I have been very glad indeed to hear that Big Jerry has been so well this summer, and I am sure that he has many more years of virile health ahead of him. I am keenly looking forward to seeing him cut a string with the new rifle.

The weather has been terribly hot in Boston this month and caused much suffering, but it is quite cool and very pleasant here by the ocean.

Every night that it is possible, I spend here with my sister's family, partly because I love to see my little namesake, even for a moment, partly to escape the city's heat and obtain some really refreshing rest. It makes me almost ashamed sometimes, when I think how comfortable I am, and how uncomfortable are the little children in the crowded city, most of whom have no woods, fields and streams like yours to play in, and many of whom never see anything out of doors except dirty, paved streets which get so hot that they burn the feet, even though the fire engine men frequently send rushing streams of water through them.

But I know that a fighter must always keep in the best possible condition, and we doctors *and nurses* have declared war on an enemy who has killed millions and millions, and never takes a day off.

I wonder how you will like the ocean when you see it. Very much, I am sure, it is so immensely big — like the sky — so beautiful, and more full of ever-changing colors than even your mountains.

They tell me that little Muriel plays beside it all day long on the fine white sand and over the rocks, while baby brother lies near by on a blanket, kicking and gurgling, and holding long, wordless conversations with the white clouds and sea birds high overhead.

This has been a much longer letter than I expected it to be, and now I must chop it off short with just five more words,

Your affectionate friend,
DONALD MACDONALD.

CHAPTER IX

THE HIGH HILLS, AND "GOD'S MAN"

Sun hath sunk in radiant splendor,
  Now the colors fade away
And the moon, with light more tender,
  Sheds its silver on the bay.

Eventide is softly casting
  O'er the earth a magic spell,
And a love-song, everlasting,
  On the night wind seems to swell.

Deeper grow the lengthening shadows,
  Darkening the heaven's blue,
One by one the stars are gleaming,
  Night is nigh, would you were, too.

DONALD hummed the words in his not unmelodious baritone, as he climbed up the forest path down which, twelve months before, he had rushed headlong, in blind anger.

The spell of the high, forest-clad hills, and the new-born night was upon his spirit. Pleasant anticipations filled his heart, and left no room for painful recollection as he hastened over the needle-strewn pathway on which the white radiance of the full moon, shining through the branches, made a tracery of silver and black.

Let men whose minds are governed wholly by

cold commonsense, and whose souls hold no spark of vitalizing imagination, scoff at moon-witchery and lunar madness. Let them declare that the earth's haunting satellite is merely a dead world which cannot even shine with its own light. Magic it *does* wield. And, just as it distorts and magnifies all commonplace, familiar objects, so it twists the thoughts of men; just as it steals away the natural colors from the things of earth, and substitutes for them those of its own conception, so it alters the hues of man's meditation.

The usually exuberant Mike trotted in silence, close to his master's heels, and now and then cast suspicious glances aloft at the tall spectre things which he knew to be trees.

Donald knew that it was rather absurd of him to be toiling up the five-mile mountain path that night, when the next morning would have done just as well; but he had thankfully thrown off the shackles of civilization along with its habiliments. For two free, full weeks he meant to live like a child of the out-of-doors, and to draw a brimming supply of new energy from Mother Nature's never-failing breasts. Every moment was precious.

As he neared the Gap, his winging thoughts flew ahead to Big Jerry's cabin and to the child-woman who had so attracted him a year before. Once more he told himself that she was nothing to him, and that now, especially, he had no right to allow her, child though she were, to hold so large a place in his heart. Yet what chance has reason in competition with moonlight?

The clearing, with the cabin beyond it, came into view. The little house was likewise a victim of the prevailing necromancy, for its rough, hand-split and weatherbeaten shingles were now a shimmering olive-silver.

Mike gave voice to a joyful yelp, and tried to crowd past his owner's legs, for he had seen, or sensed, Rose even before the latter became aware of the presence of their little friend. She was standing, alone, on the outer edge of the tiny stoop, whose darkened doorway formed a black background, against which her figure appeared, cameo-like. The flooding brightness lifted her form and face, seen in profile, into sharp relief, and the shadow which it cast on the grass made her appear the more tall and slender. Grown and subtly altered she undoubtedly was, thought Donald. The girlish curves and litheness had not departed; but they carried a suggestion of approaching maturity. Her wavy hair no longer hung unbound about her face, but was dressed in two braids, one of which had fallen forward across her breast. Shoes and stockings covered her legs; but the simple dress still left her neck and arms bare, and the flesh was robbed of its color and made alabaster, the golden threads stolen from the dark hair and replaced by a silver sheen, so that there was something ethereal, but startlingly beautiful, in the picture.

Holding the violently wriggling Mike in check, one hand on his collar, the other grasping his jaws, Donald stole silently forward until he had passed the corner of the cabin, and his own shadow had crept forward, and laid itself at the girl's feet.

Suddenly she perceived it, and turned with a question in her shadowy eyes. Her lips parted, then curved into the familiar magic smile, as she cried, "Oh, Doctor MacDonald. You've *come*."

Mike twisted free, and, with a mad bound and wiggle, threw himself on the girl, who caught him in her arms. Then, holding him against her, she somehow succeeded in extending one hand, shapely and slender, to meet the man's two eager ones.

"Oh, grandpap," she thrilled through the doorway. "Hurry out hyar. Dr. Mac hes come fer ter see ye."

A sense of vague disappointment possessed Donald as he heard her lapse into the musical, but provincial, dialect; but, seeming to read his thought that the year of study had not been able to alter it, she whispered, "I always talk like I used to, to him, for he likes it best."

"I see, and you're quite right, too," was his low-voiced reply, as he heard the old man's heavy tread crossing the bare floor within.

"Wall, wall, stranger. We air shor'ly powerful pleased fer ter welcome ye ergin," came in Big Jerry's deep and hearty voice, as he emerged from the darkness, and caught Donald's hand in the old, crushing vise.

For a few moments they all chatted happily, and then Jerry said, "Erfore I fergits hit, us wants ye ter stay up hyar this trip. Ther loft-room air yourn, an' leetle Rose hes fixed hit up special fer ye — curtains et ther window, er rag rug on ther floor, an' ther Lawd knows what else."

"Do you really want me to?" cried the newcomer in pleased surprise.

"Of course we really want you," answered the happy girl.

"Then, by Jove, I'll be only too glad to, although I had not thought of such a thing."

"I allows thet yo' kin regard this hyar cabin as yo'r home whenever yo're hyarerbouts, an' we wants fer ye ter feel thet hit *air* home," said the giant with simple courtesy.

"I can't tell you how much that means to me — real hospitality like that," began Donald, hesitatingly. "You know I . . . I haven't any real home and haven't had . . . since mother left us, and my sister was married. Of course," he added hastily, "my rooms are pleasant and comfortable, and all that; but they're only a place to work, sleep and eat in, and there isn't any of that indefinably vital something — a soul, perhaps — which makes a *real* home a sacred spot, no matter how big or how small it may be. I get frightfully lonely there, sometimes."

"I didn't allow thet a man could git lonely in the city," replied Jerry.

"'In the city?' My dear man, one can be *twice* as lonely there as any place I know of. The very life makes for shut-inness, in mind as well as body, and there are thousands and thousands of men, and women, too, there, who know scarcely a soul outside of the very few with whom their daily work brings them in contact; and *they* are mere acquaintances, not friends. They see only the four walls of the rooms in which they work and sleep, and the walled-in streets between the two.

"These very streets seem to me to typify the city's life — so hard, so filled with hurrying, jostling crowds of people, all equally intent upon their own narrow, selfish affairs, people who would think a fellow crazy if he spoke to them pleasantly, as you did to me the first time I saw you. There are thousands who never even lift their eyes to the narrow strips of sky between the tall buildings. *They* — and they only — know what real loneliness is.

"Of course I'm not one of those unfortunates," he added quickly, "for I have many friends, and am making new ones daily; but that is the atmosphere I live in fifty weeks of the year. Do you wonder that it gets on my nerves at times, and that I long to run away from it all and get into the big, open spaces in the warm heart of friendly nature?

"Do you think that I can ever feel lonesome in the forest and fields, with living things always about me which are ready to share themselves with me?"

"I reckon I haint never thought uv thet. This hyar mountain country air's whar I hev lived in contentment all my life, an' I allows thet hit's good ernough fer me ter keep on livin' in, twill I dies."

Rose remained silent, although obviously disturbed by Donald's words; but, before she could voice her thoughts, another figure quietly joined the group — a tall, stooping man, clean shaven, and with an æsthetic countenance seemingly out of its natural environment.

"Why, it's my minister man," cried Rose joyfully. "Wherever did you come from?"

"My wanderings brought me close home, and I could not pass by without calling on my two good friends in Webb's Gap."

"An' we air downright glad fer ter see ye, reverend," answered the host. "This hyar air the doctor man from the city, what leetle Rose hes told ye so much erbout."

Donald already felt drawn to the strange divine, their common interest in the girl acting as a lodestone, and he clasped his hand with friendly pressure. The other returned it less vigorously, but no less sincerely, and Donald experienced a peculiar mesmeric thrill which startled him a little.

"Perhaps I should apologize," began Mr. Talmadge in a low voice, the timbre of which still retained the resonance of early culture. "I came on this happy scene — or at least to the corner of the house — while you were speaking of life in the city, and I could not very well help pausing and listening.

"I know your feelings only too well, Dr. MacDonald. I was born, bred and worked in New York until my health became undermined by just such influences as you mentioned; and I was forced to run away, too, and seek the hills 'whence cometh my help.'"

"And deep in your inner consciousness you don't regret the change, do you?" asked Donald.

"No. Perhaps I am selfish — a shirker — and there are times when the old call to get back where I know that the need is greatest comes like a clarion. But for myself, the disaster — which once seemed like a curse — has turned out to be a blessing, as is so often the case. I have learned a great lesson, doctor."

"What lesson?" queried Rose.

"God's," responded the minister, quietly. "It may seem strange to you, my dear, but, although I was reared in a religious family, went through a great theological school, and was the rector of a city church for ten years, I never fully knew Him until I came here."

"Why, Mr. Talmadge!" gasped the girl in astonishment, while Donald said bluntly, "Do you really believe that you know Him, now?"

"I do. Not, of course, in all the fullness of His

mysterious majesty, but as a friend whose ways are no longer hidden from my eyes."

"Frankly, I wish I might say as much," said the doctor. "I, too, was brought up in a religious household, but small good it did me, for, when I became old enough to think for myself, the glaring errors and inconsistencies in my childhood belief became so apparent that I became hopeless of ever understanding the truth which might lie within that astonishing maze. I quit going to church long ago."

"Doctors are generally regarded as an atheistic lot," smiled the minister.

"That's slander. We may — in the aggregate — be agnostic. . . . I suppose that I am."

"I . . . I don't understand," said Rose in distress, "but I don't like for to hear yo' say that, Dr. Mac."

"It may not be as bad as it sounds, my child," laughed Mr. Talmadge. "An atheist is indeed a terrible person, who doesn't believe in our heavenly Father, but an agnostic is only one who confesses that he doesn't know . . . but may be quite willing to learn."

"Oh, learn . . . I mean teach him, then," she said earnestly. "You are God's man and know everything about Him, Mr. Talmadge."

"Indeed I don't — far from it, and I imagine that your friend doesn't want to hear a sermon on the mount."

"*I* do," she cried, "there's lot of things I want

to hear about, but I've always been afraid to ask you, till now."

Rather gruffly Donald added his word, "I hope that I am broad-minded enough not only to receive, but to welcome, any light on a subject which is, I imagine, the most vitally important one in life."

"Well, then, suppose we hold a little spiritual clinic for our Rose's benefit primarily, remembering that where two or three are gathered together in His name, God will be with them. And, after all, what time could be more fitting than this silent, holy night; what place more suitable than this great temple of the out-of-doors, for us simple children of His to seek understanding?"

CHAPTER X

"SMILES'" CONSECRATION

If, half an hour previous, Donald had been told that, during the first evening of his long anticipated visit to his forest of enchantment, he was to play the part of patient in a spiritual clinic, conducted by a wandering backwood preacher for the instruction of a seventeen-year-old mountain girl — as well as for his own enlightenment — he would have scoffed at the idea; yet, oddly enough, he felt no sense of displeasure or antagonism.

In the company of this unaffected man of God, the simple old mountaineer and the equally simple girl only, vanished all the self-conscious reserve and reticence which usually attacks the modern city dweller when called upon to speak of things spiritual and eternal, and which had so often bound Donald's tongue, even when his inner being cried aloud for expression.

"I hardly blame you for your attitude of mind, doctor," began Mr. Talmadge. "Although it is certain that the knowledge of God starts from Himself a ray of pure white light, the dogmas, creeds and theologies — invented by many men of many minds — have raised between it and our spiritual eyes a glass clouded with earthly murkiness, through which we now see darkly. Only as mankind grows in spiritual stature, and lifts his head above the clouds, can he hope to see the ray in all its purity and glory."

"Yes, I suppose that's so," assented Donald. "But I'm afraid that my difficulties lie deeper than the unessential differences in dogma. However, since our little friend is the one who has questions to ask, let her conduct the catechism."

Rose was speechless with embarrassment, but finally managed to say, "I reckon I'm so ignorant, that I can't say the things that are in my heart. Please, Dr. Mac., you ask the reverend the questions and let me just sit and listen. Only don't use too big words, for I want to understand."

"All right, I'll be cross-examiner, but please believe, Mr. Talmadge, that what I may say is not intended to be argumentative, but rather honestly inquisitive. I really would like to find out if any one can reasonably explain some of the many things in religion to the acceptance of which I have been unable to reconcile myself."

"I'll do it gladly, if I can. But, before you begin, let me apologize for what I said in ill-timed jest about doctors being atheists. I suppose that, in one sense, there isn't a more truly religious class of men in the world."

"I can't agree to that, either," said Donald.

"Perhaps not, but tell me this. Isn't the structure

and functionings of the human body infinitely more wonderful to you, who have made an intimate study of it, than it can be to us who have not?"

"Undoubtedly. It's the most marvellous thing on God's earth," answered Donald, unthinkingly employing an expression heard in childhood.

"There!" cried Mr. Talmadge. "He's convicted out of his own mouth, isn't he, Rose? 'God's earth', he says."

"A mere figure of speech," the physician laughed.

"A statement of fact, sir. There are mighty few of you doctors who will not, within your hearts of hearts, agree that a Supreme Being must have designed this earthly temple which we call our body, the world we dwell in, and established the laws that govern both. And, knowing, as none others can, *how* wonderfully the former is constructed, is not a doctor's appreciation of the Almighty's power bound to be sincere?"

"Granted. But that isn't being religious," Donald protested.

"It is the foundation of all true religion," was the quiet answer.

The physician was still dubious. "Well, perhaps. Still, I doubt if many ministers would agree that merely because a man may believe in a superhuman creative power, he is religious, if, at the same time he says — as I must — that he doesn't and can't subscribe to many of the things which we were taught as children to believe as 'gospel truth.'"

There was the sound of a shocked and troubled "Oh," from Rose, but the minister's composure was in no wise ruffled.

"The trouble is, I imagine, that you have mentally outgrown the willingness to accept certain statements blindly, as children and primitive minds do, and yet have made no really earnest endeavor to lift the veil and look behind it with the intent of finding out if a simple and understandable truth may not lie hidden there."

"But how is one going to get behind a plain statement of what is apparently meant to be fact, such as the description of the creation in Genesis?" demanded Donald, somewhat impatiently. "Science is absolute, and I, for one, know that the Darwinian theory of life, or one substantially like it, is true. Why, a study of human anatomy proves it, even if we did not have conclusive evidence in anthropology and geology. So, in the very first words of the Bible, we start off with a conflict between its tenets, and what human learning shows us to be an indisputable fact."

"Do we?" smiled the minister.

"Don't we?" answered Donald.

Rose sat looking first at one, then at the other, with a puzzled look in her eyes, for it was all Greek to her.

Noticing this, Mr. Talmadge said, "I guess that we've started a bit too strongly for our little listener, but we want her to accompany us from the start," and he briefly, in simple words, outlined the Darwinian theory, which brought an outraged grunt from Big Jerry. Then he turned back to Donald, and said, "Take the story of . . . well, say the prodigal son, for an example. Was that the account of real happenings, think you?"

"Of course not. Merely a parable." The other's mind reverted to the one which he himself had preached by letter to little "Smiles."

"The Bible is filled with parables," said Mr. Talmadge, simply. "Why should we regard certain stories as allegories merely, and others as historically accurate statements of fact when they are difficult to credit as such? Especially why should we do so in the face of the obvious fact that the earlier part of the Old Testament is simply tradition, handed down, orally at first, by an intensely patriotic and rather vain race? *Sacred* tradition it is, to be sure; but that should not deter us from endeavoring to analyze it in the light of reason. Besides, hasn't it ever occurred to you that in a translation from the original Hebrew, some of the finer meanings of the old words are sure to have been lost or distorted?"

"Yes, I suppose that is so."

"As a matter of fact, the Hebrew word '*Yōm*,' which, in the story of the Creation, has been translated 'day,' also means 'period.' And it is a rather interesting thing, in this connection, that the biblical account mentions an evening to each of the first six 'days,' but not to the seventh, which shows that *it* isn't finished yet. Science tells us that this last period, since the creation of mankind, has already lasted many thousands of years — although the length of time ascribed to it varies greatly — and this gives us some idea of how long those other 'days' might have been. Besides, in this case, we do not have to be 'finicky' about the meaning of the ancient word, for in the Psalms there is a verse which says that a thousand years in *His* sight are . . ."

"Are but as yesterday," Rose completed the quotation in her gentle voice. "You see, those were God's days, not ours."

"Well, I'll be . . . blessed," said Donald. "It is logical enough, isn't it? The trouble in this case, at least, was that I never consciously tried to reconcile what I regarded as the old and new beliefs."

"But, Mr. Talmadge," Smiles' perplexed voice broke in. "If human beings just developed from a kind of monkey . . ."

"The anthropoid ape wasn't exactly a monkey, although he may have looked and acted like one," laughed Donald.

"Well, but how could the Good Book say that God created man in His own image?"

"Do you remember what Paul said, in his wonderful epistle to the Corinthians? He answered your question when he wrote, 'There is a natural body, and there is a spiritual body . . . and as we have borne the image of the earthly, so shall we also bear the image of the heavenly.' What does the Bible say that God is, Rose?"

"'God is a spirit,'" whispered Smiles, reverently.

"Exactly. And Dr. MacDonald will tell you that 'spirit' comes from a Latin word which means 'breath.' When God perceived that some of the earth creatures had, according to His plan, developed sufficiently in mind so that they could rule the world, He breathed into them some of His own spirit, and thus created them in His own image — for of course a spirit hasn't form and shape like beings of flesh and blood."

"Hasn't He?" gasped the girl. "Why, there is a picture of Him, like a great big man with long beard, in my Bible."

"Merely symbolic, dear child, and I have always felt that it was a vain symbolism, in both senses of that word. You look them up in your new dictionary to-morrow. In trying hard to picture God, men have made Him in the likeness of the most wonderful things their eyes had ever seen — themselves — and just increased His size. As for the beard, that is supposed to be a sign of power and strength.

"Of course, in fact, God isn't a man or even a super-man, but a spirit, combining the spiritual elements of both male and female."

"I reckon I jest hev ter think of er somebody fer ter worship," broke in the hitherto silent Jerry. "Jest something like ther wind air er bit too onsartain fer me."

"And for millions of others," answered the minister

quickly. "Of course there isn't the slightest bit of harm in people thinking of Our Heavenly Father as a Being with a form which our eyes might see if they were only given the power to behold heavenly, as well as earthly, things. The conception of the Omnipotent as a physical embodiment has in the past been of incalculable advantage in making an appeal to an aboriginal type of mind, since it really requires some sort of material personification, which it can at least visualize, the conception of which serves as an incentive for well-doing, and a deterrent from evil doing. It is therefore infinitely preferable as a working basis to an unembodied force."

Big Jerry brought a smile to the lips of the other two men by bursting out, "Durned ef I understand. Them words air too powerful ederkated fer me."

"But," said Rose, "what you say kind of frightens me, Mr. Talmadge. If we can't ever see God, even in Heaven, how can we be sure that He *is?*"

"Have you ever seen . . . love?" queried the minister softly.

"No, sir."

"Yet you know that *it* is. You've never seen, tasted, touched or smelled thought, but you know that it exists. In the same mysterious way we know, and we shall know more perfectly hereafter, that the Great Spirit — I've always loved that beautiful Indian expression — *is.*"

"Yes," she said, somewhat uncertainly. "I *think* that I understand. But it's powerful hard to understand how I can be His little child if He isn't a person."

"I don't wonder that it puzzles you, dear. It is hard for even the oldest of us to try to imagine something entirely different from what we have actually seen with our mortal eyes, and we can hardly conceive of a spirit, or even a ghost, as something without some sort of a form, even though it be a very misty one. But the *real* you isn't the flesh that we can see and touch, but the spirit that dwells inside, and, just as some of your earthly father and mother is in your body, so you have something of God within you, which was given you at birth. We call it . . ."

"My soul."

"Yes. And as that was part of Him you are His child . . . so are we all — spiritual children."

"And Jesus? Was He His son in the same way?" whispered the girl.

"Exactly, only to a far greater degree than we can hope to be, for to Him the Heavenly Father gave His spirit in fuller measure than He ever had before to mankind, so that He might set an example to the world and teach us the way we should try to live."

There was silence for a moment, and then Smiles spoke the thought that had been troubling her. "But, Mr. Talmadge, if God hasn't any body and our spirits are like him, why heaven . . ."

Mr. Talmadge sent a glance of smiling appeal at the doctor as though to say, "Now I'm in for it.

How can I explain heaven as a spiritual condition?" Aloud he said, "I won't pretend to know just what heaven is like, but, of course, our spirits won't need an earth like this to walk on."

"But," persisted the child, "the Good Book says that there are many mansions there, and golden streets, and also that it is a land flowing with milk and honey."

"So it does, and very likely there are, in the realms of the spirit, things which correspond to those that we have known on earth, but I am quite sure that they are not *material* things."

"Ef thar haint no real heaven, thar haint no real hell," broke in Big Jerry, whose mind had been slowly grasping the meaning of the minister's words. "I reckon thar must be a place uv punishment fer sinners."

Painstakingly, as though explaining to a child, Mr. Talmadge answered, "Mr. Webb, did you ever do something wrong, because of which your conscience troubled you later?"

"Reckon I hev. Reckon I suffered the torments uv the damned fer hit."

"Did you ever burn your hand?"

"Yes, I done thet, too; powerful bad."

"Which caused you the most suffering, your conscience or your hand?"

"I erlows thet my conscience done hit."

"That is the answer to your implied question. God doesn't need to give us new bodies, and send them into a place of fire and brimstone to punish us for our sins. If the soul suffers, it is in hell, even though it may still be in our mortal bodies. That it must suffer, when we do wrong, we know. But, Mr. Webb, I do not think that it is meant to be punishment in the sense of retribution — getting even — so much as it is for correction. You know that men put gold through the fire to purge it of the dross that makes it dim and lustreless. That is what the fires of the spirit are for; that is why the Bible speaks of Hell as a place of fire. It is another parable."

"Yes, I see," said Rose, but the old man shook his head, unconvinced. Then the girl asked suddenly, "But why was God so good as to give us part of Himself and let us make it impure and suffer, Mr. Talmadge?"

"Ah, now you are getting into the depths of religion and I'd rather not discuss that until you have had a chance to think over what we have talked about already. All that I wanted to do to-night was to get both you, and the doctor, to thinking for yourselves. Come and see me, doctor, if you want to continue this discussion. I've got theories on any subject that you may mention, I guess," he laughed. "But I won't count the evening wasted — even leaving out the pleasure I have had — if I have helped to open your eyes, ever so little, to the light."

"Oh, you have . . . and mine, too," answered Rose. "I mean to think *hard*, but if I get very puzzled, I'll come to see you about it. But, anyway, I mean to be God's little child all my life — as well as a trained nurse. And I mean to help Dr. Mac., always, to be a child of our heavenly Father, too," she added, simply. As Donald arose to bid the minister good-night, his eyes were a little misty, for the girl's unaffected declaration had moved him more deeply than he had ever been moved in his life.

CHAPTER XI

ADOPTION BY BLOOD

For a little while Donald lay awake under the eaves in his loft room, but his sleeplessness was the result neither of worry or nervous tension. His mind, indeed, was unusually contented. None of the disturbing thoughts of difficult tasks on the morrow assailed it; he felt only an unwonted peace and contentment. The impressions left by the evening's talk still swayed and uplifted his soul. Yet, deep within his consciousness, there was a vague realization that it would be long, if ever, before he could hope to pattern his life by the precepts of the man of God who had so stirred him. Happily, he could not foresee how soon mortal passions were to repossess him wholly, to blot out the new spiritual light which was his.

In her little room below, Rose, too, lay awake, her youthful mind teeming with wonderful, new ideas garnered from the seeds sown by the "reverend"; but the insistent call of slumber to her tired, healthy body in time lulled her busy thoughts to rest.

. . . .

"Oh, Doctor Mac, come *quick!* Grandpappy's hurted."

Sound asleep, and even then visioning the girl whose terrified voice suddenly wove itself into the figment of his dream, when the first word fell upon his ears, Donald was wide awake, and he was half out of bed before the last was spoken.

He paused only long enough to draw on his hunting breeches and thrust his bare feet into their tramping boots — which left a hiatus of unstockinged muscular calf — hurriedly dropped down the ladder, and in two strides was out of doors.

Near the wood pile stood the old mountaineer, on his countenance expression of mingled pain and chagrin, the latter dominating. His right hand still grasped the keen-edged axe, while Rose stood beside him, clasping his brawny left forearm with both of her small but sinewy hands.

As Donald approached them on the run he noticed that the girl had sacrificed her treasured hair ribbon to make a tourniquet halfway up the old man's arm, and that blood was running down his hand and falling from the finger tips with slow, rhythmical continuity.

"Hit haint nothin' et all, Smiles," Big Jerry was rumbling forth. "Hit air jest er scratch. I don't know how I come fer ter do hit an' I reckon I ought ter be plumb ershamed. Why, Smiles, I been erchoppin' wood fer nigh onter fifty year, an' I haint never chopped myself erfore. Hit war thet tarnation knot. But hit haint nothin', this hyar haint."

"Come over to the well where we can give it a

wash," was Donald's curt command, and Big Jerry followed him obediently, while the girl hastened ahead and drew up a bucket full of pure, sparkling, ice-cold spring water. The doctor tipped it unceremoniously over the giant's arm, and, as the already coagulating blood on the surface was washed away, made a hasty examination of the slanting, ugly gash beneath.

"Superficial wound. No artery or major muscle severed," he announced, as though addressing a class. "Still, you were right in taking the precaution of applying that tourniquet, Rose. I suppose it was bleeding pretty merrily at first."

"Hit war spoutin' powerful," she answered, in her stress of excitement lapsing into the language of childhood.

"Yes, I suppose so. That is in a way a good thing in such cases, however. It automatically cleanses the wound of any infectious matter. Look, Rose," he added, as though explaining to a clinic, "see how the blood is thickening up into a clot? That is chiefly the work of what we call 'white corpuscles' — infinitely tiny little organisms whose sole purpose in life is to eat up disease germs which may get into the veins, and to hurry to the surface when there is a cut, cluster together and die, their bodies forming a wall against the wicked enemies who are always anxious to get inside the blood for the purpose of making trouble."

"I told ye 'twarnt nothin'," said Big Jerry, not

without a note of relief in his voice, however. "A leetle blood-lettin' won't do me no hurt. I'll jest wind a rag eround hit, an' . . ."

"Not so fast," laughed Donald. "In all probability 'a rag just wound round it' would do the business, for your blood is apparently in first-class condition, with its full share of the red corpuscles; but you might just as well have the benefit of the hospital corps since we are on the ground. The red corpuscles," he added, addressing Smiles, "are the other good little chaps who continually go hurrying through the body, feeding it with oxygen and making it strong. Run into the house and get my 'first aid' kit, from my knapsack, child. You'll remember it when you see it, for I had to dig it out the very first time that I saw you."

The girl hurried cabinwards, fleet as the wind, and, as the two men sat down on a woodpile to wait for her, Donald had an opportunity to take note of his ludicrously inadequate costume.

It seemed little more than a minute before Rose returned with his kit, but it was not brought by a mountain maid. In that almost incredibly short time the child had changed her gingham dress for the immaculate costume of a trained nurse, and the transformation in apparel had been accompanied by one in mien no less noticeable. Dainty and fair as a white wild rose she was, yet seriously business-like in expression. Donald was startled for a moment. It came to his mind that he was looking upon a vision of the years to come, and the picture caused his heart to beat a little faster; but, although the light of appreciation shone in his eyes, his only comment was, "Are your hands as clean as that dress?"

"Yes, doctor."

"Now how the deuce did she come to use that stereotyped response?" he wondered; then said, aloud, "Then undo that roll of gauze bandage and tear off a piece about six feet long . . . be careful! Don't let it touch the ground."

Then he immediately gave his attention to Big Jerry, and smiled with professional callousness as he caught the giant's wince when the antiseptic fluid which he poured on the wound started it smarting.

"Now for your first lesson in the scientific application of a bandage, Smiles," he said.

Very carefully she followed his directions, and at length the split end was tied with professional neatness. But, as his fingers tested the knot, the girl seized one of his hands and exclaimed, with solicitude, "Why, you're hurt, too, Doctor Mac.!"

She indicated on one of his fingers a small jagged tear from which the blood was slowly oozing.

"How the dickens did I do that?" he demanded in surprise.

"Sliding down the ladder from the loft-room, I reckon. See, there's a piece of splinter in it still."

"Right-o, Miss Detective." He turned to the old man and remarked, "It looks as though your blood and mine had been mixing, this morning. Why not complete the ceremony and make it an adoption by blood; the way they used to do in some of the Indian tribes, you know?" he added, half jestingly, and acting on a sudden impulse. "You can take me into the clan as . . . well, as your foster-son."

"Thar haint no clan nowadays, I reckon, but ef yo' wants fer ter be my foster-son I'd shor' be pleased fer ter hev ye es such, lad."

"Great. I feel like 'one of the family' already, and if you *will* adopt me as a new son — with all the privileges and obligations of one — I'll appreciate it, no joking."

As a pledge of their compact the city and mountain man clasped hands solemnly, while Rose stood by, delightedly smiling her benediction upon their act. "Why," she cried, "that makes me your little foster sister, Doctor Mac. Oh, I'm so glad!"

"Yes, so it does." Donald answered with a cheery voice, but no sooner were the words spoken than a sense of rebellion took possession of him. "Idiot!" he muttered, shaking off the feeling with an effort of his will.

"But haint . . . aren't you going to do up your hurt finger, too?" she queried anxiously.

The man seized the broken sliver with his fingers and jerked it out, examined the tiny incision and then thrust the wounded member into his mouth. "Don't ever tell any of my patients that you saw me do this," he laughed, with a return to good humor, "but that is my way of treating a minor injury . . . then I forget it. It's a fearful secret," he added, lowering his voice, "but nature, aided by sun and air, are wonderful healers, and just ordinary saliva, if a person is healthy, is both cleansing and healing."

"Thet air the way anumals cures thar hurts," remarked Jerry.

"Yes, it is nature's way, and if the blood is pure, and the cut not so deep as to make infection likely, there isn't a much better one, after all. However, Miss Nurse, you may practice your art on my finger, too, if you want."

He held his hand out, and, flushing with childish happiness, Rose bound up the little scratch painstakingly, answering Donald's brief word of commendation with a flashing smile. Indeed, experience with many nurses of many grades of ability made him aware that her untrained fingers held an unusual degree of natural knack which augured well for the future.

During a simple breakfast, leisurely eaten, the trio talked over in detail the varied happenings of the year that had passed, and Donald was as astonished as he was pleased to discover what diligent application the girl had exercised in her studying, and what results she had attained, despite the manifold handicaps under which she had labored. Her ministerial friend and mentor had truly guided her feet far along the lower levels of learning. Yet the old and well-remembered childish charm had been in no wise lessened, and the unaffected simplicity with which she dropped into the mountain tongue, when speaking to her grandfather, caused Donald to glow with sympathetic appreciation.

As they finished eating, Big Jerry remarked, "Hit air a powerful fine mornin' fer ter spend huntin', my boy. I reckon yo'll wish ter git inter the woods right smart, an' ef yo' desires ter make a day uv hit, Smiles 'll fix ye up er leetle lunch ter take erlong."

"Oh, I'm not exactly sure what I shall do," answered Donald, with slight hesitation. "Perhaps what I need most, to start with, is just plain rest, and I rather guess I'll laze around this morning, and maybe go down to Fayville to get my grip this afternoon."

"Wall, thet air a good idee. Jest make yo'rself ter home. I've got a leetle bizness ter attend to up the mountain a piece, an' I allows yo' kin git erlong 'thout me fer a while." He departed, disappearing with surprising rapidity, and left the man and girl together.

Donald sank onto the doorstep, leaned against the side post, and sucked away at his pipe with lazy contentment, alternately watching Rose as she flew busily about her simple household duties, and sending his gaze out over the broad stretch of peaceful mountainside, which lay dozing in the warm morning sun.

CHAPTER XII

THE THREE OF HEARTS

At length Donald said, abruptly, "You haven't asked me anything about Miss Treville, Smiles."

There was a perceptible pause in the girl's dish-drying, and the simple mountain ballad that she was happily humming broke off in the middle of a minor cadence. The man regarded her with curiosity as she slowly approached him, saying, "I didn't mean to be so forgetful, doctor, and I'm plumb ashamed. I should be pleased to have you tell me all about her."

"Why, I don't know as there is much to tell," he replied, a little nonplussed by the unexpectedness of the implied question. "Of course she is very nice and very lovely, as I wrote you."

"What does she look like?"

"I am afraid that I cannot hope to give a very accurate description of her, Rose. It would perhaps be easier if you had ever visited an art museum, and seen statues of some of the Greek goddesses, for people say that she looks like one of them. You see she is quite tall for a woman — almost as tall as I am myself — and . . . well, her form and the way she carries herself is queenly. Then she has hair darker than yours, and . . . her eyes are gray, I guess, although, come to think of it, I never noticed particularly. She isn't pretty like a wild-flower, but very beautiful, more like a stately cultivated bloom. When you have seen conservatory blossoms you will know better what I mean. She is very serious, too. Even when she is quite happy it is sometimes a bit hard to tell it, for she seldom really smiles. . . . I wish she would," he added, as though to himself, "she has wonderful teeth."

"Oh, she must be very lovely," mused Rose, and added with slight hesitancy, "I reckon you must love her powerful."

"Yes, of course," Donald answered, and then added, as though a logical reason for his affection was necessary, "You see, I have known Marion all her life. She is my sister's closest friend, and almost grew up in our house."

"I wish I had," said Rose, the note of envy in her voice being outweighed by the childlike sincerity which her words carried. "What does she do?"

"Do? Why, I don't know, exactly — what all society girls, with plenty of money at their disposal, do, I suppose. Of course she has clubs which she belongs to, and she goes to dances and theatres and . . . I think she is interested in some sort of charity, too." He had an uncomfortable feeling that he was failing to make out a very strong case for the woman to whom he was engaged, and at the same time wondering why any vindication of her should seem necessary, since he had always regarded her as a bit too perfect, if anything."

"Oh, that is lovely, for the Bible says that the greatest of all is charity," cried Rose, her eyes sparkling. "And does she go about helping poor, lonesome city people, and the dear little poor children? It must be wonderful to have lots of money, so that you can do all sorts of things to make them happier and better."

"Confound the child," thought Donald, although his exasperation was directed rather at himself, than at her. "It's positively indecent the way she gets inside one. Judged by the standards of her class, Marion is a splendid girl — head and shoulders above the average — yet these unconsciously searching questions of Smiles' are . . . Hang it all, I wish I had had sense enough not to open the subject."

Aloud he said non-committally, "Yes, of course it is wonderful and I know that you would do it if you were able."

"I *shall* do it," was the confident answer. "I can't give money but I can give myself." There was a moment of silence; then Rose added softly, "I guess she loves you a lot, too, you are so good to . . . to people, and do such wonderful things. When do you calculate to get married to her, Doctor Mac?"

"Married?" he repeated in a startled voice, "Oh, some day, of course; but you know how terribly busy I am, and . . ." He stopped, visualizing himself at that moment as he lolled indolently in the doorway of that mountain cabin, and wondering if the same thought were in her mind as was in his. At the same time came a welcome interruption in the appearance of a small child, brown as the proverbial berry, and bearing in her arms a large and rather dilapidated appearing doll. For an instant Donald failed to recognize her, and said, "Hello, here comes one of your little friends to see you, Smiles. Why, I do believe . . . yes, it's Lou. Come along. You're not afraid of the doctor man who sent you that doll."

Lou advanced, one finger in her mouth, the corners of which were lifting in a shy smile. Sensing the approach of another old friend, Mike bounded out of the doorway where he had lain panting in the shadow, and so energetic was his greeting that the child was very nearly upset by it, although as soon as she could regain her equilibrium she flung her little arms around the roughly coated neck, without a trace of fear.

"Mike's got er broken leg," she announced. The words gave Donald a start until he saw that she was holding out to him her doll, one of whose limbs flapped about in piteous substantiation. "Kin yo' make hit well ergin?"

Examining the injured member, whence the sawdust blood had issued through a deep incision in the cloth, Donald replied seriously, "It will require a rather serious operation, but I guess that I can mend it with the assistance of Nurse Smiles. We will hav to sew up the wound and put the leg in splints."

"Hit haint er-goin' ter hurt her much, air hit?" begged Lou, with all the solicitude of a young mother.

"No. We'll give her an anesthetic — something to put her sound asleep — and I guess that she won't know anything about it." Rose joined them laughingly, bringing a threaded needle and some bits of cloth for stuffing and in a few minutes the operation was complete, even to the application of splints, roughly shaped by Donald's jack-knife. Throughout the process the physician explained each step to Rose, who cried as they finished, "Oh, I love to do it. It's lots more fun than book studying or weaving baskets."

"Well, we might have a real lesson in 'first aid' this morning, if Lou can stay and be your little patient. Bring out that roll of bandages again."

What a merry hour they spent, helped by Mike, who insisted in doing his share by licking the patient at every opportunity. The air was so warm that Lou's little dress could be taken off, and as she giggled or screamed with merriment, Donald and Rose treated her for every conceivable fracture, sprain or injury, the former all the while explaining in the simplest language at his command the major facts of human anatomy.

Rose proved to be an astonishingly apt pupil, and after each demonstration insisted on going through both the procedure and explanation alone.

Finally, in the course of demonstrating an unusually intricate piece of bandaging, Donald put his arms about Smiles, the better to guide her hands, and impulsively drew her close against him. He could not see her face, but he perceived that a quick flush mantled her neck and delicately rounded cheek. She moved away hastily, saying in a low voice, "I reckon you oughtn't do like that, Doctor Mac."

"Why, Smiles!" came his response in a hurt tone.

"I don't mean for to hurt you, and of course I cares for you like I used to, but I guess it ain't . . . isn't . . . just right for you to put your arms around me . . . that way now. I'm most grown up now, and . . . and . . . you're pledged to . . . to some one else." During her speech the color had flamed brighter and brighter.

The man was both surprised and chagrined. He realized, of course, that in many respects Rose was indeed, 'most a woman now'—that she was far more mature in certain ways than city-bred girls of the same age; for, while they might be infinitely more sophisticated in worldly ways than she, they are still children, whereas she had already entered into the problems of life and for several years had not only been in full charge of a home, but in intimate touch with the issues of life and death in the little community. Understanding all this, he nevertheless looked upon her as a child because of the child-like simplicity which characterized her still.

"I see," he answered slowly and a little ashamed, then added lightly, "but you have apparently forgotten that you adopted me as a foster-brother this morning."

For a moment she said nothing; then the old misty smile touched her lips, and she replied, "I shor' most forgot that, and it makes it all right. Please, Doctor Mac., don't think that I didn't enjoy for you to do it."

There succeeded another brief, awkward silence. Then Smiles slipped her arm about Donald's neck with frank, childlike affection, and leaned close to him, her young, warm being thrilling his senses, as he full well realized Marion's infrequent embraces never had.

Shocked and distressed by his own emotions, Donald was the first to withdraw his encircling arm, with an intent to continue the lesson. But it was ended.

During the brief interlude Lou had stood regarding the man and girl uncomprehendingly. Now she piped up, "Smiles loves ye er heap, I reckon, doctor man, an' so does I. Ef she don't marry with ye, I'll do hit when I gits bigger."

"My, but I'm a fortunate man to have *three* fair ladies love me, and I won't forget your promise," Donald laughed merrily.

"But my brother Juddy don't love ye none," said the child, innocently bringing a cloud over the friendly sunshine in her hearers' hearts. Donald looked at Rose uneasily as he answered.

"Oh, I hope he will like me some day. We should be the best of friends, for we both care for the same two dear girls."

"Where *is* Juddy?" came Smiles' somewhat troubled query.

"Oh, he air away ergin; up in ther mountain."

The shadow deepened on Rose's face and Donald caught the sound of a distressed, "Oh."

"What's the matter?" he asked without special thought.

"It haint . . . it isn't anything . . . leastwise it isn't anything that I can tell you about, doctor Mac. I . . . I just don't like for him to go up there."

A feeling closely akin to jealousy stirred Donald's heart. Did that uncouth young mountaineer really mean something to her after all?

CHAPTER XIII

GATHERING CLOUDS

DESPITE Smiles' ingenuous proffer of a sister's affection, Donald was troubled with an unreasonable dissatisfaction over the course which the events of the morning had taken, and he knew that it was unreasonable, which made it worse. Now he suddenly announced that he guessed he would not wait until the afternoon before going down to Fayville to get his small amount of baggage.

The girl was troubled, also, without knowing just why, and she watched his departure with an unhappy feeling that somehow the changes which the year had made in both their lives had raised a misty barrier between them — intangible, but not easily to be swept away. Furthermore, young as she was, she intuitively sensed that hers was the necessity of reconstructing their friendship on a new foundation, because she was a woman. The man could not do it.

Meanwhile Donald performed his downward journey with none of the lightness of heart which makes a long walk a pleasure, rather than a task. Going down the wooded descent, where the dew still lay wet beneath the heaviest thickets, was not so bad; but, when he had obtained his grip and gun, and started on the back trail, his discomforts commenced. As the main street of the little village changed its character, first to a road and then a cart path through the fields, it grew deep with dust, and, although no air stirred, it seemed to rise, as water does by capillary attraction, until his clothing was saturated and his mouth and nose overlaid with a film of it. Overhead the sky burned, and from the brown fields, which stretched to the wooded base of the mountain, heat waves rose as though the dry earth were panting with visible breath. An insect chirped half-heartedly in the grass, and then left off as though the effort were too great, and a small striped snake leisurely wove a sinuous path through the dust ahead of him, and vanished with a faint hiss.

It was better when he struck the woods, for there was shade; but the air was more sultry and the added exertion of climbing started the perspiration and turned the coating of dust to sticky grime. Still the breeze delayed, and the fragrant odors of the woods were cloying. His luggage grew heavier and yet more heavy; his arm and back began to ache painfully.

When physical discomfort is accompanied by morose introspection, the result is certain to be unpleasant, and Donald's thoughts were in dismal grays and browns, which ill-matched the radiant colors of external nature.

Certainly Smiles was not to blame, he thought,

as he trudged up and up. The fact still remained that they lived on utterly different planes, and that he had not the slightest idea of falling in love with her, or, even mentally, violating his pledge to Marion. Pshaw, she was nothing but a child! It was foolish, absurdly so, yet somehow he felt that his world was out of joint, and, since he could not, or would not, determine just what the trouble was, he could not take active measures to bring about a readjustment.

With a conscious effort of his will he put the mountain child out of his thoughts, and attempted to analyze his real feelings for the city girl, to whom he was betrothed. He could assign no reason to the vague, but persistent, feeling which frequently possessed him, when he was apart from her, that she was not his natural mate. Her poise and reserve, which sometimes irritated him, he knew to be really virtues, in a way as desirable as they were rare in women, even of her class; her unusual beauty fully satisfied his eye; she was a reigning queen, the desired of many men and he had won her, although he hesitated a little over the word "won." Finally, he was certain that she loved him, after her fashion. Why should he, a man as reserved as he was, and one who had little time to spend on the romantic embellishments of life, ask for more? Yet there was mute rebellion in the depths of his heart, and even the memory of that milestone night, eight months before, when the spirit of Christmastide had added its spell to the influences of life-long propinquity, and they had, almost without spoken words, crossed the border and pledged themselves to one another, brought no thrill.

"I *know* that she is a wonderful woman, and a real beauty," mused Donald, half aloud. "The trouble must be . . . yes, *is*, with me. She's too wonderful for my simple tastes; that's the truth, as I told Ethel. Oh, well, perhaps I can learn to live up to her . . . but I hate this society stuff."

. . . .

Donald's return to the cabin, weary and uncomfortable in body and mind, found Big Jerry sitting heavily in a chair, with Smiles hovering about, and, from the expression on the face of each, he sensed at once that something was wrong. The old man was saying, somewhat laboriously, "Hit don't pain me . . . much, Rose, gal. Hit haint nothin' . . . ter mention. I'll jest set still hyar erwhile, an' . . ."

As the girl caught sight of Donald's big form in the doorway, her face brightened momentarily; but it clouded again with swift pain when he touched his heart with a significant gesture, accompanied by a questioning look. She nodded, then said aloud, "Here's our Doctor Mac. back ergin, grandpappy. I reckon he kin do somethin' fer ter help ye."

The newcomer attempted a cheery laugh, and said, "Well, I'm not much good unless we can turn

Time's flight backward, and make him a child again temporarily. Kiddies are my specialty, you know, and although I've a few grown-up patients, left over from the time when I took whatever came, and was thankful, I am killing them off as fast as I can."

He spoke facetiously, with the design of instilling a lighter element in the conversation; but, although Jerry smiled wryly, the girl looked so shocked that Donald hastened to add, "Please don't be alarmed, dear, of course I didn't mean that literally. And you know that I will do anything in my power to help. I only wish that I knew more about troubles affecting the heart," he added.

"Reckon the doctor down in Fayville hed ought ter say the same thing," interposed the old man. "I erlows he didn't do me no good, fer I got better es soon's I quit takin' the stuff he left me."

"Don't be too hard on him, foster father. After all, what you probably needed most was to give that big heart of yours a rest, and that is what did the business then, and will now. Well, I'll look you over anyway. I guess professional ethics won't be outraged, with the other physician five steep, uphill miles away."

While he talked he had been opening his suitcase, and now took out a compact emergency bag which experience had taught him never to go away without, and at whose shining, unfamiliar contents Smiles' eyes opened with fascinated amazement. Taking out a stethoscope, Donald bade the giant open his soft, homemade shirt, and planted the transmitting disk against the massive chest, padded with wonderful, bulging muscles.

"O-ho," he said under his breath, as he finally laid the instrument aside; for his intently listening ears had caught the faint, but clearly discernible sound of a systolic murmur, deep within.

"Air the trouble 'Aunt' . . . what the other doctor said hit was?" questioned Rose.

"Angina pectoris? He may have had a touch of that last winter of course, but my guess is that it's something a bit different now."

"I haint erfeered ter hyar the truth," rumbled Jerry, straightening up like a soldier before the court martial.

"Well," answered the doctor, "I should say that you have a touch of another jaw-breaking Latin phrase, namely, an aneurism of the thoracic aorta."

"Hit shor' sounds powerful bad," grunted Jerry. "But then I reckon thet doctors likes ter use big words."

"Right. For instance, we prefer to call an old-fashioned cold in the head, 'Naso-pharyngitis.' The worse it sounds, the more credit we get for curing it, you see. Well, 'sticks and stones may break our bones, but *words* will never hurt us,' so don't let that Latin expression worry you. Just take things a bit easy, don't overdo physically or get over-excited, and you'll be good for many a moon yet," he added lightly.

Jerry fastened up his shirt with big, fumbling fingers and walked slowly outside, while Rose, tears of pity shedding a misty luminousness over her eyes, stepped close to Donald and laid her hand appealingly on his arm, "Is it something pretty bad, Doctor Mac.?" she breathed.

"Well, it's apparently a mild case . . . so far."

"But the trouble . . . is it . . . is it dangerous?"

He hesitated an instant, then responded quietly, "Nurses have to know the truth, of course, and I am sure that you have a brave little heart, so I'm not afraid to tell you that it *is* bad. It is almost sure to be fatal, in time, but not necessarily soon. If he will take things easy, as I told him to, he'll live for a considerable time yet; but we mustn't allow him to get very greatly excited, or do any very heavy work."

Suddenly very white, but calm and tearless, Smiles answered, "I reckon I can help him better if I know all about it, doctor. I *got* to help him, you know. He's all I have now in the whole world."

"Of course you're going to help him — we both are — but . . . you have me, little sister, and your life work," he answered with awkward tenderness. "Now let us see if I can make you understand what I believe the trouble to be. In its incipient — that is, its early stages, it would be rather hard to tell from angina pectoris, for the symptoms would be much the same — pain about the heart and shortness of breath. But one can get over the latter, and feel perfectly well between attacks."

He picked up from his open suitcase a folded newspaper which he had tossed in half read, on leaving the city, and drew for her a crude diagram of the heart and major arteries.

"This biggest pipe which goes downward from the heart is called the great artery, and it and its branches — just like a tree's — carry the blood into all parts of the body, except the lungs. Another name for it is the descending thoracic aorta, and that is where grandfather's trouble is. If you knew something about automobile tires I would explain it by saying that he had a blow-out, but it's something like this. The pipe has an outer surface and an inner lining. At one time or another something happened to injure and weaken the former — disease does it sometimes — perhaps it may have been a severe strain or crushing blow on his chest."

"A big tree fell on him early last winter," cried Rose, with sudden enlightenment. "His chest is so big and strong that he didn't think that it hurt him, 'cept to lame him considerable."

"That may have caused the trouble. Well, what happens is this. The blood is pumped by the heart through that weakened pipe, and, little by little, it forces the lining out through the weakened spot, making something like a bubble filled with blood. In time that might grow until you could actually see the swelling, and all the time, the containing tissue is getting thinner and thinner. Now you can yourself guess the reason why he mustn't do anything to over-exert his heart. Hard work, or great excitement, makes our hearts beat faster, and sends the blood through that big artery with extra force and . . . "

"The bubble might . . . break," whispered "Smiles," with a frightened look on her young face.

"Yes. We call it a rupture of the aneurism, and when that happens mortal life ends."

"Oh," she shuddered slightly. "I must keep him very quiet, Doctor Mac. I am strong and can do all the work. You tell him that he mustn't do anything, please, doctor."

"I'm not sure that that would be the wisest plan, Rose. He has been so strong and active all his life it would break his great heart to be tied down like an invalid. I'm sure that he would be happier doing things, even if as a result he didn't live quite so long. Don't you think so, yourself?"

She nodded, and he continued, "Of course he is so big and strong he can do common, simple tasks without anything like the amount of exertion required by an ordinary man, and, so long as he doesn't strain himself, or get very much excited, we may reasonably expect him to live for a good while yet. Besides, as the aneurism progresses there will come a steady, boring pain and increased shortness of breath, which will themselves help to keep him quiet."

"But can't I give him some medicine?"

"The best medicine that he can possibly have will be your happy, comforting smile and tender love, my child."

She furtively wiped a stray tear from her cheek and smiled bravely up into his face, in a wordless pledge that to the administration of this treatment she would devote herself without stint.

"May I . . . may I have that paper," she answered appealingly, as he started to crumple it up, preparatory to tossing it into the fireplace. "We don't often have city papers to read, you know."

"Why, of course; I didn't think," he answered, smoothing it out and handing it to her. She took it eagerly, and had read barely a minute before she cried, delightedly, "Why, Doctor Mac. *You're* in this paper. Oh, did you read what it says?"

"Hang it," thought Donald, "I forgot all about that fool story, or I wouldn't have given it to her." But she was already reading the brief article aloud, slowly but with appreciatory expression.

EXCEPTIONAL FEE PAID BOSTON DOCTOR

DR. DONALD MACDONALD OPERATES ON MULTI-MILLIONAIRE'S CHILD

What is rumored to have been one of the biggest fees paid to a physician in recent years, was received lately by the brilliant young children's specialist of this city, Dr. Donald MacDonald.

A few weeks ago he was summoned to Newport in consultation with local and New York physicians over the five-year-old daughter of J. Bentley Moors, the millionaire copper king, and finally saved the child's life by performing successfully one of the most difficult operations known to surgery — the removal of a brain tumor.

The child had already totally lost the power of speech, and had sunk into a comatose state, the operation being performed at Dr. MacDonald's suggestion as a final desperate resort.

His associates on the case are unstinted in their praise of his skill, and declare that few other surgeons in America could have carried it through with any hope of success.

The child was completely cured, and in his gratitude her father sent the young doctor a check which — it is said — represented an amount larger than many men earn in a lifetime.

"What does 'comatose' mean, Doctor Mac.?" asked Smiles.

"It means a condition during which the body appears to be lifeless. A tumor is a growth — in that particular case here, inside the skull, which pressed on the child's brain, paralyzing, or shutting off, all the senses."

"Oh, wasn't it wonderful to do what you did . . . it was almost like the miracles our dear Lord performed, for you gave sight to the blind and raised up one who was *almost* dead. I am so glad for that little child and her dear father, and I don't wonder that he gave you a lot of money. Was it . . . was it as much as a . . . a thousand dollars?" she asked in an awed tone.

"Yes, indeed, much more than that, in fact."

"Not five thousand?"

Donald laughed. "The newspaper men, who had somehow or other got wind of the story — goodness knows how — tried mighty hard to get me to tell them how much, but I wouldn't. However, since I know that you can keep a secret, I will tell you. It was just ten times the amount of your last guess."

"Oh!" she gasped, as the result of the multiplication dawned upon her. "Why, it was a fortune, and . . . and *I* know you."

"Of course it pleased me," was his answer, "but not half as much as the result of the operation, dear. If a doctor is really in earnest, and bound up in his work, he never thinks whether the little sufferer stretched before him in bed, or on the operating table, has a father worth a million dollars, or one in the poorhouse. That is the reason why we have to charge for our services by a different standard from men in almost any other kind of work. The rich man has to help pay for the poor man, whether he wants to or not. I meant to charge that very rich man enough so that I could give myself to a great many poor children without charging them anything, perhaps; but he had a big heart and sent me that check for several times what I should have charged without even waiting for me to make out a bill. And his letter, which came with it, said that even fifty thousand dollars was poor compensation for a life worth more to him than all the money in the whole world."

"A little child's life *is* more precious than all the gold that ever was," said Smiles seriously, "for only God can give it."

CHAPTER XIV

SOWING THE WIND

THE noonday meal was a rather quiet, constrained affair. None of the three was in a talkative mood, Donald was still distrait, Big Jerry obviously in physical and mental distress, and Rose too full of troubled sympathy for conversation. Frequently Donald caught her gaze fixed on the old man's face with an expression of unutterable love; and as often, when she saw him watching her, her face lighted for a moment with a tender, compassionate smile.

The eagerly anticipated vacation and reunion had truly begun badly, and it was with a sense of relief that Donald finished the simple dinner, and announced that he guessed he would go for a little tramp in the woods, while Rose was performing her household tasks.

"Hain't yo' ergoin' ter tote yo'r rifle-gun?" queried Big Jerry, as he noticed that the doctor was leaving the house without a weapon.

"No, not this trip. I'm not in a mood for hunting. All I want is a walk, — and a stout club and Mike will be protection enough against anything in these woods. Good-by, Smiles. I'll be back before supper-time, hungry as a bear."

He left the clearing for the virgin woods at random, striding along briskly and with rising spirits, and at first unmindful of the direction that he was taking.

In fact he had, subconsciously — even in his recreation — refused to follow the easiest way, and had struck out on the up-mountain trail.

For a while Donald walked on, regardless of whither. Then the consciousness of the fact that he was in a — to him — unknown part of the mountain, and nearing the summit, brought with it a recollection of the words spoken that morning by little Lou, "Judd air erway ergin . . . up in the mountain."

Still, he kept on, for, although he told himself that he had not the slightest intention of seeking the mountaineer, or the solution of Smiles' troubled look, and most certainly was not courting trouble, purposeless curiosity impelled him higher and higher into the hitherto unexplored fastnesses. Now the timberlands lay beneath him, for, although the hardy laurel continued in profusion, albeit somewhat dried and withered, the trees were thinning out and becoming more scraggly, and more frequently the naked rocks, split and seamed, thrust themselves up through the baked soil, "like vertebræ in the backbone of the mountain," thought Donald. Now they were toned and softened by moss and lichen; now barren of vegetation, rugged and gaunt, split asunder by the ancient elements. In the distress which had come like a cloud over the sunlight of his spirits, so gayly anticipative a few hours previous, they flung a wordless challenge to the battling instinct in the man, and he accepted it with the thought that the best balm for troubled minds is strenuous bodily action.

Eager and joyous over the new game, Mike tore about, panting, and dashing from side to side through the underbrush on real, or imaginary, scents, now stopping to dig madly for a moment, then racing on to catch up with his master, who frequently had to haul him over the precipitous crags by the shaggy hair on his muscular back.

The air was cooler here, and as invigorating as wine; the sky was a transparent blue.

At last, somewhat tired of pushing his way over rocks and through virgin underbrush with no objective, he was on the point of turning to retrace his footsteps, when Mike stopped short with nose a-quiver and bristles lifting on his neck.

"What's up?" asked the man. As usual he addressed the dog as though he were a sentient being. "Trouble ahead? Some wild animal there, old boy?"

But, instead of retreating, he grasped his cudgel more firmly, and cautiously parted the thick bushes in front of him.

To his surprise, Donald found that he was almost on the edge of a sharp declivity leading down into a natural bowl-like hollow, so shut in with high rocks and underbrush that it was, in effect, a retreat almost as good as a cave for concealment. And that it was so used, or had been at some time, was made evident by the presence of a rude hut, little more than a lean-to since one end was wholly open, which snuggled against the further bank.

With growing curiosity and caution, he worked his way along the edge, for now a faint odor of wood-smoke reached his nostrils, and there came to his ears the sound of some one, or something, moving within the shelter, a presence which the dog had apparently detected much sooner than had his master.

At length he reached a point of vantage, partly hidden by a cleft rock, from which he could look fully into the interior of the shack. It was obviously not a habitation, although a fire was burning briskly within it. Near by stood a small keg or two, what appeared to be a large tub or vat, and, over the fire, was a queer metal object, the shape of which caused Donald to wonder for a brief instant if necromancy still existed, and he had stumbled upon the retreat of a mountain wizard. Almost immediately, however, the true explanation flashed through his mind.

It was a crude illicit distillery — the hidden "still" of a mountain moonshiner! At the same moment a tall man in typical mountain costume moved into view and bent over the fire.

In his interest Donald had forgotten Mike; but, at the appearance of the man, his companion gave voice to a sharp and hostile challenge.

The furtive toiler turned like a flash, and, seizing the rifle which leaned against the wall near at hand, sprang out and levelled it at the intruder whose head was visible above the rock, for he had been too much surprised to move.

"Put up yo'r hands!" he cried, and Donald complied with the order without perceptible hesitation, at the same time pushing into full sight. The man below was Judd!

For a moment neither spoke, and the silence was pregnant with serious possibilities. Then Donald regained partial control of his shaken self-possession, and with his hands still held above his head, slid awkwardly down into a sitting posture on the edge of the bank.

"Do you know, Judd," he remarked at last, with an assumption of coolness. "I thought *that* sort of thing had ceased to exist, even in these wild mountains," and he nodded toward the distillery.

"I allows thet yo' hev er habit of thinkin' wrong," was the surly response. "You haint no doctor man. Thet's er blind. Yo' be er revenuer, I reckon, an' es sich I've got ter put er bullet inter ye."

"Don't be a fool," snapped Donald, even in this dangerous predicament unable to resort to conciliatory words when addressing Judd. "I'm nothing of the sort, and you know it."

There was another spell of nerve-racking silence. Then the outlaw said slowly, "I reckon yo' speaks ther truth. Yo' haint smart ernough fer er revenuer. One er them wouldn't come er still-huntin' 'thout er rifle-gun, an' *with* er barkin' dawg."

"Well, I'm glad that's settled," answered Donald, uttering a forced laugh. "My arms are getting tired, held up like this, and, as you have a rifle and I haven't, I suggest that I be allowed to resume a more natural position."

Without waiting for the permission, he dropped his hands to the bank beside him.

Donald's action placed Judd in an obviously unpleasant dilemma. He knew it, and therein lay the intruder's best chance.

"I haint never shot er man in cold blood erfore, but I reckon I've got ter do hit now," he said sullenly. "Yo' know too damned much erbout sartain things what don't consarn ye."

"If they don't concern me — as I am willing to admit — why waste a bullet?" answered Donald, mentally sparring for time. "As a law-abiding citizen I might reasonably feel that you still ought to be put out of existence; but, it's no hunt of mine, since I'm not a federal officer. I haven't any particular desire to get a bullet through me, and I know perfectly well that you don't care for the thought of adding the crime of murder to the misdemeanor of illicit liquor making."

"I haint erfeerd ter shoot ye," blustered Judd, and added significantly, "Yo're body wouldn't never be found, and yo' wouldn't be ther first pryin' stranger what got lost in these hyar hills, and warn't never heard of more."

"Admitted. But what's to be gained in taking the chance? I'm ready — yes, anxious — to give you my word of honor that I'll forget what I've stumbled on here this afternoon. Come, be reasonable, Judd."

"Wall, ef you'll swa'r thet . . ." began the mountaineer dubiously.

"I do," broke in Donald with undisguised eagerness. "I solemnly swear never to tell a soul about the existence of this still, so help me God. There, I hope that satisfies you. You need not be afraid of my not keeping my oath, but just the same, I think you're a fool to do this. You're almost sure to be caught at it, sooner or later, and a federal prison isn't a particularly pleasant place."

"I don't reckerlect hevin' asked any advice from *yo'*," was Judd's surly reply.

"Well, I don't expect that you'll follow it," answered the other, as he scrambled to his feet. "And since we don't seem to hit it off very well together, I guess I'll be starting along."

"No yo' won't . . . leastwise not yet!" Judd's words came with crisp finality, and were reinforced by a quick movement of his rifle to the hip. "I haint through with ye yet, stranger. Last year I warned ye fair thet this hyar mountain war an onhealthy place fer ye. 'Pears like yo' didn't believe hit, but I means thet ye should this time. Erfore yo' goes I'll hear ernother sworn promise from ye, an' I reckon yo' kin guess what hit air."

"I can. And you're not going to get it. No, by God, not if you put a coward's bullet into me for refusing," burst out Donald, with his pent-up anger breaking its bounds at the other's dictatorial demands. "I agreed that what you did with your time wasn't my business, but what I do with mine, is. And I don't take orders from you in the matter, understand?"

The mountaineer's lips drew back, his body quivered, and the finger on the rifle's trigger trembled.

Above him, Donald stood equally tense and pale. He felt that he should be praying as he had never prayed before, but wrath possessed his spirit wholly, and his mind was completely concentrated on that lean forefinger, whose slightest tension meant death. Moments like these come but once in the lifetime of the average man, if, indeed, they ever come at all; but, when they do, when he suddenly finds himself face to face with some cataclysmic upheaval in human or external nature that threatens to rend the thin but impenetrable curtain which separates him from eternity, the salient characteristic of his being is unmasked and stands forth, naked. If he be at heart a coward, even though he may honestly never have suspected himself of cowardice, he will try to flee, or cringe and grovel for mercy; if his soul is stayed upon the immortal and everlasting truths, he will face what Fate may hold with the resigned fortitude which was the martyrs'; but, if he is merely a man, strong with the courage of the beast, refined and strengthened in the fires of intellect, he will be more likely to stand his ground unflinchingly and cast his defiance in the teeth of the danger which threatens, wrathful, but unafraid.

Donald was of the latter breed. He made no move; but the cords and veins in his muscular neck and hands swelled visibly, and his dark gray eyes took on a steely glint, as they bored steadily into Judd's glowering black ones.

Suddenly, with a deep oath, the mountaineer dropped the butt of his gun to the ground. Both men breathed a deep sigh, and the latter said: "No, I kaint shoot an unarmed man, even ef he *air* a skunk. But hark ye. I warns ye now fer the last time. Clar out uv this hyar mountain terday, er go armed an' ready, fer, by Gawd A'mighty, I aims ter shoot ye dead the next time I meets ye. Hit's yo' er me now."

When the other dropped his weapon, Donald had almost decided to make an attempt to clear the atmosphere by telling him again that his suspicions were utterly groundless and that, so far from having any intention of stealing the affections of the mountain child whom Judd loved, he was betrothed to another. But, at the challenge to fight, something, which he could neither explain afterwards nor control then, swept away the half-formed resolve, and the heat of primal hate sent a burning flush through him and drove cool reason utterly from its throne.

"If you didn't have that gun, you damned coward,

I'd come down there this instant, and thrash you within an inch of your worthless life," he shouted, heedless of consequences; too angry to care what might happen. And simultaneously, spurred on by his own blind passion, he slid down the bank and, with fists clenched, advanced on Judd. A yard ahead of him bristled Mike, a canine fury with gleaming teeth bared and muscles tensed for a spring. His master's quarrel was his also.

"Call off thet damned dawg, ef yo' don't want fer him ter git shot," raged the other, white with anger. "I reckon thet the time *hes* come fer me ter teach ye a lesson; p'raps then a rifle bullet won't be nowise necessary. Yo' tie up thet devil, an' I'll hev it out with ye, now." Wrath robbed him, too, of all caution and he flung his gun far to one side as Donald, with hands that trembled so violently that he could barely tie the knots, slipped his handkerchief through Mike's collar and fastened him securely to a stout bush. Then he faced the infuriated mountaineer.

"Hit's yo' er me," panted the latter, assuming a pantherlike crouch.

"Let it go at that," answered the city man, dropping naturally into a fighting position.

The veneer of our vaunted civilization is, at the best, thin, and every man, in whose veins runs red blood, has within him pent-up volcanic forces which require but little awakening to produce a soul-shattering upheaval. Donald knew that his being shouted aloud for battle — why, he didn't pause to analyze. Judd knew full well what *he* was fighting for. It was the woman whom his heart had claimed as his mate, regardless of what his chances of winning her were.

In college days, Donald had been a trained athlete, and he was still exceptionally powerful, although city life and his confining work had robbed his muscles of some of the flexibility and strength which had once been theirs, and were now possessed by those of his opponent. In weight, and knowledge of the science of boxing, he far surpassed Judd; but these odds were evened by the fact that *his* mind — thoroughly aroused though it was — held only a desire to punish the other severely, whereas Judd's passion burned deeper; blood-lust was in his heart and he saw red. Nothing would satisfy him short of killing the man who seemed to be the personification of his failure to win Smiles.

The mountaineer opened the fight with a furious rush. Donald instinctively side-stepped, and met it with a jolting short-arm blow to the other's lean jaw, which sent the aggressor to the ground.

Like a flash he was up again, wild to close with his rival and get his fingers about his throat. There, in the little natural amphitheatre, with only the ancient trees as silent witnesses, was staged again the oft-fought fight between the boxer and the battler, but the decision was not to rest on points. No Marquis of Queensberry rules governed, no watchful referee was present to disqualify one or the other for unfair tactics.

CHAPTER XV

REAPING THE WHIRLWIND

It was not long before Donald realized that, whatever had been Judd's primary purpose, he was now fighting to kill, and he sought desperately to drive home a blow which would knock him out. But, with all his greater skill, it was not easily to be accomplished. The mountaineer was tough, agile and actuated by a rage which mere punishment only increased. And punishment he took aplenty; while Donald remained almost unscathed, as he met rush after rush, and a storm of wildly flailing blows, with an unbroken defence.

Nor was it long before the other realized that absolute necessity called for him to break through that guard, and clinch with his opponent, if he were to hope to be successful in carrying out his design. Gathering his physical forces for a final desperate assault — which right and left hand blows on his already battered, bleeding face could not check — he broke through Donald's defence, and flung his sinewy arms about his rival.

For a moment both men clung desperately to one another, their breath coming in labored gasps.

Then, suddenly, the mountaineer twisted his leg

about one of Donald's, catching him off his guard, and they went heavily to the ground together.

Whatever had been the city man's advantage when they were on their feet, he shortly discovered that the woodman's great agility and crude skill in wrestling gave him the upper hand in this more primitive method of combat. Over and over they rolled, gasping for breath, and, although Donald exerted his great, but now rapidly failing, strength, more than once he felt the clutch of the other's lean, powerful fingers gripping his throat and shutting off his breath, before he could tear them free.

The end came suddenly.

During a deadly grapple — with first one man, then the other, on top — Donald called into play the last of his nervous reserve force, and, with a mighty effort, broke free, and flung Judd face downward on the ground. The latter's right arm was extended, and, grasping the sweaty wrist, he drew it up and back, at the same instant crowding his knee into the spine of the prostrate man.

Judd cursed and wriggled frantically; but only succeeded in grinding his battered face into the torn turf. It was some seconds before the conqueror could gain breath enough to speak. At last he panted out, "Now I've got you. If you move I'll dislocate your shoulder like *this!*" An involuntary shriek of agony was wrung from the defeated man's bleeding lips.

"I'll let you up when . . . ."

"Oh, ooooh!" came a startled, terrified cry from

above him. Donald lifted his eyes, and saw Rose standing on the bank where he had stood.

For an instant he remained as though turned to stone, staring at the girl with growing dismay. Finally he got slowly to his feet, instinctively gave partial aid to Judd as he too struggled up, his burning eyes also fixed on Smiles. It seemed as though the two dishevelled, dirt-covered and bleeding men typified the brute in nature, and stood arraigned there before the spirit of divine justice, for the slender girl's white dress, and no less white face, against the background of dark green, made her appear almost like an ethereal being.

Her breast was rising and falling rapidly as was indicated by the palpitating movement of her hand pressed close against it; her lips were parted and her large, shadowy eyes filled with uncomprehending fear and pain.

"What . . . what do hit mean?" she whispered.

As Judd made no answer Donald finally succeeded in summoning up an unnatural laugh and lied reassuringly, "It . . . it isn't anything serious, Smiles. Judd and I got into a dispute over . . . . over which was the better wrestler, and I have been showing him a few city tricks."

"Thet air a lie!" The mountaineer's words lashed out like a physical blow, and the crimson flamed into the other's cheeks — and those of Smiles as well.

"Hit air er lie," he repeated with a rasping voice, as he dashed the blood and dirt from his lips. "We war fightin' ter kill, an' I reckon yo' kin guess what hit war erbout," he added, flinging the last words up at the girl.

Once again Donald attempted to save her still greater distress by a white lie. "I chanced to stumble on his hidden still, Smiles, and he thought that I would betray him."

"Oh, Juddy," cried the girl wringing her hands, "I've been erfeerin' this. In course I knowed erbout hit, fer yo' showed me the still yerself, but I've been worryin', and hit war ter warn ye . . . ter beg ye ter quit fer leetle Lou's sake erfore hit war too late thet I came. Yo' must quit, oh *please*, Judd." In her eagerness she ran down the bank and toward him. "*I* knows thet Doctor Mac wouldn't tell, but hit's a warnin'."

As though hypnotized, Judd gazed into her pleading face, with his passion for her overwhelming that other one, which had so short a time before swayed him. He stepped to meet her with a gesture of hopelessness, and, realizing that he was for the moment forgotten, Donald moved softly to the mountaineer's rifle, ejected the cartridges from the magazine and pocketed them unobserved.

"I *kaint* quit, Rose," answered Judd, looking into her face with a hungry expression. "I kaint stop. Hit's my work, an' hit pays better then ever hit done. I wants ter make money . . . fer yo'. Besides, ef hit hadn't ha' been fer the white liquor what I sell ter the storeman down in Fayville, I wouldn't have been able ter sell yo'r baskets for ye. I wouldn't hev had no money ter give. . . ."

He checked his impetuous, unconsidered words too late. The girl's quick mind delved into his unspoken thought. She started and stepped back, crying, "'To give?' Judd Amos, war hit yo' thet paid me ther extry price on them baskets?"

Confused and distressed, the other remained silent until she repeated her question insistently. Then he answered pleadingly, "I loves ye, Smiles. Yo' know hit, an' so does *he*. I wanted ter holp ye, an' 'twar ther only way."

Even while Donald — rejoicing in the opportunity to regain his self-possession — had stood apart from the other two, none of the conversation had escaped him. With his wrath now fanned to flame afresh by Judd's apparent falsehood, he, too, burst into hot words without pausing to consider the effect of them on the girl, "What? You dare attempt to curry favor with her by lyingly claiming credit for the additional money her work brought, you cur? You didn't know that I held the cards to call that outrageous bluff, too, did you? You didn't know that I bought every one of those baskets, and told the storekeeper what price to pay for them, did you?"

No sooner had the anger-impelled words left his lips than Donald felt heartily ashamed of himself, and wished that he might unsay them. Half afraid, he turned his eyes toward the girl to find his fears realized. Her eyes were flaming from her deathly white face, and a mingled look of hurt pride and bitter scorn struggled for supremacy on her lips.

"Yo' . . . yo' think I would accept yo'r charity?" she cried. "Yo' think I would take money gifts from any man? I allows ter pay ye both every cent uv thet money; and I hates ye . . . I hates ye both."

For an instant she stood trembling with anger and mortification, then turned and sped up the bank and away into the woods.

Judd sank down with a muffled groan, but Donald, shocked at the result of his ill-advised and hasty words, forgot his late adversary and sprang in pursuit, crying, "Smiles. Dear child, wait. I want to talk with you, to explain. . . ."

He ran over rock and crag blunderingly into the forest in the direction she had taken, and, as he disappeared, Mike, who, during the combat, had continually raged at his leash in futile frenzy, made a last desperate effort, snapped the leather collar, although the effort drew a yelp of pain from him, and tore after him.

He passed his master and overtook the fleeing girl, sagaciously sensing the situation; but, as she paid no heed to his appealing barks and tugs at her skirt, but merely ran the faster, he turned back to await his lord. Body-weary and discomforted, Donald likewise gave up the chase as the sound of Smiles' flight grew more distant and died away.

Eventually she too dropped into a walk, and

finally stopped altogether, with a deep, gasping sob. Throwing herself down at the foot of an ancient tree, she pressed her flushed face hard against the rough bark, her mind in a wretched turmoil.

For the first time in Smiles' young life her eyes had been opened, and she had looked upon the brute passions of men, had tasted the bitter gall of trust abused, had felt an anger which brought with it the desire to hurt another as she herself had been hurt.

Stabbed to the quick of her soul, she lay on the moss-bedded roots of the impassive tree, her body quivering with soundless, shuddering sobs.

She hated herself, the two men — and Judd less than Donald, for she had known and excused his short-comings, while in her childish eyes Dr. MacDonald had been all that was noble, a superman, an idol whose feet were now clay. She hated the world where such things were possible.

For a long time Rose lay as she had fallen, hardly moving, and when — pale and dry-eyed — she did arise to return to the cabin through the twilight shadows, something beautiful, but indefinable, which had gone to make up the fresh, childlike charm of her face, had vanished.

Meanwhile, Donald walked heavily on with bowed head, heedless of the direction he took. The sound of rushing waters finally struck upon his ear, and his heated, dirt-covered body turned instinctively in their direction. A few minutes brought him to the river at a point where it tore through a narrow ravine of rock, in dashing cataract and noisy rapid. Donald, with increasing lameness, made his way painfully along the craggy bank until it descended to the river's edge, and, kneeling beside the leaping waters, he plunged his bruised, aching hands and face into them gratefully.

As he stood up again at last, his ears caught faintly above the river's tumult the distant crack of a rifle, followed immediately by another sound nearer at hand on the bank above him.

It was the agonized yelp of pain from a dog. Donald sprang erect, his heart seeming to lift with a convulsive action, and crowd his throat. He well knew that canine cry, now filled with mortal agony.

Almost blind with reborn rage and fear, Donald sprang up the steep bank, scrambling, stumbling, heedless of boughs which lashed across his face, and rocks which bruised his legs. He reached the top, and, parting the bushes, found what he had sought — and feared to find. On the stubbly grass lay little Mike, whining and biting at a spot on his side where the tawny hair was already matted and dark with flowing blood.

Made speechless by the clutching pressure in his throat, and suddenly dizzy from a mist which rose before his eyes, the man bent and lifted the panting animal — his bosom friend and faithful companion through many days and nights — in his trembling arms.

Mike painfully turned his head and licked his master's drawn face. The next instant came the sound of crashing underbrush, and, through vistas, Donald saw a man approaching them on a lumbering run. It was Big Jerry. His beard and clothing were dishevelled, and, as he drew near, his deep, gasping breaths became audible. From his ghastly gray and working face his deep eyes looked forth with an expression which spelt pain of body and wrack of mind.

Donald stood up, with the dog clasped to his breast, and a terrible expression on his countenance.

"Mike . . . my friend . . . shot . . . he is dying," came his words, in an unnatural voice. "God have mercy on the man who did it. I shall not!"

The giant's frame seemed to collapse visibly; two big tears started from his eyes and ran down the furrows of his cheeks as he moved closer and laid his big, shaking hand on the dog's head.

"*I* done hit," he answered dully.

Mike licked the wrinkled hand which moved in slow caress over his jaws.

"You?" whispered Donald in amazed unbelief.

"Gawd help me, yes. I shot him . . . I wish hit hed er been myself," returned the old man, between breaths which came in deep, body-shaking gasps.

Slowly the doctor bent, laid his chum back on the ground, and knelt beside him until the fast glazing eyes — which never wavered from his — closed forever, and the pain-tortured little body lay still. Big Jerry, too, sank down and dropped his massive head onto his hands, while his frame rose and fell with convulsive heaving.

"Hit war this erway," he began to speak at last, and told his story in broken, laboring sentences. "I war erhuntin' with . . . with yo'r rifle-gun in the woods thar beyond ther ravine. Jest es I war startin' fer the cabin, I seen . . . I seen a man erstandin' hyar on the bank, er peerin' down towards the river, thar. I looked whar he war erlookin', an' seen ye down thar, bathin' yo'r face in ther water. The man war ertotin' a rifle-gun, an' uv a sudden he drapped ter his knee an' raised hit, an' I knowed he war kalkerlatin' ter shoot ye.

"I tried fer ter shout, ter cry out a warnin' ter ye, but my voice hed somehow lost hits power, an' wouldn't kerry above the noise of the falls. Thar war but one thing fer ter do, an' hit called fer powerful quick action.

"Yo' war my foster-son, an' ef 'twar yo'r life er his'n I allowed I knowed whar my duty lay. But I didn't aim fer ter kill him. . . . I wish ter Gawd I hed. 'Taint boastin' none fer me ter say ter ye thet I aimed only fer ter shoot the arm what war holdin' the gun.

"In course hit takes time fer ter tell ye all this, but I acted like I thought. Then . . ." he paused, and went on only with a supreme effort, "then, jest as I started the trigger-pull, I seen . . . I seen leetle Mike spring out o' the bushes straight at . . . at the man. I *seen* him, I tells ye, erfore I fired. My mind told me not ter pull thet trigger, an' . . . an' I done hit. My aim war true, but . . . . " he stopped altogether.

"The man," asked Donald at length, through clenched teeth. "What happened to him?"

"He turned et the crack of my gun. He . . . he seen me, and run off inter the wood thar."

There ensued a long silence. Then Donald's hand stretched out and grasped that of the sorrowing giant.

"Jerry," he said steadily. "Don't feel so bad, it wasn't your fault. You did all that man could do. You were trying to . . . to save my life, just as . . . as Mike was, God bless the little dog. He must have realized that Judd was following me by the exercise of a sense beyond our knowledge, and rushed back to attack him — for my sake."

"Yo' said . . . yo' said . . . 'Judd.' How did yo' come ter know 'twar him?"

With new and deepened remorse, Donald sadly outlined the chief incidents of the quarrel, without, however, mentioning the discovery of the still, or the immediate cause of the combat.

"Gawd help us all ef er new feud hes broken out hyar," said Jerry solemnly, as he finished. "But yo' air my friend, enjyin' ther hospitality of my roof, an' from this day Judd Amos air my mortal enemy, even though he be my next neighbor."

Donald sadly removed his coat, and, wrapping it around the body of his chum, arose, and the silent, painful journey home was begun.

CHAPTER XVI

THE AFTERMATH

SUPPER was over. With kindly hands night had laid her deep purple mantle over the new-made mound back of the cabin, hiding it from the grieving gaze of the three who sat before the door in painful silence beneath the star-pierced dome of heaven. In the poignancy of her own sorrow, and her overwhelming sympathy for Donald, when she had come to a realization of the meaning of the bundle which he brought out of the woods and laid so tenderly down on the grass before the cabin's stoop, every vestige of Smiles' anger had instantly vanished.

"Oh, the pity, the uselessness of it," cried Donald's heart, as his thoughts again and again turned back to the tragic series of events which had made the afternoon a thing of horror. The bitter culmination, — the death of Mike, poor, courageous, self-sacrificing little Mike — was the most needless of all, for, although he had not mentioned the fact to Big Jerry, Donald knew that in all human probability Judd's rifle was empty of cartridges. And, although Jerry himself uttered no word of complaint, the physician knew, only too well, that the gripping excitement, against which he had warned the old man only a few hours earlier, had brought its inevitable aftermath. The giant's breath came with labored, audible gasps, and his very appearance told the story of the increased pain within his breast. For these disasters — as well as the mortal enmity of the young mountaineer and the heart-ache of the innocent girl — he, and he alone, was to blame. Donald groaned under his breath.

The silence was finally ended by Smiles crying out bitterly, "Oh, Doctor Mac, I can't understand why grandfather pulled that trigger, and shot dear little Mike. He saw him spring at Judd."

"It wasn't in any wise his fault, dear heart. He could not possibly have helped it. You see our brains are telegraph stations from which the nerves run like wires, carrying messages to all the different parts of our bodies. Big Jerry had sent a command to his finger, ordering it to pull the trigger, and the muscles had started to obey. The second message countermanding the first — quick as it was — came too late to halt the purely muscular action; that is all."

"Another good evening, my friends," came a cheery voice, and the mountain minister approached out of the shadows, and joined them. "I am just back from a journey into the wilderness, like John the Baptist's, and . . . Why, what's wrong? Do I see the ghost of a sorrow sitting amid this group, which should be so happy?"

"Oh, Mr. Talmadge," cried Rose, jumping up and stepping to his side as he paused. "Many ghosts are here to-night. I think that you took God away with you on your journey, for His spirit has not been in Webb's Gap this afternoon."

"Tell me, what has happened, my dear?" he answered quietly, as he seated himself within the circle.

Then, step by step, the whole unhappy story was haltingly poured into his ears, save only that Smiles consciously refrained from mentioning the cause which Judd had — by implication — given for the quarrel and Donald kept his promise and made no allusion to his finding of the still. Since the minister asked no questions and made no comment concerning the cause, it is fair to assume that he guessed the truth and wisely held his own counsel. When he had brought the patchwork recital to an end, the doctor laughed with a bitter note.

"You see how much good the brief glimpse which I had last night of the eternal light did me! Before one full day has elapsed, I sound a lower depth in primitive, brutal passion then I ever had before in my life. I am sick at heart when I think how quickly and easily I could forget everything which goes to make up civilization. There was no excuse for it — that's the worst part. I was infinitely more to blame than Judd, even leaving out of consideration the fact that a greater degree of self-restraint and forbearance should reasonably have been expected of me, a city-bred man, than of him, a more primitive son of the hills."

Donald placed his elbows on his knees and buried

his face in his hands with a stifled sound, which might have been groan or curse, and very gently Smiles' hand stole up in the darkness and stroked his tumbled hair, until the man's own fumblingly sought and held it close, to find mute comfort in her warm clasp.

"Perhaps I understand better than you think the reasons which underlie these most unhappy events," answered the old man slowly. There was no rebuke in his quiet voice.

"Although it is true, doctor, that the deeper we get into the heart of primal nature, the closer we get to the heart of nature's God, it is equally true that the nearer we also get to the primal in man.

"I cannot help feeling that the city's laws and conventions trammel the spirit in its free exercise of self, which is ill; but yet the inbred realization of those very laws and conventions, and the fear of consequences if they are broken, act as a salutary check on the primitive passions inherited by every one of us from our savage ancestors.

"Of course, I know that, in places where men are crowded together, such man-made laws and conventions are wise and necessary; but the life which results is not — cannot be — full and natural as it may be in an isolated place like this, when honest obedience is paid to the still higher laws of God — and it is for *that* obedience which all of us must strive constantly.

"You failed in the test to-day; but, believe me,

there are many in these mountains who, lacking all the advantages of training and education which are yours, meet it. Their lives are lived under nature's higher laws in perfect sincerity, and, although they might not conform to the standards of so-called civilization, they are surely purer in God's sight than those of millions who pattern theirs by printed precept."

"I reckon," murmured Smiles, "that St. Peter had to put many black marks on three books to-day . . . yes, mine too, for I was wickedly angry. It was hate that made me run away from Doctor Mac, and if I hadn't done it, M . . M . . . Mike wouldn't have been shot." She leaned her head against Donald's arm, and cried softly.

" 'The wages of sin is death,'" said the minister. "And he paid the penalty for you, Dr. MacDonald, sacrificing himself because of his great love. Poor little Mike. Such faithful animals as he must have souls, and his is now in its own paradise."

No one spoke for a little, and then Mr. Talmadge continued to muse aloud.

"Mere repentance, such as the doctor now feels, is not enough. You remember the parable of the woman who drove the evil spirit from her fleshly temple, and swept it clean, but failed to fill its place with another guest, and seven other devils came and repossessed it? So it is always with human life, Dr. MacDonald. Nature abhors a vacuum, and so does the spirit. If a man does not fill his soul—swept free of past evil by repentance — with that which is actively good, the repentance is of little avail."

"Yes, yes, I can readily understand that, for it has a parallel in bodily illness," answered Donald, somewhat impatiently. "We all know that, when the sick physical being is freed of its disease, it is left weak and an easy prey for new troubles. We can bring back to it the strength to resist by giving nerve- and tissue-building food and tonics, but how is the spirit to be . . ."

"How persistently the earth-man kicks against the pricks," cried Mr. Talmadge. "Child, your friend will not lift his eyes from the maze of doubt. You pledged yourself to help him. Help him now."

Her face suddenly glowing with light, Rose turned to Donald eagerly, and said without hesitation, "Oh, Doctor Mac, don't you see? The answer is so clear, so simple that even I know it. The dear God spirit is everywhere, just waiting for you to call it to your aid. Please pray to Him to give you new strength so that you may not be weak again, and I will pray, too."

"Yes," supplemented the minister, "'Whence cometh my help? My help cometh even from the Lord, which hath made heaven and earth.'"

Donald was strongly moved at the eager interest in him which these two displayed. Shifting uncomfortably he replied, "I need His help, I know; but . . . but I guess I have forgotten how to pray for it."

"Open your heart with sincerity, and He will enter and bestow the strength you need in order to take up your task anew, and carry on until your purpose here on earth has been accomplished. That is all that prayer need be, for He is ever more ready to give than we to receive. Verbal petitions are vain and empty things; honest communion with Him *is* prayer."

He arose, content to say no more, and to leave the sorely troubled spirit of the stranger to Smiles' tender ministrations. "I am deeply sorry for you in your distress, Dr. MacDonald, but although there is small comfort in the remark, I cannot help but feel that what has happened was ordained to complete your lesson, so that you may leave these hills with a new understanding and higher purpose in life. Good night, and God be with you all."

CHAPTER XVII

THE PARTING PLEDGE AND PASSING DAYS

"DOCTOR MAC.," began Smiles timidly, at length. "I'm sorry for what I said to you this afternoon, and I want to take it back. I guess when you're angry you don't see things as they are, and I'm sure that you were only being very, very kind to me when you . . . you bought those baskets. I love you for it, really I do, and if . . . if you want me to keep the money, and it would hurt your feelings if I . . ."

"Of course I want you to keep it, dear. Yesterday you took me for a foster-brother, and I hope that you will always let me do for you as I would for a real flesh-and-blood sister."

"I promise, and I will always do the same for you if I can, dear Don," she whispered softly, adding, "but somehow to-night — oh please don't laugh at me now — somehow to-night I feel more like . . . like a mother, than a sister to you."

"And I truly think you are — a spiritual mother, little woman. I need you much more than you need me, I guess."

"Do you know," he went on, after a moment, "I am beginning to believe that I was wrong this afternoon when I said that . . . that Judd lied about adding to the money he received for your baskets. Of course I have no way of making sure, unless you have kept accounts, but I actually begin to think that he did."

"I *know* it," she replied promptly; but with a troubled voice. "Judd has been very wicked, but he doesn't lie. I think that he meant it the way . . . the way you did, too; but he's different and I mean to give it all back to him." There was another pause, and then Smiles said gently, "Donald, it makes my heart ache like, to tell you this, but I've got to now. I want that you should go away early to-morrow morning."

"What?" he burst out angrily, springing to his feet. "And have him believe that I ran away from him again? No, how can you ask it, Rose?"

"It isn't that. We know, and *he* knows now, that you're not afraid of him. But this mountain is his home, and, if you stay here, there is sure to be more trouble, and I couldn't bear that, Don. Even if one of you wasn't . . . wasn't hurt in the body, wicked thoughts would hurt your souls. I know it is so, and you *must* go . . . but, oh, how I am going to miss you."

For a moment Donald stood tense; then his body relaxed weakly and he answered, "Yes, you are right, Smiles. It *is* up to me to go; but I know that some day these clouds are going to be lifted somehow, and we shall see each other again and be happy together."

"I know it, too," she answered, with a sob catching her breath. As she spoke, the clouds, which had been covering the moon for some time, broke, letting the cool, white light flood the mountain side like a promise, and her face lit up with the old wondrous smile. "Of course we will," she cried. "Why, I mean to be your own special nurse some day, and help you always. Good-night, dear Don."

She turned and ran quickly into the cabin, so that he should not see the tears which followed the smile.

"Rose war right erbout yo'r goin', — I reckon she air allus right," came Big Jerry's voice. "Yo' hev got ter go; but I'm ergoin' ter miss ye powerful, likewise, lad."

"But I'll see you again, too, before long. I've got some of my sense back, and I mean to write Judd that I am engaged to a girl in the city — not that I want his friendship after what has happened, however — and I will be down here again, for a few days at least, when the atmosphere has cleared — perhaps early this winter."

"Taint likely yo'll ever see me ergin on earth, son," Jerry said heavily. "Reckon I'm most done fer."

"Your heart? Is it very bad?" queried Donald.

"I allows hit's nigh ter bustin'," was the steady response. "But mebbe I'll last some while yet — I hopes so, fer leetle Smiles' sake. I haint blind ter what hes happened, an' I knows thet the time air comin' when she's es plumb sartain ter fly erway from this hyar mountain es a homein' dove; fer she hes heard the call uv her city blood, an' hit haint ter be denied. But I reckon she haint ready ter leave the old nest yet, so I aims ter stay on erwhile longer . . . fer her, though hit haint goin' ter be in no wise easy fer ter do."

The younger man knew not what answer to make to this affecting declaration; but the necessity of a reply was forestalled, for Big Jerry stepped closer and continued earnestly, "Since yo' wished fer ter be a son ter me, I air ergoin' ter treat ye es sich, an' tell ye something thet I've done fer the leetle gal, an' thet she don't yet know erbout.

"Back in the spring when I seen thet her mind war made up ter be a nurse, an' I knowed thet my own time war comin', I sold the timber rights ter these hyar woods ter a city lumber company fer a thousand dollars. They haint ergoin' ter cut fer some years yet, an' by thet time I won't be hyar ter grieve, an' Smiles won't neither.

"Thet money, an' a leetle more what I hev saved, air ter be hern . . . hit's in er savin' bank down ter the city now. But thet haint all I wants ye ter know. The reverend drawed a last will an' testiment fer me, leavin' this hyar land ter her — she haint blood kin of mine, yo' know, nor adopted by law — an' I reckons hit will be val'able some day, fer a city stranger told me oncet thet thar's coal on hit. So my leetle gal haint ergoin' ter start her new life penniless, an' . . . an' now I wants ter name ye ter be her guardeen till she air growed up. I hopes yo'll accept ther charge, fer I trusts ye, son."

"Accept? Indeed I will, and it makes me mighty happy to realize that I mean something to both of you. I've been playing that she was my sister, but now she will really be as much to me as though she were."

The two men clasped hands again in full understanding, and as a symbol of a trust bestowed and accepted.

. . . .

At sunrise the following morning Donald once more turned his face toward the valley, whence he had climbed lightheartedly less than two days previous. He had come with a beloved companion. He went alone, save for crowding memories — some bright, but far more black as storm-clouds and shot with malignant flashes of lightning.

His vacation — a travesty on the name — was ended; the castle which his dreams had built on this remote mountain was a shattered ruin. Yet, through the dark series of crowding events, ran a fine thread of gleaming gold, and Donald felt that it had not been broken by his departure. No, it was spun by Destiny to stretch on and on into the unseen future, at once for him a guide-line to a higher manhood, and a tie binding his life to that of the girl whose pathway — starting so far removed from his — had so strangely converged with it.

To continue his hunting trip in another location, with Mike no longer his companion in it, was unthinkable. The empty spaces made the void in his heart unbearable, and he at once returned to Boston and joined his family at their summer home, to their amazement and delight.

But the man now returned to them after little more than a week's absence was vastly different from the one who had left. All marked the alteration in him, and over and over in family council tried, vainly, to account for it, for Donald had withheld far more than he told of his experiences, and minimized what he did tell.

But he knew, as well as they, that a new chord had been struck within him, and by its vibrations his whole life was being tuned anew. Something of the old boyishness and impetuosity was gone, a new purposefulness — not of the will but rather of the spirit — had supplanted it and engendered an unwonted serenity. Was it born of the words of the strange mountain prophet, or the impelling appeal of the no-less-strange mountain child, whose mysterious smile, though seen less frequently than on his first visit, still cast a spell over his senses, even in memory? He could not say.

Whatever uncertainties had disturbed his heart before, when his thoughts had turned upon her, none now remained. The die was cast. Smiles had made her place in his life, and would always occupy it, but merely as a dear charge and comrade. Half-child, half-woman, she still appealed to him in both capacities as perhaps none other ever had; yet he could now admit that fact frankly, and at the same time tell himself that there was, there could be, nothing else.

With the mists of uncertainty dispelled, and his mind purged of the passions which had, so unexpectedly, possessed it, Donald's life returned to its old ruts. His work absorbed him as before, he accepted Marion as more fully a part of his life than she had previously been, and, in so doing, found an unexpected contentment. If, at times, he still felt that she was not all that he might desire, at least she was of his class and he understood her thoroughly.

"My work furnishes enough of romance for me," he sometimes thought. "And, if I want to remain a civilized human being, I had better stick to the life in which I was brought up. I never suspected how much of a 'cave man' I was until I got into the heart of the primitive. Whew! Supposing I had killed Judd that afternoon! There were a few moments when it would have been a pleasure to have done it. Or supposing he had killed me! He wanted to, right enough. Puck was right."

And so, while the months passed, Fortune smiled on the brilliant young physician, and daily laid new tributes of wealth, honor and affection at his feet.

. . . .

In the mountain cabin it was otherwise.

Changes, born of the travail of tragic happenings,

cast their ever-lengthening shadows over Smiles' life, blotting out the golden sunlight of childhood, and overlaying it with the deeper tones of womanhood.

Judd, her companion since baby days, she no longer called "friend," and he, for his part, steadily avoided her and the cabin which had once been a second home to him. Big Jerry, uncomplaining ever, day by day grew more feeble and pain-wracked, and so became more and more a dear burden to her. Only Mr. Talmadge, of her real intimates, remained unchanged in his relations with her, unless it was that in his deep and understanding sympathy he brought her greater spiritual and mental comfort than ever. The other neighbors were kind always, in their rough, well-meaning way; but he was her chief guide and comforter, and in him, and the books which Donald conscientiously sent to her every few weeks, she found the strength to carry forward.

So, in the never-ending tasks which her daily life provided, and which she performed with distress in her heart, but a smile on her lips, Rose saw the weeks come and go, bringing in their slow-moving, but inexorable, train, autumn, fall and another winter.

CHAPTER XVIII

THE ADDED BURDEN

It was mid-winter. The twilight sky — cold and pale, more green than blue — brought the thought of new-made ice. Stripped long since of their verdure, the wooded Cumberlands lay, like naked, shivering giants, across whose mighty recumbent torsos the biting winds swept relentlessly.

In contrast with the desolation without, inside Big Jerry's cabin all was as bright, warm and homelike as a merry fire, the soft glow of the evening lamp and the presence of the heart of the spot — the girl herself — could make it.

Thankful for the blessings of the cheery home and her grandfather's presence in it still, and softly humming an old ballad which he loved, Rose was busily engaged in preparing an early supper, when she was interrupted by the sound of a low, uncertain knock on the door.

She opened it, wonderingly, and the firelight leaped out into the night and disclosed the unshaven face and gaunt form of Judd.

Save on rare occasions, and then at a distance, she had not seen him since that fateful day on the mountain's summit, when his passionate love and hate, intermingled, had driven him to commit the great offence against the unwritten laws of the feudal clan, by attacking one upon whom the sacred mantle of hospitality had been placed, by which act he had incurred Jerry's enmity, and made himself love's outlaw.

The months had dealt harshly with him. Not only was his clothing frayed and soiled; but his face was so unnaturally pale that the deep-set eyes beneath their lowering black brows seemed to burn like embers, and there were many new lines on his countenance not graven there by wind and weather.

Shocked at the change in him, and suddenly filled with womanly compassion which sounded the knell of anger, Rose called, gently, "Judd! Why, Judd! Come in."

He shook his head. "I reckon I haint welcome in this hyar cabin, Smiles, an' taint on my own ercount thet I comes ter ye."

"Why, what is the trouble?" was her startled inquiry.

"Hit . . . hit air leetle Lou. I erlows she's sick er somethin'."

"Lou? Tell me quick, Judd. What is the matter with her?"

"I don't rightly know." The answer was made with obvious distress. "She haint been her sunshiny self fer quite some time, an' ter-night . . . wall, she air actin' so sorter . . . queer, thet I got skeered."

"I'll go over home with you at once," said Rose, as she hastily caught up and drew a shawl about her head and shoulders. "Grandpap," she called softly through the door to the old man's bedroom, "I'm ergoin' out fer er leetle time. One of ther neighbors air sick. Don't fret, fer I'll be back right soon, dear."

There was a brief, rumbled reply; and, closing the door behind her on the warm comfort within, the girl joined the mountaineer in the crispy evening, now almost dark. She shivered a little, and he marked the involuntary act, and drew back a step.

In silence they walked rapidly up the narrow path, slippery from a recent fall of light snow. Once Rose slipped, and instantly Judd's sinewy arm was about her waist, steadying her. Then, as she regained her balance and started forward, it tightened and drew her suddenly to him in a passionate, crushing embrace. She made no effort to struggle free, or voice her heart's protest against this outrage, but stood with her body rigid and unyielding within the circle of his arm until he slowly released her, mumbling, "I reckon I air plumb ershamed of myself, Smiles. I didn't go fer ter do hit, an' I knows thet I haint deservin' ter tetch so much es ther hem of yo'r skirt."

She did not answer, and neither spoke again until his cabin was reached.

When the door was opened, Smiles caught sight of the child sitting motionless on a stool near the fireplace. Her lips were parted and in her eyes was an odd look of semi-vacuity.

"Lou!" cried Rose, pausing in alarmed astonishment.

A light of recognition sprang into the child's eyes, she stood up a trifle unsteadily, and said, with a low throaty laugh of delight, "Hit air my Smiles. I awful glad ter see . . ." She started toward her friend; but her course suddenly veered to the left, waveringly, and her wandering gaze fell upon the now sadly battered doll lying in one corner. "To see ye, Mike," was the ending of her sentence, as she trotted to Donald's gift and began to cuddle it.

"Yo' haint erbeen ter see Lou fer er long, long . . ." The piping voice trailed off into silence.

"Why, Lou, sweetheart. What is the matter? Don't you know your own Smiles?" pleaded the deeply distressed girl, as she gathered the child to her breast.

The baby's hands dropped the doll unceremoniously and sought her friend's cheeks. Looking up with big eyes into the face drawn close to her own, she replied in a strangely slow, hesitant manner. "In course I remembers ye, Smiles. Yo' air the nurse what lives with . . . with thet thar doctor man . . . in the big city, whar air monkeys thet . . . clumb sticks an' . . . an' doll babies what close thar eyes . . . an' say . . . an' say . . . My head hurts me, Smiles, hit do."

She lay still in the loving arms for an instant, and

then wriggled free and, sliding to the floor, picked up and began to rock the doll again, the while crooning a wordless lullaby.

With anxiety growing akin to terror, Smiles felt the irregular pulse, as Donald had taught her how to do, and pressed her hand to the pale cheek and forehead.

"She *is* sick, Judd, and I'm kind of frightened, too. You can't take care of her here, and I mean to take her home with me, right now. I reckon you had better go down to the village and get Dr. Johnston, quick."

The man had started, with words of protest trembling on his lips; but, as his look turned on his little sister, as she now leaned drowsily against the girl's knees, he stifled them unspoken, while a spasm of pain crossed his worn face. With a dull nod of acquiescence he held out his arms to receive the child, whom Rose had lifted and wrapped in a blanket from her little bed that had been brought in near the fire.

The return journey was quickly and silently made, and, delivering the slight bundle to Smiles when her cabin was reached, Judd set off into the night, concern lending wings to his feet.

"Grandpap, hit's Smiles back ergin'," called the girl softly. "An' I've brought leetle Lou Amos. She haint feelin' right well, an' I allows I hev got ter take keer of her here."

The old man uttered a low growl of protest, which caused Rose to run to him and tenderly lay her hand on his lips, with the words, "Hush, grandpap. The baby haint in nowise ter blame fer . . . fer what Judd done. In course we hev got ter keer fer her."

Big Jerry nodded an abashed assent, and said no more.

Smiles undressed her new charge, who struck uncertain terror to her heart by drowsily talking on and on, in snatches of unrelated sentences running the gamut of her limited experiences and with the childish words often failing, half formed. She put the baby in her own bed, and, after the belated supper had been eaten and cleared away, and the old man made as comfortable as possible for the night, Smiles lay down beside the baby, whose silence and more regular breathing indicated that she was at last asleep.

The morrow's sun was well above the valley horizon before Judd returned with the country doctor, and again the former refused to enter the cabin. While the physician remained, he paced back and forth, back and forth, with weary, nervous strides; but even in his stress of mind he unconsciously kept out of view from the window in Big Jerry's room.

At last Rose and Dr. Johnston reappeared, and, breathing hard, Judd hastened to join them.

"It's brain fever, the doctor says, Judd," said Smiles at once. "He's left some medicine for me to give her, and you know that I'll nurse her for you like she was my own baby."

"Air hit . . . air hit *bad*, doctor?" asked the mountaineer, with a catch in his voice.

"Well, of course it ain't an . . . er . . . exactly easy thing to cure, but I reckon she'll get well of it. By the way, Amos, how long has she been a-goin' on like that?"

"I kaint rightly say, doctor. She hes acted kind er strange-like fer quite er spell, now thet I comes ter think on hit; but I didn't pay no pertickler attention to hit ontil er day er two back," answered the man contritely.

"Hmmm," said the doctor. "Oh, I guess we can pull her through all right, and I will get up here as often as I can. Well, I reckon I'll be stepping along back."

. . . .

But little Lou did not fulfil the country practitioner's optimistic prophecy. The change in her condition, as day after day crept by, growing longer and colder, was almost imperceptible; but it was steadily for the worse. The mountain winter closed in with unusual rigors, and Smiles' cabin continued to be a hospital where she passed her hours ministering equally to the keen-minded, but bodily tortured old man — whose heart pained constantly and with growing severity, and whose breathing became daily more labored — and the child whose mind steadily became more clouded and her physical functions more weak.

Like a gaunt, miserable dog which had been driven from his home, Judd haunted the cabin. When she stole out one morning, to speak with him about Lou, Smiles cried, "Oh, if Doctor Mac. were only here now! *He* would know what to do, I'm sure."

Judd's hands, blue with cold, clenched so violently that the knuckles grew a bloodless white, and the look of pain, lying deep down in his eyes, changed to a flash of burning hate.

"Don't never speak thet man's name ter me, gal."

The words were spoken in a harsh voice and he strode abruptly away.

At more and more infrequent intervals, the village doctor made his toilsome way up the slippery mountain side, sat regarding the little patient with a hopelessly puzzled look, and finally departed, shaking his head; but he never failed to leave behind him another bottle of obnoxious medicine on the chance that if one did not produce an improvement, another might. Even to the girl it was all too apparent, however, that he was aiming blindly into the dark.

There came a time when the child spoke scarcely at all, save to moan piteously something about the pain in her head; her emaciated legs barely carried her on her uncertain course; her vague, sweet eyes turned inward more and more; and it was with the greatest difficulty, and only by the exercise of infinite patience that Smiles could feed her. The little mountain blossom was wilting and fading slowly away.

On the afternoon of the first day of January Dr. Johnston spent a long time at the cabin, striving against the impossible to solve the problem which confronted him like an appalling mystery, far too deep to be pierced by the feeble ray of science at his command.

At last he arose with a gesture of finality, and announced to the anxiously waiting girl, "I reckon I'm done. I won't go so fur as to say that a city specialist might not be able to help her; but hanged if *I* can. The trouble is too much for me, and I guess Lou is just agoin' to die."

Sudden tears welled into Smiles' luminous eyes, and ran unheeded down her cheeks, now unnaturally thin and wan.

"Hit haint so," she cried in a choked voice. "Lou haint ergoin' ter die, Dr. Johnston!"

Suddenly she stopped, as her thoughts flew backward on the wings of memory. Her eyes grew larger, a strange light came into them. Then, speaking slowly, almost as though the words were impelled by a will other than her own, she added with a tone of absolute certainty:

"Yo' allows *yo'* don't know what the trouble air, but *I* does."

The doctor was startled and looked as though he thought that he was about to have another patient on his hands.

"Hit air a brain tumor thet she hes got, I knows it, an' I knows one of the few doctor men in this hyar country what kin cure hit. He air *ergoin'* ter cure hit fer me, an' leetle Lou haint *ergoin'* ter die."

Uncertain what to make of this outburst, the doctor departed rather hastily. Smiles caught up her shawl and ran immediately to Judd's lonely, cheerless abode, which she entered without a thought of knocking. She found the man sitting dejectedly before a feeble fire.

He sprang up, voiceless terror apparent in the look which he turned upon her white face, but, without pausing for any preliminaries, Rose said, "The doctor, he's been ter see our little Lou again, Judd. He allows thet he can't do anything more for her, and thet she has got ter die."

The man — whose whole world was now centred in the child to whom he had, for a year, been father and mother as well as brother — sank down on his chair and buried his face in his hands.

"I knowed hit," he muttered in a dead voice.

"Hit haint so," cried the girl, who had by this time wholly relapsed into the mountain speech, as she frequently did still, when laboring under the stress of emotion. "Hit haint so, Judd. We kin save her. We hev *got* ter save her."

"Thar haint no way." The words were tuned to despair.

"Thar *air* a way. Thar's one man who kin save Lou's life fer ye, an' we must get him ter do hit."

She had mentioned no name, but Judd sprang swiftly erect, fists clenched and shaking above his head. "Do yo' think thet I'd be beholden ter *thet* man, after what I done ter him? Do yo' think thet

I'd accept even my sister's life et his hands? I hates him like I does the devil what, I reckon, air ergoin' ter git my soul!"

"Judd!" cried the girl, "yo' don't know what yo'r ersayin'. Hit's blasphemy. Ef Doctor Mac. kin save Lou's life — an' he *kin* — yo'd be a murderer, — yes, a murderer uv yo'r own flesh an' blood, ter forbid him."

Spent by the force of his previous passionate outburst, the man sank tremblingly back into the chair again.

"I kaint do hit, Smiles," he answered piteously. "I kaint do hit, an' hit's a foolish thought anyway. He wouldn't come hyar. Hit takes money fer ter git city doctors, an' I haint got none."

"He will come ef I asks him, an' I hev money, Judd," she said with a pleading voice.

"No, no, no. Ef Lou dies, I reckon I'll kill myself, too; but I forbids ye ter call the man I wronged, an' hates."

Slowly the girl turned away, with a compassionate glance at the bent, soul-tortured youth, went out of the cabin, and softly closed the door.

CHAPTER XIX

"SMILES'" APPEAL

It was snowing when she stepped outside, — a soft, white curtain of closely woven flakes rapidly dimming the early evening glow and bringing night-shades on apace. The wind, too, was rising; its first fitful gusts drove the snow sweeping in whirling flurries across the open spaces, and then whistled off through the leafless trees.

Rose shivered. The wind greeted her boisterously. It clutched her shawl in hoydenish jest, tore one end of it free from her grasp, and ran its invisible, icy fingers down her neck.

The cabin of the nearest neighbor — Pete Andrews — was only a few rods distant; but, before the girl reached it in the face of the momentarily increasing storm, she was panting, and her face, hair and clothing were plastered with clinging flakes.

"Mis' Andrews, I hates ter ask er favor of ye such er powerful mean night; but I needs help," said Smiles, as soon as the door had been opened, letting her in, together with a whirl of snow which spread itself like a ghost on the rough floor.

"Yo' knows thet I'd do enything in ther world fer ye, Rose gal. I reckon I owes ye my life since when . . . when Gawd Almighty tuck my baby back ter thet garden er His'n in Paradise," answered the frail, weary-looking woman, whose eyes quickly suffused with tears.

"Hit haint repayment I'm askin' of ye, but er favor, Mis' Andrews. I wants ye ter help me save ther life of another mountin flower, what's nigh faded plum erway."

"Lou Amos?" asked the woman. She had already turned to get her own shawl.

"Yes, hit's leetle Lou. She air powerful sick, an' I wants fer ye ter stay ter-night with her an' grandpap, ef yo' will. Thar haint nothing ter do but stay with them."

"In course I'll do hit fer ye, Smiles," was the ready answer, and her lank, slouching husband nodded a silent assent, as she turned to him.

"But what air yo' reckonin' ter do? Yo' kaint go nowhar in this hyar storm. I don't recollect hits like on the mountain, no time."

The girl did not answer; but held the door open while the other stepped out, only to catch her breath and flatten herself against the cabin's wall as a sheet of mingled sleet and snow struck her. By continually assisting one another, the two made their way slowly over to Jerry's home; and, when they paused within its shelter, Rose held her companion's arm a moment, and said, "Thar haint no use tryin' ter prevent me, Mis' Andrews, cause I'm ergoin' ter do hit. I'm ergoin' down ter Fayville, an' send a telegram message fer er city doctor thet I knows, ter come hyar an' make Lou well. Don't go fer ter tell grandpap whar I've gone er he'll worry erbout me, an' thar haint no cause ter. The storm's et my back, an' hits all down hill goin'. I hates ter tell a lie ter him, but I allows I've got ter, this one time."

In sudden terror over the mad plan, the older woman began to protest; but Rose shook off her detaining hand, and put an end to the sentence by leading the way hastily into the cabin.

"Thar's a leetle child what needs my help, an' I've got ter take keer of her fer er while, grandpap," Smiles said at once. "Mis' Andrews hes come over fer ter stay with ye and Lou, now haint thet kind uv her? I'll git back es soon es ever I kin, but don't yo' fret ef hit haint erfore yo' goes ter bed . . . or even till mornin' time."

She furtively obtained a few bills from her precious store, kissed the old man's haggard, wrinkled cheek, and the white forehead of the baby who lay on the bed, almost inert save for the restless moving of her head from side to side, and the low moans which came with almost every breath, and hurried out into the storm.

In later years Rose could be induced to speak only with the greatest reluctance of that journey down the snow-swept mountain path — for the blizzard was as fierce as it was rare — and even the recollection of it brought a look of terror into her eyes.

There was flying horror abroad that night, and

the demented trees quivered and tossed their great arms so wildly that they cracked and broke, to fall crashing in the path. Yet, accomplish the five mile long, perilous descent, in the midst of lashing sleet and snow, over a slippery, tortuous path, she did. With her clothing torn by flaying branches and clutching wind, and drenched by icy water as the snow melted; with her hands and lips blue, and her feet numb; with her wavy hair pulled loose from its braids and plastered wetly against her colorless cheeks; she eventually stumbled into the rude building which contained the railroad and telegraph office at the terminus of the branch line at Fayville. Then she fell, half unconscious, into the arms of the astonished agent, who came to the door when he heard her stumble weakly against it.

"Good God, child, where did you come from?" he cried.

Smiles' lips moved faintly, and he caught an echo of the words which she had been repeating mechanically, over and over, "She haint ergoin' ter die!"

"I reckon she ain't, if human will can save her . . . whoever *she* is," muttered the man, as he laid the exhausted girl on a rude waiting bench, poured between her bruised lips a few drops of smuggled whiskey from a pocket flask, and then unceremoniously cut her shoe lacings and removed her sodden, icy boots.

After a moment, she sat weakly up, and — punctuated by gasps drawn by exquisite pain — managed to pant out, "I've got to send a telegram . . .

to-night . . . now. Oh, *please,* Mister, don't wait for anything."

"There, there. We'll take care of your message all right. Don't worry, little woman," he answered, reassuringly. "But I ain't agoin' ter send a tick till you're thawed out. My missus lives upstairs, an' she'll fix you up."

He half-carried, half-helped the weary girl up the narrow stairs, and, having surrendered her into the charge of a kindly and solicitous woman, hastened to rekindle the wood fire in the stove. As its iron top began to regain the ruddy glow which had scarcely faded from it, Rose crept near, holding out her bent, stiffened hands.

"Now, take it easy, little girl," cautioned the agent. "Not too close at first."

"And take off your dress and stockings, dear," said his wife. "Don't give no thought to him, — we've got three daughters of our own, most growed up."

The agent departed, with a heavy clamping of feet on the stairs, and gratefully — but with hands which were so numb that she had to give up in favor of the woman — Rose obeyed; and soon her teeth stopped their chattering, and the red blood of youth began once more to course through her veins, while her drenched, simple undergarments sent up vaporous white flags which indicated that the watery legions of the storm king were fast surrendering to their ancient enemy — Fire.

The older woman wrapped a blanket about the girl, as her husband came upstairs again with a pad of telegram blanks, and said, "Now, I'll write out the message you've got to send for you, if you want me to."

"Thank you, sir. I'm obliged to you and your missus. I reckon you can put the words better than I can, for I haint . . . I have never sent one before. It's for Dr. Donald MacDonald, who lives on Commonwealth Avenue, up north in Boston city. And I want to tell him that little Lou Amos is most dying from a brain tumor. And tell him that she is nearly blind and 'comatose' . . ."

"That word's a new one to me, how do you spell it?" interrupted the agent, with pencil plowing through his rumpled hair.

"I . . . I guess I've forgotten. Spell it like it sounds, and he'll know. And tell him that I will pay him all the money I've got, if he'll only come quick."

"How shall I sign it? It has to have your name, you know."

"Say it's from his foster-sister, Rose."

Laboriously the man wrote out the message, and the floor was littered with discarded attempts before he was satisfied; but in time the distant, slow clicking of the telegraph key below was sending not only the child's eager appeal to its destination many hundred miles north, but a message of renewed hope into the heart of Smiles.

"It will cost you more'n a dollar," said the man, as he appeared again. "But if you haven't got that much, why . . ."

"I've got it right here," responded the girl, turning on him for an instant a glowing smile of gratitude for his halting offer. "I'm truly more'n obliged to you, sir . . . and your wife. I reckon God meant that you should be here to-night to help save the life of a dear little child," she added simply.

"Now I'll just put on my things and be startin' back home."

"Startin' home? Well, I reckon not. You're agoin' to stay right here to-night, and let my woman put you straight to bed. That's what you're agoin' to do."

Smiles' protests were all in vain, and soon the weary body and mind were relaxed in the sleep which follows hard on the heels of exhaustion.

. . . .

It was close on to midnight when Dr. Donald MacDonald reached his apartment after a rare theatre party with his fiancée. His day's work had been exacting, and he was doubly tired. The thought of bed held an almost irresistible appeal.

As he inserted his latch key in the lock, he heard the telephone bell in his office ringing insistently; his heart sank, and cried a rebellious answer.

Combined force of habit and the call of duty caused him to hasten to the instrument, however, without stopping to remove hat or coat, and to his ear came a small, distant voice saying, "A telegram for Dr. Donald MacDonald. Is he ready to receive it?"

"Yes . . . Hold on a minute until I get a pencil. . . . All right, go ahead."

"It is dated from Fayville, Virginia, January 1, 1914. 8:30 P.M. Are you getting it?"

"Yes, yes. Go on," cried the man, with increasing heart pulsations.

"'Dr. Donald MacDonald, Commonwealth Ave., Boston, Mass. Lou Amos dying of brain tumor almost blind and 'k-o-m-o-t-o-s-e'" — she spelt it out —'Come at once if possible I will pay.' It is signed, 'Your foster-sister Rose.' Did you get it? Yes? Wait a moment, please, there is another one dated and addressed the same. The message reads, 'Girl came alone down mountain in howling blizzard. Case urgent. Signed, Thomas Timmins, Station Agent.' That is all."

"Thank you. Good-night," said Donald mechanically, as he replaced the receiver.

Through the partly open folding door he could dimly see that enticing bed, with his pajamas and bath robe laid across it. It seemed to him as though it were calling to his weary body with a siren's voice, or had suddenly acquired the properties of the cup of Tantalus. He hesitated, and moved a step toward it. Then the vision of Rose as he had last seen her, with the ethereal smile trembling on lips that struggled bravely to laugh, and in deep misty eyes, came between it and him.

Still clad in hat and overcoat, he seated himself at the desk and called up first the information bureau of the South Terminal Station, then his young associate, Dr. Philip Bentley, in whose charge he was accustomed to leave his regular patients when called away from the city for any length of time; and finally a house used as a semi-club by trained nurses.

When his last call was answered he asked, "Is Miss Merriman registered with you now? This is Dr. MacDonald speaking."

After a wait of several minutes, during which he felt himself nod repeatedly, a sleepy voice spoke over the wire, "This is Miss Merriman, Dr. MacDonald. I'm just off a case."

"Good. I'm lucky . . . that is if you're game to take another one immediately."

"Yes, doctor. Do you want me to-night?"

"No, to-morrow . . . this morning, that is, will do. I shall want you to meet me at the South Station, New York train, at seven o'clock."

"Yes, doctor. What sort of a case is it?"

"Same as the last you assisted me in — brain tumor. But we're going further this trip . . . the jumping-off place in Virginia. It's up in the mountains, so take plenty of warm clothes."

"Very well, doctor." Then there came a little laugh, for these two were excellent friends now, and the query, "Another record-breaking fee?"

"I'll tell you to-morrow," he replied. "Don't forget, seven o'clock train for New York. Good-night."

"Good-night, doctor."

Donald turned away from the desk, and for a moment stood motionless.

"God bless her brave, trusting, little heart," he said half aloud.

And he was not thinking of Miss Merriman.

CHAPTER XX

THE ANSWER

MORE than once Rose caught herself wondering if, after that day was done, she would ever be able to smile again. In obedience to the doctor's prescription for Big Jerry, which it was ever her first duty to fill, she never looked towards him — as he sat bent over before the fire, eyes heavy with pain, breath coming in deep rasps, but lips set firmly against a word of complaint — without sending him a message of love and compassion through the intangible medium of that smile. Yet, as the weary hours dragged on with plodding feet, it seemed to her as though each new one was not an interest payment on a fund of happiness stored within her heart, but a heavy dipping into the principal itself.

Before she had taken her early morning departure back up to the mountain over the sodden, slippery path, she had received a telegram that Donald had sent off as his last act before yielding to the lure of bed, and which brought her the hope-engendering word that he would be with her as soon as swift-speeding trains could bring him.

But that was yesterday. By no possibility could he reach them before the coming evening, and surely never had the sun taken so long to make his wintry journey across the pale blue sky.

Hour after hour Rose sat by the bedside of little Lou, and tenderly stroked her cold small hands while she hummed unanswered lullabies, each note of which was the chant of a wordless prayer. The sufferer lay so white, so utterly still, save for the periods when her every breath was a faint moan or she suddenly shook and twisted in a convulsive spasm, that time and again the girl started up with a cry of terror frozen on her lips but echoing in her heart, and bent fearfully over to press her ear close against the baby's thin breast. As often it caught the barely discernible beat of the little heart within.

The baby's eyes, now piteously crossed, had turned upward until the starlike pupils were almost out of sight. There were long periods when only the occasional twitching of the bloodless, childishly curved and parted lips, or the uneasy moving of the golden crowned head on the pillow, betrayed the fact that the spark of life still glowed faintly. Could she, by the power of will and prayer, keep that spark alight until the one on whom she pinned her faith should arrive, and fan it back to a flame by his miraculous skill? That was Smiles' one thought.

The violet shadows of evening began at last to tinge the virgin whiteness of the out-of-doors, and Rose caught herself starting eagerly, with quickened pulse, at every new forest sound. The crunching tread of Judd, who paced incessantly outside the window, grew almost unbearable. She counted the steps as they died away, and listened for them to return, until her nerves shrieked in protest, and it was only by an effort that she curbed their clamoring demand that she rush to the door and scream at him; bid him stand still or begone.

. . . .

Through the shadows Donald was once again making his way up the now familiar mountain side. To have climbed up the footpath with Miss Merriman and their essential baggage would have been impossible, and he had, after much persuasion, finally succeeded in hiring a man in Fayville to drive them up in a springless, rickety wagon. This had necessitated their taking a much more circuitous route, and what seemed like an interminably long time.

During the railway journey from the Hub, he had told his companion all of the relevant facts, and much of the story of Rose, and the nurse's sympathetic interest in the recital had made her almost as anxious as the man himself to arrive at their destination and answer the girl's cry for aid.

Once she had voiced a doubt as to the wisdom of leaving his urgent practice and taking such a trip on so slender grounds.

"But how do you know that it *is* brain tumor, doctor, or that there is either any chance of saving the child's life, or any real need of a surgeon? At the most you have only the conclusion of a country doctor who can hardly be competent to determine such a question."

"I have considered all that, Miss Merriman," he had replied, shortly, and then added, as though he felt that an explanation were due, "Frankly, when I made up my mind to go, I wasn't thinking of the patient so much as I was of my foster-sister. Perhaps she won't appeal to you as she has to me; but I really feel a strong responsibility for her future, and I don't want her faith in m . . . . in physicians to be shattered. You see, I have held up the ideal of service, regardless of reward, as our motto." He sat silently looking out of the car window for a moment, while the nurse studied his serious, purposeful face and mentally revised her previous estimate of him. Then he went on, with an apologetic laugh, "Besides — Oh, I know that it sounds utterly preposterous, but there are times when a man's groundless premonitions are more real to him than any logical conclusions of his own. This is one of those times."

The subject dropped.

Donald had, in addition to a fortnight's compensation in advance, given Miss Merriman a return ticket and sufficient money to cover all necessary disbursements, and told her that she must, of course, look to him for any additional salary. Under no circumstances, he said, was she to accept what Rose was sure to try and press upon her.

At length the plodding horse turned into the little clearing before Jerry's cabin, and, as it appeared, the watcher outside, his face twitching, slunk silently away into the forest, where his racked soul was to endure its hours of Gethsemane.

Rose heard them. She hastened to the door, and her white lips uttered a low cry which spoke the overwhelming measure of her relief.

"I just *knew* you'd come!" she said, as the man, numbed with cold, swung his companion to the ground. The girl gave her a quick glance of surprise; but her eyes instantly returned to the doctor's face with an expression which Miss Merriman decided was as nearly worship as she had ever seen.

Donald did not return her greeting in words at first; but, after he had paid the driver, so liberally that the latter was left speechless, and they had entered the cabin, he held out his strong arms to her. Smiles swayed into them and pressed her face against the thick fur of his coat with an almost soundless sigh that told the whole story of anxious waiting and the end of the tension that had left its mark on her childlike face.

"This, Miss Merriman, is my little foster-sister, Rose. And Miss Merriman is a nurse who has come to help us," said he, as he released her, and passed on to greet the old giant, who had slowly pulled his shattered, towering frame from his chair, and now stood with a gaunt hand held out in welcome, while a ghost of his one-time hearty smile shadowed his lips. Big Jerry's flowing beard was now snow-white, and Donald was shocked at the change which had taken place in him.

Their greeting was brief and simple, as between men whose hearts are charged, and, as soon as he had eased him back into his seat, Donald spoke with a quick assumption of his professional bearing.

"Now, about our little patient. How is she, Rose?"

"Close to the eternal gates, I'm afraid," whispered the girl, with a catch in her voice. "Oh, Donald, we cannot let her . . ." she turned abruptly and led the way to the door of her tiny bedroom. The doctor stepped inside and looked briefly, but searchingly, at the child who lay there, silent, and the semblance of Death itself. With her lips caught by her teeth, and her hands clasped tightly together to still her trembling, Rose watched him.

His next words, spoken as he stepped back into the cabin and shook himself free of his greatcoat, were brusquely non-committal. "And the doctor? Where is he?"

"The doctor? Why, he . . . he isn't here; he hasn't been here for days. He doesn't even know that you were coming . . . that I had sent for you."

"What? But I don't understand, child. Of course he ought to be here." Donald's voice was so sharp that it brought the tears, that were so near the surface, into Smiles' eyes, perceiving which, he hastened to add more gently, "There, there, of course you didn't know; but I can hardly hope to diagnose . . . to determine what the trouble really is, or where the growth, if there is one, is located, unless I get a full history of the case from him and his own conclusions to help me."

"But . . . but, Donald, he didn't *have* any conclusions. He said it was . . . was brain fever, first, and then he gave up trying and told us that Lou had just got to die. Besides, *I* know the . . . the history. . . . " She stopped, with a little wail of distress.

"'Brain *fever!*' Then who . . . . the telegram certainly said 'tumor.'"

"Yes, yes. *I* said that. Oh, I can't tell you why; but I just *know* that it is, Donald, for little Lou has been exactly like you told me that baby up north was — the one you saved by a . . . . a miracle. Oh, don't you remember? It was in the paper."

Her sentences had become piteously incoherent; but their significance slowly dawned upon him. To Miss Merriman the conversation was somewhat of an enigma, and she stood aside, regarding Rose with an expression half bewildered, half frightened. Had this strange child summoned so famous a physician, whose moments, even, were golden, to the heart of the Cumberlands on her own initiative and on the strength of her own childish guess, merely? It was incredible, a tragic farce.

Perhaps something of similar import passed swiftly

through the man's mind, for he placed his large hands upon the girl's slender shoulders, and, for an instant, sent a searching gaze deep into her eyes, now luminous with unshed tears, as he had first seen them. They looked up at him troubled, but frankly trusting.

"Do you mean, Rose," his words came slowly, "that you sent for me without a doctor's suggestion and advice; that you did it on your own hook?"

She nodded. "I just couldn't bear to have her die. She is all that . . . that Judd has got in the world, now, and I knew that you could save her for him."

His hands felt the controlled tension of her body, and he impulsively drew her close to him. When he answered, his voice was strangely gentle.

"It's all right, little doctor. I'm glad that you did, and only hope that I can help. Now, let's all sit down here before the fire — how good it feels after that bitter ride, doesn't it, Miss Merriman? — and you will tell me all that you can about the baby's trouble — every single thing that you have noticed from the first, no matter how little it is. You see, that only by knowing exactly how the patient has acted can the surgeon even hope to guess where the trouble has its seat. Once before I told you that a nurse has got to face the truth, understandingly and bravely, and I may as well tell you about some of the difficulties which lie in the path that we must tread to-night. Your faith has been almost — sublime, dear. I wonder if it would have failed if you had known how like a child in knowledge — a child searching in the dark — is a surgeon at such a time as this?"

"I . . . I don't believe that I understand, and you kind of frightened me, Don. I thought that all you would have to do would be to . . . . to cut out that awful thing that is stealing away Lou's precious life. Wasn't that what you did for that other little child?"

"Yes, but . . . how am I going to explain? If there is a tumor, as we think, I'll do my best to take it away; but, in order to do that, I have, of course, got to go inside of her skull right to the brain itself, and the trouble might be here, or here, or here." He touched her now profusion of curls at different cranial points. "That is the riddle which you and I must solve, and I have got to look to you for the key. The human brain is still a book of mystery to us. Some day, physicians will be able to read it with full understanding; but so far, we have, after thousands of years, barely learned how to open its covers and guess at the meaning of what lies hidden within."

Rose had edged close to Miss Merriman on the rough bench before the fire, and, with the older woman's arm about her, now sat, wide-eyed and wondering, while Donald talked. As he kept his gaze fixed on the glowing heart of the fire, he seemed, in time, to be musing aloud rather than consciously explaining.

"This much we have learned, however; that certain parts of the brain control all the different actions or functions of the body — I've called it a telegraph station once before . . . ." he paused, and both thought of little Mike in his last home under the snow . . . . "with different keys, each sending its message over a separate wire. So you see that, if we can learn exactly what the message has been, I mean by that just how certain parts of the body have been affected — Miss Merriman would call them the 'localizing symptoms' — we can often tell almost exactly which key is being disarranged by the pressure of a foreign growth, such as a tumor. Do you think that you can understand that, Rose?"

She nodded slowly.

"That is the first, the great and most difficult thing for us to do. The rest depends, in part, upon the mechanical skill of the surgeon, but far more upon Fate, for there are certain kinds of growths which may be removed with a fair chance of success — it is only that, at present — and others . . . but we won't consider the others. Lou is young, and in one way that is in our favor. If there *is* a tumor, there is less likelihood of infiltration," he added, glancing at the nurse.

Rose opened her lips as though to ask a question, and then decided not to, but her expression caused Donald to say, "Come child, don't look so frightened."

"But I didn't know . . . it's so . . . so terrible. How can any one live if his head is cut open like that?"

"It sounds desperate, doesn't it," he answered,

lightly, "But with our anesthetics, which put the patient quietly to sleep, and our new, specially made instruments, the trained and careful surgeon can perform the operation quite easily — as far as the mechanical part goes, I mean. But, you can see how all-important it is for you to tell me just how Lou has been affected. I know what a good memory you have; make it count to-night."

With her breathing quickened, and eyes shining from pent-up excitement, Rose began. Simply and painstakingly she recounted everything which she had observed about the baby's strange behavior from that painful night when she had brought her from Judd's lonely cabin, through the long days in which she had steadily weakened and failed, to the time when the invisible hand of Death seemed to have begun to pluck at the thread of life itself.

Donald listened intently, without a word of interruption, until she suddenly broke off her recital with the words, "Oh, I can't think of anything more, truly I can't; and I'm so afraid . . . afraid that it hasn't been enough to help."

Miss Merriman's encircling arm closed comfortingly about the girl, and she patted the head which turned and burrowed into her shoulder, but she said nothing, waiting for the man to speak. He mused for a moment, and then his words came with the crisp incisiveness of a lawyer in cross-examination.

"As she lost control of her legs and began to waver and stumble when she tried to walk, did she seem to turn, or fall, to one side more than to the other? Think!"

The anxiety deepened in Smiles' eyes; but she answered without hesitation, "No, I don't think so. It was more as though her little body was plumb tuckered out."

"And her hearing? Did that fail?"

"No, not until just toward the last, anyway. Even when she couldn't seem to answer me, somehow I was quite sure that she understood, when I spoke, or sang, to her. She would kinder smile, but, oh, it was such a pitiful smile that it 'most broke my heart."

"She seemed to understand, eh?" He paused, and the room was very still, except for Big Jerry's stentorian breathing. "Can you say quite certainly — don't be afraid to answer just exactly what you think — can you say, then, that, aside from the general weakness of all the powers of her little body and mind, the headache and occasional sickness, the most noticeable thing in all her strange behavior was that she wasn't able to talk clearly, and this increased until she wholly lost the power of speech which happened before she became as . . . as I see her now?"

"Yes, doctor."

Donald turned abruptly to the nurse. "Barring the use of technical phraseology, and a possible expression of his own, probably valueless, conclusions, could any doctor, such as is likely to be practising in Fayville, have given me any more information, or told it better?"

"No, doctor."

At these unexpected words of praise the girl's smile appeared mistily for a moment, and then quivered away.

There was silence again in the cabin, while the man turned his thoughtful gaze back to the fire, which had now turned to glowing orange embers. A far-off look, alien to his keen, masterful face crept into it. Finally he seemed to shake off his new mood, and spoke with a queer laugh.

"I told you on the train that I was the victim of an uncanny premonition. I guess that Horatio was right about there being many things outside the ken of our limited philosophy. What psychic whisper from a world whose existence we men of 'common sense'" — he spoke the words sarcastically — "are loath to credit; what inspiration, born of the memory of that story of the case of the Bentley Moors' child in New York, which I told her in words of one syllable six months ago, was it that brought the light of truth to this girl's mind, when the village doctor utterly failed to catch so much as a glimmer of it?"

"Then you think, doctor . . . ?" began Miss Merriman.

"My diagnosis coincides with Smiles', — a tumorous growth on the brain, probably upon the third left frontal convolution . . . . right here," he said in explanation, as he touched his forehead between the left eyebrow and the hair. "Rose, you have done excellently. Now we, too, will do what we can, and we shall need your help in full measure to-night. I know that it is going to be bitterly hard for you, perhaps the hardest thing that you will ever be called upon to do in all your life; you've got to be a woman, and a brave one. I'd spare you if I could, but . . . ."

"But I don't want to be spared, Donald," she interrupted, eagerly.

"I know, and I trust you more than I could any grown-up woman here in the mountains. It's hardly necessary to tell you again, that a nurse is a soldier, and must be not only brave, but obedient. If we decide to . . . to go ahead I will be, not your friend, but your superior officer for a while, and, if my orders seem harsh and even cruel, you must not hesitate, or feel hurt. You understand that, don't you, dear?"

"Yes, doctor. I understand."

She spoke bravely, but her voice trembled a little.

"Good. Before I make my final examination, Miss Merriman and I have got to change our clothes. She will use your room and I the loft; but first let us bring Lou's bed out here by the fire."

It was done.

"Now," he continued, "while we are getting ready, there are a number of things which you have got to do, and you will have to work fast. First, make grandfather comfortable in his room, and build up this fire. Then heat up as much water as the big kettle will hold, and see that a smaller one is scoured absolutely clean. Start some water heating in that, too. Finally, undress Lou completely, and wrap her in a blanket. Can you remember all that?"

"Yes, Donald . . . yes, doctor."

Donald smiled, and added, "One thing more. Partly fill a pillow-case with sand, or dirt, if it is possible to get any. Perhaps the ground in the wood-house isn't frozen so hard but that you can get it."

She nodded wonderingly.

In a quarter of an hour her duties were completed and Miss Merriman and Donald had appeared, clad in their spotless white garments of service. Rose, likewise, was in her play uniform, which was now considerably too small for her, and her appearance in it would have caused a smile if it had not been more provocative of tears.

Six months earlier the doctor and nurse, assisted by others of the most skilled and highly trained that the metropolis afforded, had prepared to perform the same desperate service in humanity's cause, within the perfectly appointed operating room of a modern city hospital. How different was the setting now!

In the rude, but homey room of the mountain cabin, lighted only by old-fashioned lamps and lanterns and the pulsating blaze of the fire in the cavernous fire-place, whose colorful gleam touched with gold the scoured copper of pot and kettle, the three workers, in the immaculate garments of a city sickroom, bent intently over the naked form of the nearly insensible child, to whose alabaster body the leaping flames imparted a simulated glow of warm tones.

The general examination was brief, and made in silence. Then Donald drew the covering over the little body as a sculptor might the cloth over his statue, and straightened up with a look in his gray eyes that was new to Rose.

He spoke in curt sentences. "Of course the case is far more desperate than our last, Miss Merriman. It's the proverbial 'one chance in a thousand.' On that single thread hangs the child's life."

Suddenly he startled Rose by giving a short, mirthless laugh, and, turning away, he began to speak in an undertone, as though unconscious of the presence of the other two, for, despite his previous calm, the thought of what was in prospect had keyed up his nerves to a pitch where they quivered like the E string of a violin.

"Good God, what a colossal nerve a man is sometimes called upon to have in this world. Of course she'll die in twenty-four hours if I *don't* operate; but only a fool — or a genius — would tackle *this* operation under such impossible conditions. Practically none of the things here that science says are necessary. 'A fool, or a genius.'" — He suddenly smote his hands together, and said, "I hope that I'm a fool for to-night. God takes care of them . . . and drunkards. I wish I had a strong slug of Judd's white whiskey, it might steady my nerves.

"Where *is* Judd?" he snapped out, aloud, turning to Rose.

CHAPTER XXI

A MODERN MIRACLE

"I DON'T know. He was here when you came, but I saw him going up the mountain into the woods. But I'll answer for him; I'll take that chance, doctor. She is nearly as dear to me as she is to him, and I know that she is going to die, unless . . . unless . . ."

"I knew you'd say it. Well, we'll operate, Miss Merriman."

Donald's voice was calm, impersonal again, and his tone had a steely quality, as though his lancet or scalpel had become endowed with a voice, and spoken.

Silently, and with practised hands, the nurse began to unpack his bag and lay out upon a sheet, which she obtained from Rose and spread over the rough table, the many strange instruments, bottles, rolls of bandages and sponges in their sterile packages.

"Have you any baking soda — saleratus, Rose?"

She nodded.

"Good. Put about a teaspoonful in the smaller kettle, and boil these instruments for ten minutes, while we are making the final preparations. I want some hot water, too."

He turned away, and for a moment stood looking up at the calm heavens in which the stars made openings for the white eternity beyond to shine through. Something in the scene bore his thoughts back to that summer evening when the mountain man of God had tried so earnestly to minister to his own disease. Snatches of sentences re-echoed in his memory. Then he stepped back to Smiles' side and his voice was soft, as he said, "I suppose that, whenever a surgeon begins an operation like this one, he has an unformed prayer deep in his heart, though he may not realize to whom he prays. There was never more occasion for one than to-night, Rose. I know that the Great Healer is nearer to you than to me. Ask Him that my hand may not falter."

She nodded again, sweetly serious.

Once more his accustomed bluntness of manner returned, and he snapped, "Oh, why in the devil didn't I have sense enough to bring another assistant?"

"I am here, doctor," answered the girl.

"Yes, yes, I know." He regarded her with the old, searching look. Then, to the nurse, "It's only one of the many chances we have got to take. When you put the patient under the anæsthetic you will show Rose exactly how it is administered, for she will have to keep her unconscious without any further aid from you after I begin to operate. We have *got* to trust her, Miss Merriman," he added shortly, as he caught the expression of grave doubt which the nurse could not keep from appearing on her countenance. "See that she washes and sterilizes her hands thoroughly. That hot water, Rose. I want a basinful."

She supplied it, then departed to do the rest of his bidding, and for some moments was kept so busy that she did not realize what the other two were doing at the bedside, other than to note that Donald had raised the head of the bed by blocking up the legs with firelogs, and covered it with a rubber sheet such as she had never seen before.

When she did, however, return to the side of the little sufferer, whose face was far whiter than the clean, but coarse, sheet which covered the emaciated body, a low cry of protest and grief was wrung from her lips. Already most of the lovely ringlets of spun gold, which had won for the baby Donald's characterization of "Little Buttercup," gleamed on the rough floor, and the ruthless but necessary sacrifice was being continued.

There were tears on her cheeks as she aided the doctor to scrub the shorn scalp, until the child moaned and turned her head from side to side.

"He is my commanding officer. He told me that I must always remember that, and obey," whispered Rose to herself, as Donald, in his abstraction, began to snap forth his orders in a manner and tone which, for a moment, made her shrink and quiver. His words were often unintelligible to her, until Miss Merriman, silent-footed and efficient, translated them into action, as, before the wide eyes of the mountain child, there began to unfold the swift drama of modern surgical science at its pinnacle, amid that fantastic setting.

Strange words, indeed, were those which now fell on her attentive ears, many of them far outside the bounds of her limited vocabulary; yet, stranger still, she soon began to grasp their meaning intuitively, and her quick native perception, keyed high by emergency, led her often to anticipate the physician's wish, and act upon it. More than once she won a look of surprise from the older woman.

Donald's directions to Miss Merriman were curt and incisive; but soon he did not limit his speech to them. Rather he seemed to be uttering his thoughts aloud; the old habit of making a running explanation for the benefit of a clinic or the better understanding of an assistant was subconsciously asserting itself, and it was to Rose as though she were listening to the outpouring of a fountain of knowledge, whose waters engulfed her mind and made it gasp, yet carried her along with them. It was all a dream, a weird, impossible nightmare to her; the familiar room began to assume a strange aspect, and the man's words came to her as do those heard in a sleeping vision — real, yet tinctured with unreality.

"In this case the elastic tourniquet will stop the blood flow as effectively as the Heidenhain back-stitch suture method, I think, Miss Merriman, and it will be much simpler. I'm glad I brought it. Have you the saline solution, and the gauze head-covering ready?"

"Yes, doctor."

"Then you may administer the ether — use the drop method, and don't forget to show her just how to regulate it.

"No blood-pressure machine," he muttered. "Oh, well, we've just got to trust to her being able to stand it, and . . ."

"And to God," whispered Rose.

He glanced quickly up, as though he had already forgotten her presence, and added, gently, "Of course."

The small pad of gauze, which Miss Merriman laid over the baby's face, grew moist; a strange, pungent odor began to fill the room. As she bent over to watch intently what the nurse was doing, Rose suddenly found herself beginning to get dizzy.

"Stand up, Smiles," came the sharp command. "Here, hold this handkerchief over your mouth and nose. Now, take the bottle yourself . . . so . . . a drop on the pad . . . now. Yes, that's right, just as Miss Merriman has been doing. Little Lou is wholly unconscious, we must keep her so.

"Remember, now your test is beginning, and I expect you not to fail me. A great deal depends on you, Rose. You are a soldier on the firing-line now, and you are going to keep up, whatever happens. It may be for half an hour, but you will keep up, for me, for Lou, whatever happens. Remember! *Whatever happens!*"

He looked fixedly into the unnaturally big eyes which were turned up to his like two glorious flowers, and she nodded. With a pang of regret he noticed how thin her face was, and how white, — so pale that the color had fled even from the sweet, sensitive lips which smiled ever so faintly at him, and then at the nurse, as the latter made the quiet suggestion that she try to keep her eyes always fixed on the pad of gauze, and not let them be drawn away from it if she could possibly help it.

But at first she could not, and so she saw the pitiful little head, stripped of its golden crown, first covered with a clinging veil of wet cloth, over which, from behind the ears to the top of the forehead, a circular band of rubber tubing was adjusted and drawn tight into the flesh — "to stop the blood, like I did for grandpappy when he cut his arm," she thought. Then the head was gently raised and settled into position on the sand-filled pillow, which cradled it firmly.

Only the gurgling breath of the mercifully unconscious baby, and the crackling of the fire, broke the silence as the surgeon adjusted and posed his patient's head, as an artist would his model's.

A piercing light flashed before the girl's eyes, and she saw that now Miss Merriman held a strange-looking black tube, which shed a circle of concentrated sunshine on the gauze-covered head. It was her first experience with a flashlight, and she marvelled at its power.

Now there came another dart of light, thin and fleeting, and she knew that a knife was poised in mid-air. Involuntarily she closed her eyes tight; a shudder ran through her. Donald's voice spoke impersonally, and steadied her.

"I shall expose the third left frontal convolution of the brain through the fronto-parietal bone, and, in making the osteoplastic flap, I intend to leave a wide working margin above the size of the opening which may actually be necessary in order the reach the growth. It has got to be fully exposed at once. I can't afford to delay, under the circumstances."

The gleam of the scalpel held her unwilling gaze with the fascination of horror; she drew her breath with a sound between a shudder and a sigh as it descended. . . .

"I *must* keep my eyes on the ether pad," came the command from her whirling brain.

Many nights thereafter, Rose was to start up from troubled sleep with strange sounds and stranger words echoing in her brain — words like "bevelled trephines," "Hudson forceps," "elevators," "Horsley's wax," "rongeurs," "clips" and "sponges," — but during the actual operation she was scarcely conscious of them, and her principal feeling was one of dumb rebellion which grew until she found herself almost hating *this* Donald, who could speak with such unconcern and apparent callousness, at such a time. As well as she could, she willed her swimming gaze to remain fixed on the pad which she must keep moist. The difficulty of the task had suddenly become increased, for the pad seemed to become an animate thing. Now it appeared to retreat into the distance, and again it came floating back until it seemed about to smother her. There was a droning note in her ears; the words spoken by the other two sounded mixed and indistinct.

Of only one sentence, repeated monotonously in Miss Merriman's clear voice, was she really conscious. "Rose, a drop of ether . . . a drop of ether . . . a drop of ether."

She wanted to speak, to ask them if the room were not frightfully hot; but she could not.

Rose had never fainted in her life, but she had once seen a neighbor swoon, and she realized vaguely that, as the minutes passed, her consciousness was slowly slipping from her. The air was close and heavy with strange smells. She felt as though she were swaying like a pendulum. The old, familiar objects grew grotesquely large and hazy; the deep shadows in the corners multiplied, and began to dance a solemn minuet, advancing, retreating; advancing, retreating. . . .

"Another drop of ether."

She took a fresh mental grasp on herself, and held Duty, like a visible thing, before her eyes.

Again that queer, far-away voice.

"Look, Miss Merriman. Can you see that neoplasm under the membrane? Ah . . . now the flat dissector . . . no, the blunter one . . ."

The voice trailed away into nothing, and another recalled her failing senses, with the battle cry:

"Rose, another drop of ether."

Then it began again, "Thank heaven, there is no infiltration, the growth is well localized and encapsulated. Steady, steady. . . . Ah, very pretty."

The word caught her flickering thoughts, and angered her. How could any one use it about anything so awful?

There was another misty moment. Then, "The operation is, in itself, a success, I think. . . . Now if the child's vitality . . . I never did a better one . . . another sponge . . . excellent . . . Are the sutures ready? . . . Quick, take the ether bottle, Miss Merriman!"

Suddenly the girl felt a painful grasp on her arm. Some one was shaking her roughly.

"Rose," came the same strange voice, "we need some more wood for the fire. Go out to the woodpile, and get some."

CHAPTER XXII

VICARIOUS ATONEMENT

In happy ignorance of the fact that the order had been given merely to get her outside, Smiles stumbled to the door with blind thankfulness, and, as soon as she had closed it behind her, crumpled up in an unconscious heap on the snow.

Within doors, the nurse was saying, "I think she's fainted, doctor. I heard her fall."

"Probably," was the callous response. "Don't worry about her, the cold will bring her around. We've got to get these sutures in. But, say, hasn't she been a brick?"

Donald's prophecy was correct. Rose came to her senses a moment later, and, trembling and sobbing uncontrolledly, stumbled through the darkness to the woodpile, and sat down on it. For a time she was powerless to move, but when, at length, she did re-enter the cabin, with an armful of wood, although her face was drawn and white, her self-control was fully restored.

Already the surgeon and nurse were bathing off the sewn wound with antiseptic fluid, and it was not long before the little injured head was wrapped in the swathing bandages which covered it completely, down to the deathlike, sunken cheeks.

The period of coming out from under the merciful anæsthesia ended, the drooping flower was restored to its freshly made bed, the evidences of what had occurred removed, and then Smiles turned to her beloved friend with a pleading, unspoken question in her eyes.

"I can't tell you yet, dear. I have . . . all of us have done our mortal best and now the issues are in higher hands than ours. I hope . . . But come, tell me, Rose, what made you feel so sure that the trouble *was* a tumor on the brain. Was it merely a guess, based on what I had explained to you?"

"No. I . . . I just *knew* it. I reckon that God told me so," was her reply.

"Well, God was certainly right, then," smiled Donald, glad of any chance to relieve the tension. "Do you want to see the growth? See, it is as large, nearly, as a walnut. Do you wonder that, with this thing pressing more and more into her brain, Lou was robbed of her power to talk and act?"

The girl broke down at last and wept hysterically, which caused Donald to look as uneasy as any mere man is bound to in such a circumstance; but Miss Merriman came to his rescue with comforting arms, and the words, "There, there, dear. Cry all you want to now. It's all over, and Dr. MacDonald will tell you that if she gets well — as we believe that she will — little Lou will be as healthy and happy a baby as she ever was in her life. He's taken out that wicked growth, kernel and all, and it will never come back again. Will it, doctor?"

"Almost certainly not. Rose, we couldn't have done without you to-night. You have been the brave little soldier that I told you to be; but I'm afraid that it has been a terrible strain for you. Of course, it was an exceptional operation, rare and dangerous; but it has given you a pretty vivid idea of what trained nurses have to go through frequently. Has it changed your mind? Do you still think that you want to go ahead and give your life to such work?"

"Would you ask a real soldier if he wanted to quit, or keep on fighting, after he had been in one battle, and seen men killed and wounded? It's got to be done, hasn't it, if the poor sick babies and grown-up people are to be made strong and well again? And I've just *got* to help do it, Donald."

He gave Miss Merriman a significant look; but his only response was, "Well, unless you want another job — that of bringing back to life people who have starved to death — you had better get us a bite to eat and some of your strong coffee. My internal anatomy . . ."

"Oh, I plumb forgot. You haven't had a thing to eat — nor poor granddaddy, either. I'm so ashamed I could *die*."

. . . .

Two hours later, after she had finished making the old man as comfortable as possible for the night,

Rose rejoined the other two in the main cabin. She came just in time to catch Donald in the act of half-heartedly trying to conceal a deep yawn.

As he, in turn, caught sight of her sympathetic smile, he said, "We have given our patient a mild sleep inducer; and now, Rose, I want you to go up into my loft room right away, and get a long night's sleep yourself. You've been under a mighty heavy strain to-day; there are many other hard days coming, and we can't have another patient on our hands."

The girl nodded, sleepily; but she had not taken one weary step before a different thought struck her, and she turned back to cry, contritely, "But you . . . and Miss Merriman. There won't be any place for you to sleep, or for her either. Oh, what can we do?"

"Just forget about us, my child. I shan't undress to-night, anyway, and can roll myself in my big fur coat and camp out in your little room, since Lou must stay out here where it is warmer. And as for Miss Merriman . . . if I catch her so much as closing her eyes for one minute, to-night, I'll wring her neck."

The nurse laughed; but Smiles' lips set, purposefully. "I forgot again. Of course some one has got to sit up with little Lou, and I'll do it. Why, Donald, poor Miss Merriman has been traveling and working all day long, and she's just tired to death — she must be. Of course she has got to get some rest. You go right up into the loft room, dear . . ." and she began to push the nurse gently toward the ladder.

"Rose," cut in the doctor, sternly, although his eyes held a pleased twinkle, "you're apparently forgetting one thing — that I'm boss here for the present, and that my nurses must learn to do as they are told, without arguing. I'm sorry for Miss Merriman, too; but she knows just what to do if anything happens, and you don't — yet. Besides, it won't be the first time that she has stayed up twenty-four hours at a stretch, will it?"

"No, indeed — nor forty-eight," answered the nurse, as she smoothed the pillow under the little patient's head. "I shall want you fresh and strong to help me with the 'day shift,' Smiles dear. And, as the doctor says, orders are orders."

The girl's tired eyes suddenly filled again, this time, with hurt, rebellious tears, and a pout, almost like a child's, appeared on her lips as she turned and moved slowly toward the ladder in the far corner. Donald watched her with sympathetic understanding and the thought, "She must think me a brute"; but, before he could speak the word of consolation which was on his tongue, she whirled about, just as she had when sent to bed on the first night of their acquaintance, and running back, threw herself into his arms. As she clung to him passionately, sobbing without restraint from weariness and the break in the tension which had kept her up for so long, she whispered, "Oh, I love you so, dear Don. You have been so good, so good to me, and I'm so very happy."

"Well, well," answered the man huskily, as he patted her shoulder, "you certainly have a funny way of showing it; but, after all, women are queer creatures. I'm happy, too, dear — happy to be here and to have been able to help you. And now," he concluded, lightly, "my happiness will be complete if you will just let me see that sunny smile on your face, as you obey that order which I have had to give you three times already."

The tired girl, for the moment more child than woman, leaned back in his arms and looked up at him with an expression so transcendently appealing that it was only by the exercise of all his moral force that he was able to restrain the impulse to crush her to him. He saw that the nurse was regarding him with a peculiar expression, and as she, in turn, caught his eye and turned hastily away with a little added color in her cheeks, Donald recovered himself, lightly kissed the forehead so close to his lips, and said, "Now for the fourth, and last, time, '*go to bed.*' Good-night, little sister."

This time Rose actually departed, and, after the physician had given Miss Merriman a few final directions, and bidden her call him instantly, if anything appeared to be going wrong, he said good-night to her also, and stepped toward the little room which he was to occupy. On reaching it he paused, for there had come a low, uncertain knock on the cabin door.

Lest it be repeated more loudly, and disturb the quiet into which the room had finally settled, Donald forestalled the nurse's act, hurried softly to the door, and opened it a few inches.

He started. There, leaning dejectedly against one of the pronged cedar posts on the tiny stoop, was a spectre figure, ghastly of countenance — Judd's. The doctor read in it the awful anguish of uncertainty which had driven the mountaineer, against his will, back to the cabin which held for him either hope or blank despair — and the man he hated.

Donald slipped outside, and closed the door softly behind him. He touched the inert form on the shoulder, and said in an undertone, "Come with me away from the house, Judd."

The other followed him, with dragging feet and sagging shoulders, his obedience being like that of a whipped dog. As he reached the rock before the gnarled oak, which, in happier days, had been the target for Big Jerry's first practice shot with the rifle that was later to play a part in the tragedy of Mike's death, Donald stopped and faced the man who had sworn himself his mortal enemy. The sight of the rock had re-awakened bitter memories; but they perished still-born as his gaze turned on the dimly seen figure beside him.

"Judd," he began, almost kindly, "you know why I came here this time?"

The other made an indistinct sound of assent.

"I . . . I operated on your little sister's brain, to-night. Wait. It was absolutely necessary, if she were to have even a single chance for life. She was dying, Judd. The operation was a desperate one — a last resort. I can't promise you anything certainly, but she's still alive, and I honestly believe that she is going to live — and get well."

For an instant the listener stood motionless. Then his pent-up emotions broke their bounds in one deep, shuddering breath, and he sank down beside the boulder, flung his tensed arms across it, and buried his face on them.

At last he spoke, hoarsely, and without raising his head. "I done my damnedest ter kill ye, an' now yo' . . . yo' saves Lou's life fer me. I reckon I don't know how ter thank ye, er repay . . . but . . . my life air yourn ter take hit, ef yo' likes."

"Nonsense," was the sharp response. "And as for thanks, why I don't want any. I did it for Smiles' sake."

The kneeling body quivered once; but, when the answer came, it was uttered in even tones. "Yes, I reckoned so. Yo' hev the right ter do things fer her, an' I . . . I haint. She . . . she warnt fer me . . . never. I warnt never worthy uv her."

"She isn't for me, either," said Donald. "And besides, I'm no more worthy of her than you, Judd. I should have told you long ago — I was a fool not to have done so — I'm going to marry another girl, — a girl at home whom I have known all my life."

"Do Rose know hit?" came the mountaineer's quick, suspicious query.

"Of course she does; she's known it for a year. Judd . . ." he seated himself beside the younger man. "I want to tell you that I was altogether to blame for . . . for what happened up there last summer. I should have told you then, and . . . and I'm sorry."

"No, hit war I who war ter blame."

"Well, let's both try to forget it, now. You owe me nothing for to-night; but you owe Rose a debt of gratitude that you can never hope to pay in full, my boy."

"I knows hit. I kaint never pay even part uv hit."

"I think that you can."

"How kin I?"

"I don't pretend to be much of a preacher, but I can say this as a man, Judd. By trying to live the kind of a life she would have you live. She wants to be your friend."

"I haint fit ter be named friend uv her'n, after what I done," he replied, dully.

"But *we're* going to forget all about that, and certainly she won't hold it against you, lad. I heard your Mr. Talmadge talking about . . . about religious things, once, and I think that, if he were here now, he would tell you that Smiles and little

Lou, together, have made what . . . what the Bible calls 'atonement' for what . . . for what you did. Smiles' love and your baby sister's suffering have brought us together; each has had a chance to realize and confess that he was wrong and had been wicked; and now the way is clear for us to be . . . friends. At least I'm willing, if you are, to shake on that."

Judd sprang to his feet, and his lean hand shot out to grasp the one which Donald held out to him in the darkness. And their firm clasp was a seal to the bond that the quarrel between them was ended for all time.

"Rose will be glad, Judd. I can't let you see Lou to-night; but come to-morrow morning . . . come early before I leave, and we'll tell them all about it, and start things all over again. Good-night, my boy," said Donald, heartily.

And there was a new light on the face of each man, as one returned to Jerry's cabin, and the other strode, with restored hope, to his own abode, which had been once so cheerless.

CHAPTER XXIII

TWO LETTERS

THE FIRST

BIG JERRY'S CABIN,
January 15, 1914.

My dear Dr. MacDonald,

Although this is theoretically only my semi-weekly report, made in accordance with your instructions, I feel in the letter-writing mood, for a wonder, so I *may* overstep professional bounds, and become loquacious — if one can do that with pen and ink.

Rose talks about you so continually that I am actually myself beginning to regard you as an intimate friend, instead of an austere and somewhat awe-inspiring "boss." I should probably not be brave enough to say that to your face; but I find that my courage rises in adverse ratio to my nearness to you.

First, however, for my report. The little patient is still convalescing in a highly satisfactory manner, and with a rapidity which speaks volumes both for her own strong constitution and this mountain as a health resort.

The wound remains perfectly healthy and is healing without suppuration or parting — which "speaks volumes" for your skill. I am quite certain that the scar will be merely a thin white line, and not in the least a disfigurement. The silk stitches are ready to be removed and the others nearly dissolved.

Yesterday that funny, countrified doctor, from down in the village, came up to see her — fame of your operation having spread. He "reckoned" that the child's recovery was nothing less than a miracle, and that he takes his hat off to you. I told him that most physicians did.

He also "allowed" that, if I wanted him to take out the stitches, he could do it, but I "reckoned" that I could attend to that a little better than he. Was that *lèse majesté?*

I did my best to be very humble, and said, "Yes, doctor" constantly, and he tried to appear very professional; but I think he stood a little in awe of me. You don't know how I enjoyed the feeling.

But, to return to our report. Lou is gaining strength rapidly; I let her get up and play about longer each day, and have reduced the bandages to the minimum. It was most affecting when they were removed from her eyes. I forgot that I was a nurse, and cried with Smiles until the child cried, too, without having the slightest idea why. She is such a sweet, merry little imp that I do not wonder that you felt more than mere professional interest in her case. Every one here loves her.

Indeed, I am enchanted with the place and people, and have made up my mind to stay on a week or ten days after I call myself off the case, and take a vacation which I really owe to myself.

Poor Big Jerry is wonderful — so pathetically patient under his suffering, which is now acute. I am afraid that he cannot last many weeks longer, and, more than once, I have had to give him a hypodermic to deaden his pain. Somehow he reminds me of a huge forest tree that has been struck and shattered by a lightning bolt.

Then there is Judd. Rose says that he has been very, very wicked; but that only adds to his fascination in my eyes, and if he should decide some day to snatch me up and carry me off bodily to a cave, I don't think that I should struggle or scream *very* hard. However, I'm afraid there is no chance of that, as he apparently doesn't know that I exist.

He puts me in mind of a mountain eagle, with those overhanging brows and piercing, coal-black eyes of his; but I must admit that he is disappointingly tame when he looks at Smiles — as he does most of the time, to my furious jealousy. Alas, the eagle then becomes a sucking dove. *She* is apparently oblivious to the obvious fact that he is madly in love with her. Poor Judd!

Last, but by no means least, there is Smiles herself. I wish that I could adequately express my thoughts about her, but I can't. However, I no longer wonder how a mountain child like that could have captivated you so, as I did when you first described her to me.

She is adorable. For the life of me I can't understand how a girl, bred in this wilderness, could have such a fine soul and personality — not to speak of her intellect, which daily startles me more. But, of course, she is of cultured stock — she *must* be — and I have always believed that the forces of heredity are paramount to those of environment. Do I sound like a school-mar'm? Well, that is what I am.

It may surprise you to learn, as much as it does me to realize, that I have turned back to schooldays with an enthusiasm which I never felt when I was going through them, and that I spend more time as a teacher than as a nurse. Smiles simply *absorbs* education — I never knew anything like it — and I am as confident as she that her dream of going through the "C. H." and becoming a trained nurse, will come to pass. And won't she make a wonderful one? Be warned that when she *does* go north I intend to dispute with you the right to regard her as a protégé.

I couldn't love her as I do, already, if she were not so

completely human, and it amuses me immensely the way she wheedles the natives and keeps them in good humor by using that comical mountain lingo — although she can speak as grammatically as any one, when she wants to. She just smiles at one of them, and says, "Now haint thet jest *toe* sweet of ye," and they fall down and worship.

Don't be surprised if you hear me say some day, "Wall, doctor, thet air shor' er powerful preety operation, an' I air plumb obleeged ter ye fer thet yo' let me holp ye with hit." I'm catching it, too.

I hope that you will forgive the liberties which I have taken in writing like this, but I had to do it.

Sincerely yours,
GERTRUDE MERRIMAN.

P.S. You were right in your conjecture. Since you would not accept the whole, or any part of Smiles' precious savings — and your refusal nearly broke her heart until I made her understand that physicians never charged *members of their family* — she wanted me to take it.

THE SECOND

WEBB'S GAP,
Jan. 22, 1914

Dearest Doctor Mac,

My heart is broken. Dear granddaddy died last night. Of course I know that it had to be, and that he is so much happier now in the spirit body, and with Ma Webb (he talked about her all yesterday, and I really think that his soul was speaking with hers); but he was so dear to me that I can hardly bear to think that he has gone away.

Wasn't he a splendid man, Don? I am sure that there could not have been any better, nobler men, even in the city, and I know that you loved him, too.

Before he died he told me all the wonderful things that he had done for me, although I did not deserve it — how he had left me all that money and made you my guardian. I am so glad for that.

He was in terrible pain toward the end, and I don't know what I should have done without dear Miss Merriman who stayed on purpose to help me. I think that God sent her here special. And she has helped me in so many other ways too — especially with my studying. She is sure that I will be able to pass that awful examination, although it frightens me. Oh, if I *can*, I can take that hospital training and be a nurse at last, for I am rich now. Just think, dear granddaddy left me *more than a thousand dollars* — and I have my basket money, besides!

And so, dear Donald, the first part of my great dream is really coming true. It isn't just the way I dreamed it, for I didn't mean for granddaddy to be dead; but I guess things never happen just as we plan. When we look forward to something pleasant, which we want very much to happen, we never think that there may be unhappiness mixed with it — perhaps it is better that way, for if we did we wouldn't work so hard to make it come to pass.

I am afraid that I have not said that very well; but I feel that it is so, now. I am going to Boston; I will be near you, and will learn to do the work I love; but now I realize that I could never, never have done it until granddaddy went away. So that is the shadow on my golden dream.

And last night there came the great sorrow that I have been dreading so many months; and yet I know that he is happier, and I have you and Miss Merriman, and the work I am going to do, to make me forget — not him, but my sorrow — and take the pain from my heart.

Little Lou is almost well again, and both she and Judd are going to stay with Mrs. Andrews the rest of the winter. And, oh, Doctor Mac., he has promised me never to make white liquor again.

I have saved the best news for the last. *Miss Merriman is going to take me to Boston with her.* She says that her family have taken an apartment in the city, and that I may live with them until I get into the hospital. This makes me very happy, and I hope that you will be pleased, too.

I know that everything is going to be very different there in Boston, and that you are so busy that I cannot see you very often, and, besides, when I do get into the hospital I must be careful to remember that you are a very great doctor and I am only one of many probationers (Miss Merriman told me the word). But, although we cannot be chums like we have been, you must never forget that I am always

Your loving foster-sister,

SMILES.

CHAPTER XXIV

NEW SCENES, NEW FRIENDS

So another leaf was turned in the Book of Fate, and Smiles' life underwent another metamorphosis as complete as the one fifteen years previous.

There was a sudden severance of all old ties, save that of memory, an abrupt entrance into a new existence, so utterly different from the one that she had known that it could scarcely have seemed stranger to her if she had actually been translated into another sphere.

Yet that same Fate, which had tried her heart in its crucible fires, and found its gold as unalloyed as her smile, now smiled, in turn, and Rose was deeply appreciative of that fact. She knew that in Gertrude Merriman she had found a friend who was a blessed comforter for her in her days of trial; in truth, the nurse was destined to be more than that, a wise counsellor as well. Herself a girl of breeding, a college graduate, and a product of the same mill through which the mountain child had set her heart and fixed her mind upon going, she would be able to smooth many a rough spot from that path which Donald had pictured in his allegory, draw the thorns from many a bramble.

For the first time Rose parted from the friends whom she had known practically all her life, and from the rugged, picturesque mountain which had been home to her, and turned her face toward a new life. Like a child venturing into the fairyland of dreams, she journeyed with her companion through the teeming cities of the East, Miss Merriman so arranging it that they should spend a day in each, for — with wisdom born of experience — she realized that such travel was in itself a broadening education, and that, moreover, in the new wonders and new delights which each hour held, Smiles' grief would find its best assuagement.

There was another reason in Miss Merriman's mind for making the trip a leisurely one. She knew that the girl was as far from being ready to step into the new existence, without material readjustment in her manners, as she was already mentally removed from the old. To be sure, she possessed a natural grace of manner which could not but charm any one who met her; but she was almost as free from external conventions as one of her own wild birds, except for the few which she had unconsciously acquired by her association with the older woman, and with Donald; and, in her love for, and pride in, her protégé, Miss Merriman wanted Rose to be able to fit, without embarrassment, into whatever company she might find herself.

Hers was a comparatively easy task, for Smiles took to "manners" as readily as a chameleon adapts its exterior to suit the color of its surroundings. In the woods she had learned to mimic the note of the birds or the chattering of the squirrels; in the hotel dining-room she copied the behavior of her companion just as faithfully, and if, on occasion, she found herself perplexed as to the proper use of some strange implement of eating, she frankly, and without a thought of embarrassment, sought information on the subject. People regarded her with open amusement, sometimes; but more often their gaze spelt admiration, and Rose was happily unconscious of both kinds of glances.

Furthermore, in obedience to instructions from Donald, contained in a special delivery letter which reached her just before they started North, and in which he purported to be speaking and acting as the child's guardian *ipso facto*, Miss Merriman fitted her charge out with a simple, but complete, wardrobe, to Smiles' never-failing surprise and delight that so many pretty things should be all her own.

When the two were ready to leave the metropolis — whose size, splendor and feverish bustle left Smiles mentally gasping — the nurse sent a telegram to Donald, and one raw February evening found him impatiently pacing the South Terminal Station, awaiting the arrival of the train from New York.

Six months before, the prospect of some day being Smiles' guardian had seemed vaguely pleasant. Now it was an immediate fact, and the responsibilities engendered, the possible difficulties attendant on it, lay heavily upon his mind. He, too, thanked Heaven for Miss Merriman.

The train gates were opened at last, and Donald hastened down the long platform, his eyes searching eagerly for those whom he sought. They fell first upon the nurse, just descending the steps, then turned and stayed upon the graceful, slender figure which followed her. Was it really Rose? Could that young woman, clad in a simple black travelling dress and long coat which, even to his masculine perception, appeared modishly stylish and amazingly becoming, be the mountain child whom his memory clothed in home-made calico? Her face was unwontedly pale beneath the small, close-fitting black hat, yet it was so utterly sweet that Donald felt his pulses start again with the old strange thrill.

If his mind harbored any idea that she might run into his embrace, it was doomed to disappointment, for, with the habiliments of city civilization, Smiles had acquired its reserve. Her greeting was a very demure and somewhat weary one, — it both pleased and irritated him, somehow. Indeed, she spoke scarcely a word, and it was not until they had finished dinner in the quiet, homelike hotel, whither Donald had taken them, that her new shyness began to yield to his presence. Then the story of the marvels which her eyes had beheld came pouring forth with all the old-time childlike eagerness.

When they were nearly ready to leave, Miss Merriman said, with a half real, half assumed show of firmness, "Now, Doctor MacDonald, since I am off duty I can speak my mind plainly, and I mean to. I know that you are Smiles' guardian; but you can't have her. She's mine, and she's going to live with my family until she enters the hospital. So there."

Donald breathed a mental sigh of relief, and responded, laughingly, "And I, apparently, haven't anything to say about it! Oh, very well. I've lived long enough to learn that there is no use arguing with a woman, so I yield gracefully, although I'm afraid that it is establishing a bad precedent. If I begin to take orders from you like this, it is going to be hard to put you back in your place and to act the rôle of stern superior myself. I warn you, though, that I mean to get even with you on our next case, so prepare yourself to be bullied frightfully.

"You see what a horrible disposition I really have, little sister," he added, smiling at Rose, who informed him that she was not in the least frightened, and to prove it, slipped her hand into his for a moment with the childlike confidence that he loved.

So it was arranged; a taxicab bore them to the homey little apartment in the Fenway, where Smiles was taken to Mrs. Merriman's maternal bosom, and, after humbly begging his ward from them for the next afternoon, when he meant to introduce her to his family, Donald departed, whistling.

Tired, but strangely contented, Rose was at last shown to her dainty pink and white bedroom, with its inviting brass bed, beside which she knelt for a long time in thankful prayer. Nor was it strange, perhaps, that her pillow was moist with tears of gratitude and happiness before she fell asleep.

Smiles awoke early. The air in the room was very cold, but during her trip northward she had learned the mysteries of steam radiators, and she sprang up, closed the windows, and turned on the heat with a little silent laugh as her thoughts travelled back to the rude cabin on the mountain. In memory she saw herself crawl shiveringly from her bed, in the cold gray of a Winter daybreak, clad only in a plain night-gown, to build a blaze in the big stone fireplace so that the room might be warm for Big Jerry when he awoke. The smile faded from her lips, and they trembled slightly as she whispered his name. Poor grandpap, he had suffered sadly from the cold during those last few months when he could not keep the circulation up in his massive body by accustomed exercise.

Below her lay the still sleeping city. Snow covered the untenanted portions of the Fens, and hid its ugly nakedness with a soft mantle, which seemed to hold a silken sheen, as the first flush of morning touched it. How strange all her surroundings appeared. Gone was the far sweeping expanse of forest-clad mountain side, stretching off to the sunrise; in its place lay a level space closed in by substantial buildings of marble, granite and brick — the Art Museum, Latin School and clustered hospitals, — their walls changing from ghostly gray to growing rose and gold.

She drew a comfortable dressing gown — the gift of her new friend — about her girlish form, and sat down by the window in the familiar posture with her chin on her cupped hands. By Miss Merriman's description of the view which the window gave upon she recognized the creamy brick building of the Children's Hospital, snuggled like a gentle sister by the side of the impressive marble walls of its big brother, the Harvard Medical School, and, as the light grew gave definition to its outlines, she felt as though it were actually drawing nearer to her. In imagination she went to meet it; she entered its doors and took her place among those who toiled there with loving hearts and skilful hands; and thus Miss Merriman found her, half an hour later, when she, similarly clad, came to bid her little guest good morning. With silent understanding, which is born of true companionship, she drew the girl into her arms.

"I'm not going to let you do a single thing but rest this morning," she said at length. "You look pale and tired still — like a very white rose — and I want you to appear your very sweetest when you go to meet Dr. MacDonald's family this afternoon, dear. Come, let's decide what you shall wear. The black silk that we bought in New York?"

Smiles hesitated. "I think that . . . would it be all right if I wore that pretty white woollen one?"

"Why, yes, if you like, but it is very plain and simple."

"And so am I," laughed Rose a bit unsteadily. "I want them to see me just as I am, and . . . . Oh, how I hope that they will like me!"

"Never fear. They will," answered Miss Merriman, giving her a reassuring kiss.

Nevertheless, it was a very quiet and timid Smiles who sat beside Donald in his coupé at four that afternoon, as he drove to the richly sombre home on Beacon Street, where had dwelt many generations of Thayers. He, too, although he attempted to be jovial, was strangely uneasy.

"You chump!" he said to himself. "You're more disturbed about whether this child will make a good impression, than you would be over performing a major operation. Supposing that Ethel *doesn't* go wild about her, what of it?"

A trim maid ushered them into the drawing room, where softly shaded lights were already burning, for the afternoon was dull and gray, and they gave a mellow homelike appearance to the mahogany furniture, rich tapestries, oriental rugs and costly paintings. Ethel, Mr. MacDonald, Senior, and little Muriel were in the room when Donald entered with the girl's slim hand held tightly in his, for she had slipped it there impulsively, just as he stepped through the broad doorway.

"This," he said simply, "is Smiles."

They all arose, and Ethel stepped quickly forward with outstretched hands. She had told herself that she meant to be very kind to the little savage to whom her brother had taken such an astonishing fancy; but now, something in the slender form and the half-frightened expression in the pale, sweet face caused her to forget everything else except that the stranger was alone and ill at ease. Both her arms went out to Rose with a motherly gesture, and, as she drew her within them, she said, "Why, my dear child."

"Yes, she *is* a child," broke in Muriel, eagerly seizing one of Smiles' hands. "I thought that she was a grown-up woman; but see, she wears her hair down on her neck just like a school girl."

Let it be said that Miss Merriman had caught the note struck by Rose that morning, and had arrayed her to appear as young and simple as possible.

"A child? Of course she is," echoed Mr. MacDonald in a hearty voice. "My dear, Donald has told us so much about you that I feel almost as though I had known you all your life. But," he added with little wrinkles forming at the corners of his kindly gray eyes, "I would like to have seen you, as my son did first, in that one-piece calico dress. He described the picture that you made very graphically."

"Oh, look, mother. She's going to *smile*. Remember how pretty Uncle Don told us she looked when . . . ."

Rose's shyly budding smile changed to silvery laughter in which all the rest joined, and with it was sealed the bond of an enduring friendship. Then baby Don was brought down from the nursery for inspection and, before he had been contentedly curled in the newcomer's arms many minutes, he was actually trying to lisp "Mileth," which Ethel proudly pronounced to be the first articulate word in his vocabulary, if those universal sounds, which doting parents have ever taken to mean Mother and Father, be excepted. He liked it so well that he insisted upon repeating it over and over, with eyes screwed up tight and mouth opened very wide, which gave him so comical an expression that every one laughed, including himself.

Manlike, Donald had planned to get all the meetings over with at once, and had asked his sister to invite Marion in for afternoon tea and to meet his "protégé and prodigy" — as Ethel had phrased it in her invitation. He had, however, purposely refrained from mentioning the fact to Rose, and when Miss Treville entered, stately as a goddess, very beautiful and a trifle condescending in manner, as she extended her white-gloved hand and said, "So this is little Rose," the girl felt a sudden chill succeed the warmth of hospitality which had served to banish all her timid reserve, had brought a glow of happy color to her cheeks and a sparkle to her luminous eyes, and had made her as wholly natural as she would have been at home among her simple neighbors of the mountains.

Donald felt the psychological change, and sensed the reason for it; but although, in a clumsy manner, he did his best to restore the atmosphere of comradeship, he knew that he was failing. Marion also tried, and tried sincerely, to bring Rose into the conversation; but the girl had become embarrassed and silent, and to her own surprise the society woman vaguely realized that she, too, was embarrassed and not at her best. She tried to shake off the feeling with the thought that it was absurd that one who had been at ease in the presence of royalty should feel so in that of a simple mountain girl; but she could not wholly banish the feeling or the impression that the girl's deep, unusual eyes were looking down beneath the surface, which she knew was perfectly appointed — had she not, for no reason at all she told herself, taken special pains in dressing? — and that, although there was something of awed admiration in her frank gaze, it also held a suggestion of something which was not entirely approval. Donald felt it, too, and it irritated him; so much so that he was frankly glad when his fiancée announced that she must depart to attend a social engagement. Perhaps it was because he was ashamed of such a feeling that he kissed her with unusual warmth, as he handed her into the waiting motor car, and he found himself flushing deeply, without reason, when he returned to the drawing room and saw Rose standing by one of the windows, looking out at the departing limousine with its two liveried attendants.

"She is very beautiful," the girl whispered to him, as he joined her.

There was another guest that afternoon, who came in, unexpectedly — a young man, in appearance

Donald's antithesis, for, although he was of more than medium height, he was slender and almost as graceful as a woman. Wavy light hair crowned a merry, boyish face which, with its remarkably blue eyes, was almost too good looking for a man, although saved from a hint of weakness by a firm, well-rounded chin.

"Called at your office and learned that you were loafing on the job again, and that I might find you up here, visiting a baby — for a change," he ran on, as he entered after the manner of one who feels himself perfectly at home. Then he caught sight of Rose, blushed like a girl himself and stammered, "Oh, I beg pardon. I didn't know that I was . . . ."

"You're not," laughed Donald, seizing the newcomer's hand with a vicelike grasp. "Come in. I've told you about my little mountain rose, and now is your chance to meet her, for here she is. Smiles, this is my closest friend and associate, Dr. Philip Bentley — the man who steps into my shoes when I am summarily ordered to board the next train for the Cumberland Mountains, or elsewhere."

"Who steps into his practice, perhaps, but not into his shoes, Miss Rose," added the other. "I could not fill *them*, figuratively or physically."

"Go ahead, make all the fun of me that you like," answered Donald. "I'm not ashamed of having a broad understanding."

"You would not think Dr. Donald's boots large if you could have seen my Granddaddy's," interposed

Smiles, pretending to think that reflection was being cast upon her idol. "I could get *both* my feet inside one of them — really I could."

"I don't wonder," answered Philip with a return to seriousness. And the girl hastily tucked her diminutive shoes underneath her chair, as she saw the man's gaze fastened upon them.

For nearly an hour she lived in unaccustomed delight, as she listened to the merry badinage of this group of educated city dwellers and, although it was something new to her, her quick mind soon realized that Philip was a most entertaining conversationalist, with a wit like a rapier which flashed and touched, but never hurt, and that Donald, in his slower way, possessed a dry humor which she had not suspected. At the end of that time a telephone call came for Donald which sent him forth, pretending to grumble over the lack of consideration of modern children, who insisted upon getting sick at the most inconvenient times, and of their parents, who permitted it.

"Your loss, my gain," chuckled Philip. "I'll be only too pleased to take Miss Rose home."

"Indeed, I'll not allow such a thing," promptly responded Ethel. "Rose stays here for dinner, and *you're* not invited. This is to be strictly a family party."

"'Family?' Is Don going to be a Mormon, then?" challenged Philip.

It was Rose, who — blushing prettily — answered,

"I hope not, for he is my brother, too, by blood adoption." And she told the story.

"Then why can't *I* be? I'm ready, nay, anxious, to shed quarts and quarts of blood to attain a like relationship," persisted Philip. And thus the conversation ran on through dinner, for Ethel relented and allowed Dr. Bentley to remain, and, as Donald was again summoned away, it was he who, after all, took Rose to the Merriman apartment.

"Oh," she cried, in telling Gertrude all about it, "I think that it was the happiest evening I ever spent, or it *would* have been if Big Jerry might only have been there, too."

A slight suggestion of a smile passed over the face of the older woman as she pictured the mountaineer in a Beacon Street drawing room. Rose saw, and interpreted it.

"Grandpap would not have been out of place there, or in a king's palace. He *was* a king, Miss Merriman."

"Yes, dear, he truly was," the other responded seriously.

There was a pause.

"Isn't Dr. Bentley nice," said Smiles, softly. "He must be splendid, for Dr. Donald likes him a lot."

"He likes *you* a lot, too! My, aren't we vain?" smiled Gertrude.

"Oh, I didn't think how that was going to sound!"

Rose's distress was real and the other hastened to say, "Yes, Dr. Bentley is splendid. We used to call them 'David and Jonathan,' for they were always together, and, before Dr. McDonald become engaged, we said that neither would ever marry, since they couldn't marry each other. Now I suppose that Dr. Bentley will be looking around for consolation. Perhaps . . . ."

"Don't be silly," laughed Smiles. But she became suddenly silent again.

CHAPTER XXV

THE FIRST MILESTONE

THREE months sped by and were gone like a dream.

Day after day, until should come that longed-for, yet dreaded test, Rose studied with a diligence that delighted the private tutor whom Donald, through Miss Merriman, had secured for her — a young woman who found herself astonished by her pupil's avidity in seeking knowledge.

The passing days were not, however, wholly dedicated to the books which held for Smiles the key to the citadel she sought to possess.

Other doors and other hearts were open to her, and, because of her simple charm, Donald's family welcomed her as a visitor whose every advent in the city home seemed to bring a fresh breath from the hills and open spaces. Little Muriel, who had loved her unseen, worshipped her on sight, and Ethel, happy in Donald's betrothal to Marion Treville, would have been glad to have had her with them far more often than she would consent to come.

Long walks she took, too, regardless of weather, swinging freely along on voyages of discovery; losing herself often in Boston's impossible streets, only to find her way back home with the instinct for direction of one bred amid forests, trackless, save for infrequent blind and tortuous paths. And soon the historic, homey city cast its strange spell over her heart, and claimed her for its own.

Spring came at last, not the verdant, glorious, festal virgin of the Southland, but the hesitant, bashfully reserved maiden so typical of New England, and Miss Merriman finally reported to Donald that their joint protégé seemed to be fairly prepared for the test which she had come so far to take.

There are no rules, born of reason, which cannot yield to reasonable exceptions, and, although the entrance requirements of the training school were as exacting as its course, and as strict as its standard, a standard which had long since made it the peer of any in all America, some of the purely technical ones were waived upon the request of the idolized chief junior surgeon on the staff, for Donald went personally to the Superintendent and explained the case to her, and she agreed to allow Rose to take a special examination; but she shook her head when he mentioned the girl's age.

"Of course you know what the requirements are in that respect, doctor," she said. "We make exceptions, yes; but, if she enters now, she will be by far the youngest girl in the school. I think that, before I give you my decision, I shall have to see and talk with her."

Accordingly, that afternoon he took the rather

frightened Smiles to the Superintendent of nurses, and left them closeted together.

"Dr. MacDonald has told me about you, and your ambition, Miss Webb," said the Superintendent kindly. "You have been very courageous; but you are very young, even younger than I thought. Now I want you to tell me frankly just what your life has been, so that I may judge as to your other qualifications, before deciding whether it is wise for you to take the examinations."

Rose began hesitatingly; but, as the other drew her out with judicious questions, she told her story with simple directness, and, before long, the Superintendent had come to a realization that the little mountain girl — whose life had, for so long, been one of unusual responsibilities — had already acquired an uncommon maturity of judgment. Although she was still some eighteen months below the prescribed age for entering, she received the other's hesitating permission to make the essay.

It would be difficult to decide who felt the greater nervousness during the period of Smiles' written examination, and the time which had to elapse before word came as to the result — Rose, Miss Merriman or Donald. It was the last who heard first. The Superintendent invited him into her office, as he was passing through the hospital corridor one day, and said, "I am sure that you will be pleased to hear that Miss Webb has passed her tests with flying colors, doctor."

A warmth of pleasurable relief passed through Donald; but he managed to reply formally, "I *am* pleased; but I hope that you didn't ease up any because of anything . . . er . . . on my account."

"No, we didn't," was the response. "I'll admit that both your account of what Miss Webb had done, and the girl herself, appealed to me so that I was prepared to mark a bit leniently, if necessary; but it wasn't. I really don't see how she managed to garner so much education in so short a time."

"'Where there's a will,'" quoted Donald, with inward satisfaction over the fact that his ward had fulfilled his prophecy, and he stole a few minutes out of the busy morning to motor to the Merrimans' apartment to bear the joy-bringing tidings personally to little Rose, whose eyes shone happily and whose lips smiled their thanks, but who — perversely, it seemed to him — gave Miss Merriman the reward which he felt should have been his.

Dreams do come true sometimes, if they *are* true, and so at last arrived a bright May morning when Smiles folded away her little play uniform forever, and — by right of conquest — donned the striped pink and white gingham dress and bibless apron of a probationer, within the doors of the newly built home of that old and worthy institution which had had its inception, more than sixty years before, in the loving heart of Nursing Sister Margaret.

There Rose entered into a new life, as different from that of the old physical freedom of the hills, and personal freedom from restraint, as could well be imagined, for, as Donald had told her, she was now mustered, as an untrained recruit, into a great modern army; and discipline is the keynote in war, whether the battle be against evil nations or evil forces.

From half after six in the morning until ten at night, when with military precision came "lights out," her life was drawn to pattern. It was not a hardship for her, as with some others, to arise at the early hour; and the brief prayer and singing of the morning hymn, in company with her fifty-odd sister-probationers and pupil nurses, impressed her strongly the first time in which she had part in it, and never failed to strengthen and uplift her for the day's toil. Times were to come aplenty, to be sure, when the old call of untrammelled freedom stirred her senses to mute rebellion; but, as often, her all-absorbed interest in the work silenced it speedily.

Right at the outset Rose experienced the same shock which hundreds of other would-be nurses have had. She, mistress of a home for years, was obliged to learn to clean, to scrub, to make a bed! For two whole months of probationary training she had to labor at the bedside or in the classroom, doing the commonplace, practical tasks which, to many, seemed merely unnecessary drudgery; but, if she occasionally felt that Donald's prophecy was coming true with a vengeance, more often her level little head held a prescient understanding of how important this unlovely foundation was to the structure which should some day be built upon it.

And, although the Superintendent said nothing to Smiles, she noted with secret appreciation that her new pupil possessed, in addition to her sustaining enthusiasm, a no less valuable thing — the innate ability to use her hands by instinct and without clumsy conscious effort. Had not this girl, who was scarcely more than a child in years, for a long time been both a homemaker and an ever-ready nurse to all those who became ill within the confines of the scattered mountain settlement?

The second milestone was reached at last. Rose was one day summoned alone into the Superintendent's sanctum, and the door was closed to all others. A little later she came out with tears adding new lustre to her shining eyes, for the talk had been very earnest and heart-searching; but they were tears of happiness, for upon her gleaming curls now sat the square piqué cap which was the visible sign that she had safely traversed the first stretch of the long, hard road. To be sure, she knew well that even this, the so dearly desired cap and pale blue dress which went with it, did not make her fully a pupil nurse, yet that afternoon it seemed that life could never hold for her an honor more precious.

The afternoon on which this momentous event occurred was one of liberty for Rose, and she hastened with the news to her dear Miss Merriman, the precious cap smuggled out under her coat; but, after they had rejoiced together, and she had admired its reflection in the glass, she suddenly became doleful, and wailed in mock despair, "Oh, doesn't it seem as though I'd never, *never* be a real nurse. Why, now I've got to *leave the hospital*" — the tragedy in her tone almost caused her friend to break into laughter — "and study all sorts of awful Latin things. She opened a catalogue and read aloud, "'Physiology, bacteriology, chemistry, dietetics,' and goodness knows what else over at Simmons College, for *four whole months.* I shall simply die, I just know that I shall!"

Miss Merriman gently explained the necessity for each of them; but wisely refrained from further frightening her by adding that a full year's course was to be crowded into those sixteen weeks.

In due time these, too, were over, the awe-inspiring examination passed, and Smiles was accepted as worthy of a place among the pupil nurses. Like an athlete she had finished her preliminary training, and was ready for the long, gruelling race toward the goal, two and a half years distant.

Hard work though it was, Rose found all her days sunny ones, and only one cloud partly obscured their brightness. Donald she saw on rare occasions only, as the demands upon his time doubled and redoubled, and of course their brief meetings at the hospital demanded strict formality of intercourse. Deeply as he felt for her, he was a physician first, last and all the time, and as uncompromising in his own ethics as he was in his requirements of the nurses.

Yet, if she saw him seldom, there was another whom she saw increasingly often. Dr. Bentley's attitude towards Rose was also strictly professional; but he never failed to bow and speak pleasantly when he met her in the corridors or wards, and she instinctively felt that in him she had found another real friend.

Rose was too much a child of nature to be given to thinking much about men; but there were minutes, just before sleep came at night, when her mind would visualize Donald's strong, kindly face, which seemed to look down at her with an expression almost fatherly, and she would whisper a little prayer that she might help him as she had resolved to, that night on the mountain top. And at such times another face, light, where his was dark, came, not to supplant, but to supplement it.

CHAPTER XXVI

THE CALL OF THE RED CROSS

DESPITE the enthralling interest of her new work and surroundings, it seemed to Rose, during the year after she gained entrance to the temple of her desire, that her life was standing still, while all things else were speeding by her at a breakneck pace.

It had never been so before. Even in the isolation and simplicity of her former home she had felt that she was a part of it all. It had seemed to her, somehow, as though her existence had been patterned after her own turbulent mountain stream, which danced along through sunshine and shade, with here and there a ravine and cataract, here and there a rapid or impeding boulder in its course; but always moving, moving. Then, suddenly, it was as though that swift little river had fallen into a broad, quiet basin, walled in, where it moved forward almost imperceptibly. True, it was daily gaining greater depth and fulness as it gathered to itself the tributary waters of knowledge and experience, and Smiles was not insensible to this fact. But it was difficult to remember it always, for the outer world of events was moving forward so fast.

The very day upon which her probationary period came to an end and, with a smile on her lips, a song in her heart, she placed the cherished cap upon her gold-brown curls, there came, from the heart of the swiftly piled up, lowering clouds, the blinding flash which shattered the peace of the world and started the overwhelming conflagration into the seething, bloody-tongued vortex into which nation after nation was sucked irresistibly. The world had become the plaything of the Gods of Wrath.

Black days passed, shuddering things of horror to Rose, when she had time to allow her mind to dwell upon them, and her keen imagination to picture the atrocities which the fiend was committing upon the helpless babies of Belgium and France.

Then, in answer to the cries and lamentations from overseas, the banner of the Red Cross was shaken forth anew, like a holy standard, and, like crusaders of old, doctors and nurses flocked beneath it for the battle. From her own hospital home went physicians and graduate nurses to dedicate themselves afresh to service. The call reached and wrung the heart of Rose. She could not go as a nurse, she knew; yet the need was so great that it seemed to her that somehow she must answer; but she resolutely closed her ears to it and fixed her eyes the more steadfastly upon the rocky, shut-in path which she had set forth to climb.

It was a raw, bleak evening in late November when she made her final resolve. At noon Donald had met her in one of the corridors and stopped to speak with her. His face, she thought afterwards, had appeared unusually serious and determined, even for him, as he said, "This is your afternoon and evening off duty, isn't it, Rose? I want to talk with you, if you haven't made any other plans."

As it chanced, she had been eagerly anticipating a visit to the theatre with Miss Merriman, who was home for a few days between cases; but something about his manner caused her to tell a white lie without hesitation.

"Good," he said. "I'll call for you in my car and take you to Ethel's for dinner. Be ready at six o'clock."

All the rest of the day Donald's presence had been strangely close to her, and she found herself wondering what it portended; but not until the pleasant family meal was over, and he was taking her home, did she learn.

When they came out of the house they found a baby blizzard sending the first snow of the season, as light and dry as tiny particles of down, whirling and eddying through the broad street. As Rose stood in surprise at the top of the brownstone steps, a dry vagrant, left from one of the trees which was tossing its gaunt arms protestingly, came tumbling down to become stem-entangled in her hair. With a laugh, she dashed for the motor car and, when she had sprung inside it, she was panting a little, for the thieving wind had taken advantage of her lips being open in laughter to steal away her breath, so that Donald was sensible of her quickened heart beats as she leaned against him while his big but deft fingers removed the leaf almost tenderly from its imprisoning mesh.

"Doctor Bentley would make a pretty speech about getting caught in my hair," challenged Rose with a teasing pout.

The next instant she drew quickly back, for Donald's arms were almost about her. He as quickly recovered himself, with the words, "But you can't expect pretty speeches from a brother."

"You have been a dear big brother; I don't know why you have been so good to me, Donald. Do you know what this snow reminds me of? That awful night on the mountain when I went down to Fayville to telegraph for you — and you came." For a moment they both sat in silent memories, then Rose added, "Dear little Lou, I wonder how she is getting along now . . . and Juddy, too. Isn't it a strange thing, Donald, that one can forget the old things so quickly — no, not forget, either; but have them forced into the background of the mind by new surroundings and new friends. Sometimes, all those years on the mountain seem to me like a dream. I used to see the people there, Grandpap, Mr. Talmadge, Judd and all the rest, every day, they were a part of my life, and now they have been completely withdrawn and who knows if I shall ever see any of them again? They hardly seem real to me."

"Yes, strange, perhaps, but it happens many times in the course of a life." He paused, then added hurriedly, "I suppose that in a few months you will be saying the same thing about me — 'I used to see him every day, he was a part of my life, but now he is only in the background of my memory, and doesn't seem real.'"

There was a note almost of bitterness in Donald's voice; but Rose was too stunned by his words to notice or attempt to analyze the manner of their utterance.

"Donald, what . . . what do you mean? You're not . . ." She gasped, and laid her hand with an impulsive clutch on his arm.

"Look out! Don't interfere with the motorman," he laughed more naturally, as the car swerved almost into the curbing. "Yes, I am. I'm going away . . . almost immediately."

"Away? Where?"

"To France."

"Oh, Don, you mustn't; you can't. You're needed here so much."

"They need me over there more, little Smiles. I've realized it, and felt the pull, for days; but it didn't become insistent until yesterday, when I received a letter from a chap whom I have known for years. He's always had a good deal more money than was good for him, and been a sort of social butterfly. I liked him, although I didn't believe that he had a serious thought in his head, didn't think that he was capable of one, but . . . here, read what he has written me," he concluded abruptly, as a temporary block forced their car to a stop beneath an electric light on Massachusetts Avenue. "The first page doesn't matter; it merely contains a description of how he happened to be caught in Paris by the outbreak of the war, and got mixed up in volunteer rescue work through a spirit of adventure."

Rose turned to the second sheet and, holding the pages close to the glass in the door, through which came enough snow-filtered light to illumine them, read.

"I am beginning to understand, now, something of what you meant when you used to talk so enthusiastically about your confining, and, as it seemed to me, often thankless work. I never knew what real satisfaction was until I began to get mixed up with this volunteer Red Cross work. Coming from the source that it does, you will probably be surprised and amused at the statement that, when I look back on the old, superficial, utterly useless life that I formerly led, I actually thank God for the foolish whim that brought me to Paris in the fall, and the equally whimsical decision that led me to volunteer my services as an auto driver. The work has stirred something inside of me that I didn't know existed, and, if I come through this scrape (we're working in villages pretty close to the front a good deal of the time), I'll come home 'poorer, but wiser.' Yes, they've touched my pocketbook as well as my heart.

I suppose the papers give you some idea of conditions here; but no verbal description can begin to do it justice; the need is simply overwhelming and hourly growing greater. Think of it, old man, there are thousands upon thousands of babies and little kiddies of Belgium and northern France homeless, many of them orphaned, most of them sick and all helpless and with their lives — which have every right to be carefree and happy — filled with sorrow and suffering.

France has been glorious in the way she has met the staggering, almost insuperable difficulties which everywhere confront her, but how could she be expected to meet this incidental problem when she was so overburdened with the crushing pressure of the battle for her very existence. It has been a mighty lucky thing for her that the Red Cross was ready to take it off her shoulders, and she has turned to *us* (How does that sound? Can you imagine me doing anything useful?) with tears of appeal and gratitude. That isn't a figure of speech. I have actually seen the Prefect of this Province, who would rank with the governor of one of our states, and who is a brave, capable man, cry like a woman over the seeming hopelessness of the ghastly problem. I have heard him say that he — that France — was helpless, and beg us in the name of common humanity to do what we could.

Believe me, we're doing it, and I'm proud of my countrymen and women who have gone into this thing with the typical Yankee pep; proud of the American Red Cross and just a bit proud of myself. You used to make fun of my vaunted ability to stay up half the night, and be fresh as a daisy the next morning. It's serving me in good stead now. I can't begin to tell you about the work we have done already and are doing; it is a task to overwhelm the courage, but we are 'carrying on,' as the Tommies say.

New children, by the scores and hundreds, are brought into the hospital bases daily, and many of them have been living for weeks, and even months, filthy in cellars of Hun-shattered villages which are almost continually under fire. They are generally sick, naturally, indescribably dirty and, in fact, mere wraiths of childhood. God, Don, it gets me when I imagine my own nephews and nieces in their places!

We clean 'em up, give them help and something to live for. We have already established hospitals, schools and nurseries in ——— and ——— and our ambulances and 'traveling baths' go out daily to give aid to the less needy in the neighborhood. Can you picture *me* acting as chauffeur for a magnified bath tub for Belgian babies? That's what I'm doing, now!

Get into the game, old man. We need you over here, and the kids of the disgustingly rich at home will be the better for not having a doctor to give them a pill every time their little noses run a bit. Pack up your saws, axes and other trouble-makers in your old kit bag and climb aboard a ship bound for France."

Donald saw that there were tears in Smiles' deep eyes as she silently folded the pages, and replaced them in their envelope.

"Of course you ought to go," she said simply. "I spoke selfishly. But oh, Don, I don't know what I shall do without you; you're the only 'family' I've got. I don't see you very often; but I know that you are here in Boston, and I guess that I have got the habit of leaning on you in my thoughts. You know I called you a tree, years and years ago."

"Yes, I remember, an 'oak,' wasn't it? I thought that you meant that I was tough," he laughed. "The idea of *you* leaning on any one is funny, Rose." Then he added, with some hesitancy, "I've been thinking . . . Would you like to go over there, too, Rose? I could take you . . . that is, I am quite sure that I could arrange for you to do so, not as a Red Cross nurse, of course, for they have to be graduates; but as a volunteer helper in one of those base hospitals. It would be a wonderful experience, and you would be performing the kind of service that you like best. It would not be time wasted, by any means."

She started, and her lips parted eagerly; then the light slowly faded from her eyes and she shook her head slowly.

"I would love it. It would be glorious, Don, and I should be working with you, perhaps, but . . . No, I must keep on doing as I have planned. I can't falter or fail now, Don. There is going to be greater need every day, not for helpers, but for trained workers. When this awful war is ended and the weary, weary world turns back to peaceful pursuits, its hope and salvation will lie in its babies. Won't it, Don? I would like to help those babies over in France; sometimes I dream of being a Red Cross nurse and helping the poor, wounded soldiers; but I am sure that it is better for me to keep on making myself ready to serve the coming generations to the best of my fully trained ability. Don't you think so, too, Don?"

Her words had rung firm and true until the last question, when there crept in a note which seemed to his ears to carry an appeal for him to disagree, and argue with her; but the man answered, "Yes, dear. You are dead right, and I felt certain that you would say what you have said. You have got to stay until you are trained; I have got to go, because I am. You see that, don't you?"

"Yes. Oh, I shall miss you awfully, Don; I can't tell you how much. But I want you to go. And I mean to pray for you, and the poor little babies over there, too. I'll write you as often as I can; as often as you want me to."

"That's fine," he answered heartily. "But, as I told you once before, don't feel hurt if I answer only occasionally. I have a suspicion that there will be plenty of work for me to do over there."

"Yes, I'll understand. Besides, you will have to write to . . . to Miss Treville more than to me. Are you . . . are you going to get married before you go?"

"Married? Good Lord, no . . . that is, I hadn't even thought of it," he said with a forced laugh. "Why, I haven't even told her yet that I am going."

"You haven't? You told me, first?"

"Well . . . er . . . you see I had to tell you, because . . . because I . . . I hold a position of trust in respect to you, and have got to make arrangements for your future. Big Jerry told me to use my own judgment about your money, and I believe that you are fully competent to take care both of yourself and of it.

"Here," he drew a small package from his side

pocket, "is a bank deposit and check book, for I have already had the account transferred from my name, as trustee, to you individually. Now it is up to you to prove that you are a careful little business woman. With more than a thousand dollars in the bank you may feel quite like an heiress, but I warn you that a big city is a glutton and its avaricious maw is always open for money. Be warned by one who knows. If you need any advice of any nature that a man can give better than Miss Merriman, I want you to promise to call on Phil . . . Dr. Bentley, that is, for I mean to put you in his charge. You can trust him just as you do me."

"I know that," answered Rose frankly.

"Well, here we are, little sister. Don't tell any one what I have just told you, for I want to make all my preliminary arrangements before I astound the world with the announcement of what I am going to do."

"You needn't laugh," answered Rose. "I guess that it will dismay plenty of Back Bay families who have babies."

There was a catch in her voice as she bade him good-night, and she was not sorry for an excuse for running into the hospital, offered by the mellow notes of a distant church clock tolling the hour of ten. It was the signal for "lights out" in the bedrooms, and this was appreciated, too, for it made it possible for her to undress in the dark, and the pale moonlight which came in through the window, as the moon played hide and seek behind the broken masses of storm clouds — for the blizzard had ended as quickly as it had come on — was reflected on two glistening tear drops on her flushed cheeks. In the darkness her roommate could not see them and be led to ask questions.

The two girls, one the self-educated, unknown child of the southern mountain side, the other the college-bred daughter of one of New England's oldest families, had become fast friends and generally exchanged whispered confidences until the sleep which comes of physical exhaustion speedily claimed them; but to-night Rose was in no mood for conversation.

The last thread which bound the old life to the new was soon to be broken, and she felt lonelier, more nearly homesick, than she had since leaving Webb's Gap.

"Perhaps I shall never see him again," she half whispered. "But I shall never, *never* forget him, he has been so good and meant so much to me. And I shall always love him." She saw that her roommate was asleep, softly raised the window-shade to let in the moonlight that she loved, and, clad in her simple nightdress, short sleeved and cut low at the neck, seated herself before the mirror to brush her wavy mass of hair, and, as she leaned forward, and it fell about her face, tear bedewed and made almost childlike again by its frame of tumbling curls, she smiled faintly in recollection. "I look the way I used to in my homemade, one-piece dresses," she breathed. "Just as I did that afternoon when he first saw me. 'Yo' looked so funny a-fallin' over thet thar dawg, an' a-rollin' on the floor.' What a way to greet a famous physician — only I didn't know it then."

For a moment she sat like this, her thoughts far away from the northern city; then a faint blush mantled her face, and she hastily jumped up and shut out the soft light by pulling down the shade.

CHAPTER XXVII

THE GOAL

You cannot, by a bridge of sighs, attain the future's golden
 years,
But try a bridge of rainbow hopes erected on substantial
 piers
Of honest work, and you will find it leads you surely to the
 goal.
'Tis God that gives the dreamer's dreams, as radiant as
 the morning,
But, if the will to work is weak, they often die a-borning.

If this were a romance, instead of the simple account of the pilgrimage and development of a girl from childhood to womanhood, it would be permissible to say, "three years pass by in swift flight," or "drag by on weary feet," as the case may have been, and then resume the action.

But in everyday life, character is built out of everyday incidents, big and little, all of which have place in the moulding of it, and, since the years of Smiles' training within the Children's Hospital were vital ones for her, it is essential to touch briefly upon some of the occurrences which filled them.

On the other hand, it is by no means necessary to describe that period at length. It is doubtful if, in later life, she will herself look back upon the many days so filled to repletion with exacting, though interesting, tasks, as other than a dead level, for constant repetition of a thing, no matter how gripping it may be, produces a monotony. But there were special incidents — sometimes trivial in comparison with the importance of her sustained labor — which formed the high lights in the picture, and the memory of which will endure through all the after years. By recounting a few of these, and letting our imaginations fill in the interims, we can accompany Rose on her journey to the goal of her desires.

. . . .

The day after Donald had taken her into his confidence regarding his plans, Rose made up her mind to keep a diary.

"Even though he may be thousands of miles away, I mean to keep myself as close to him as possible by writing him as I would talk to him, about *all* the things which happen in my life, and, unless I set them down as they happen, I shall forget," she told Miss Merriman, after the seal of secrecy had been removed from her lips.

"Perhaps *you* can succeed in keeping one. *I* never could," laughed her friend. "Each January First I start a new one, and register a solemn vow to keep it up longer, at least, than I did the one the previous year. If I follow that system until I am three hundred and fifty years old, I will complete just one before I die."

Smiles accepted the implied challenge, and, day by day, with few omissions, the dated pages bore new testimony to her application in performing a self-appointed task. The plan bore fruit, too, for Donald, in his rare replies to her confidential letters, which went to him each fortnight, was able to praise her as the best of correspondents, writing once, "You have an exceptional gift for making incidents seem real and people alive, in your letters, and of realizing that, with us who are so far away from home, it *is* the little things which count. Ethel, alas, is hopeless in this respect. She writes me faithfully; but invariably says that nothing has happened except the usual occurrences of everyday life, and thereby utterly misses the great fact that it is just those very things that the lonely exile most longs to hear about. I would actually rather have her write that they had baked beans on Saturday night than that so-and-so had given a charity whist at the Vendome."

Yet many a sentence went into the diary that was never copied or embellished for Donald's eyes. Some of them had to do with him, or her thoughts of him; some were too intimate for another to see.

December 6th, 1915.

"My dear Donald has gone. I think that I have not felt so utterly lonesome since granddaddy died. And I could not get away to say good-by to him — I could have cried, only I didn't have time even to do *that*. It doesn't seem right, when he has been so dear to me, that I should have had to part from him in the hospital corridor with others around, so that all I could do was press his hand an instant and wish him a commonplace, 'Good luck and God-speed.' Still, it probably wouldn't have been any different if we had been alone. I couldn't have done what my heart was longing to do, everything is different now. I don't believe that I enjoy being 'grown-up.' What an unpleasant thing 'convention' is. Why, I wonder, must we always hide our true feelings under a mask? I suppose it is lest the world give a wrong meaning to them; but if I *had* kissed him, the way I used to, I'm sure that Donald would have understood. He knows that I love him as dearly as though I were truly his sister, instead of a make-believe one."

Here the page bears a number of meaningless hieroglyphics, and then the words, stricken out, "I wonder."

"He looked so manly in his uniform, and so distinguished, although I suppose that he isn't really *handsome* — at least, not like Dr. Bentley. *He* isn't so wonderful as Don; but I think that he is more understanding. He seemed to realize just how I felt this morning, and he was as sweet and considerate as a woman when I bungled things awfully in the operating room. The head nurse gave me a deserved call down, however, and it was perhaps just as well that she did, for my mind needed to be 'brought back.' Only my body was in the hospital, and the *real me*, as Mr. Talmadge said, was back in the cabin, helping Donald operate on Lou, all over again. I cried like a little fool — the first time I have done it here — but my tears weren't for the poor baby on the operating table. They were memory tears. . . .

"Poor little thing, he had to die, and he was the first one whom I have seen pass on to the eternal garden of

God's flowers since I have been in the hospital. Oh, it hasn't been a happy day at all. . . .

"I wonder if Donald could have saved him? My brain answers, 'No.' Dr. Bentley did all that lies within the power of science, I am sure. But somehow . . . ."

. . . .

Christmas night.

"If Donald might only have been here in person to-day, it would have been perfect. I think that he must have been, in spirit, for I 'felt' his presence quite near me several times; I confided as much to Dr. Bentley and he made an atrocious pun on the word 'presents.' I wish he wouldn't; it is the only thing about him that I don't like, but he will make them. Wasn't Donald thoughtful and dear to have bought a Christmas gift for me during those overcrowded days before he went away? — a whole set of books, beautifully bound, but better still, beautiful within. Books are the same as people, I think. We like to see both attractively clothed, but in each it is the soul that counts. . . .

"What a lot of presents I received — from Miss Merriman and her mother, Mrs. Thayer and little Muriel, and, oh, so many of the girls here. I don't know why they are all so good to me — because I am looked upon as a lonely little savage, I suppose. And then there was that one from Dr. Bentley. The idea of a simple mountain girl from Webb's Gap having five whole pounds of candy at once!

. . . .

"The funniest thing happened to-day, and I must not forget to write Donald all about it. He is sure to remember little red-headed Jimmy, who has to spend so much of his time in the hospital. Has he imagination enough, I wonder, to picture him sitting up in bed in the snow-white ward, with his flaming auburn hair and bright red jacket calling names at each other? I love the old custom to which the hospital still clings of putting all the little patients into those red flannel jackets on cold days, for it makes the wards look so cheerful — like Christmas fields dotted with bright berries. Jimmy is a dear, and so imaginative that I believe he *lives* every story that I tell him of the Cumberlands — certainly he likes them better than fairy stories. This afternoon, I had finished telling him about how grandpappy shot the turkey for Dr. MacDonald, and I found him looking up at me with his big blue eyes, which can be as serious as a saint's or as mischievous as an imp's. 'Your face is most always laughing, Miss Webb,' said he. 'I think I shall have to call you Nurse Smiles.' My roommate, Miss Roberts, happened to be in the room and heard him, and now it's all over the hospital. Everybody is calling me it, unless the superintendent or some of the older doctors are around. How odd it is that he should have struck on it, and given me my old nickname again. . .

"Dr. Bentley called me Smiles when he left after his evening visit."

. . . .

May 17th, 1916.

"This has been a day of days for me. First I received a long and wonderful letter from Donald. It seemed like old times, for it was as kindly and simple, too, as those which he used to write to me at Webb's Gap. I wonder if he regards me as still a child? I suppose that I really am one, but somehow I feel very grown up, and much older than many of the girls who are years older than I. They constantly surprise me by acting so young when they are off duty. . . but I love it in them.

"To-day I entered into the second year of my training. I wish that I had the power to set down on paper my feelings when I received that first narrow black band for my cap. I suppose that I had some of the same 'prideful' sensations that dear granddaddy did when he was very young, and cut the first notch in the stock of his rifle-gun. But how much better *my* notch is! It means that I am fast getting able to save lives, not to take them. I must always remember that — it will give a deeper meaning to the symbol. And now my room is going to be moved down a story — I'm so glad that Dorothy Roberts is to be with me still — and I can move in one table nearer the front wall in the dining room. That wall sometimes seems to me like a goal that I have got to reach before I will be safe, just as in a children's game of tag, and, when I get tired and discouraged — for I do, at times, little diary — it seems as though there were many, many things stretching out invisible hands to catch me before I get to it. Donald was right about the path being no road of roses. . . . Come, this will never do; I'm supposed to be happy to-night, and besides, now I've got to live up to my nickname again.

. . . .

I wonder how much I really have changed in the year? a good deal, I'm sure. I remember that at first I used to laugh to myself over the 'class distinctions,' such as I have just been writing about; that was when I was fresh from the mountain, where every one called every one else by his or her first name — and also when I was in the lowest class myself. Once I was even bold enough to tell Dr. Bentley that I thought they were foolish, but he reminded me — as Donald had — that we are an army here, and that in an army a private can't eat and sleep with a captain, or a captain with a general. Now I don't mind the rules and regulations at all, for I have learned the lesson of discipline, and I know that, even if we do have to be strict in our conduct toward the older nurses and the doctors, we are all — from the senior surgeon down to the lowliest probationer — really one in a great spiritual fellowship, as the prayerbook says, and all working together in the same great cause.

. . . .

August 19th, 1916.

"Little diary, I have been neglecting you lately, but now you and I must collect our thoughts, for we have got to write a long, long letter to Donald and tell him all about the vacation — the first that I ever had.

It was the first time that I was ever really at the seashore, too, except that one afternoon in June when Dr. Bentley took me down to Nahant in his car. Weren't the Thayers dear to have me as their guest at beautiful Manchester-by-the-Sea? Ethel (I wonder if Donald will be pleased to know that his *real* sister has asked me to call her by her first name?) insisted that they did it for my own sake, but I know that it was really on his account. They were two weeks of wonder for me; but I wish that he might have been there. How they all miss him — even Dr. Bentley. I think that there is nothing finer than such a friendship between two men. Why, he even calls on Donald's family still. He came to Manchester twice in the fortnight that I was there. Dr. Bentley wants me to call him 'Philip,' when we are not in the hospital, and I do . . . sometimes. It seems perfectly natural, even though he is much older than I — he is over thirty; but I suppose that is because at home we called almost every one by his first name. (We are rambling, little diary. I don't believe that Donald would be particularly interested in the fact that I call Dr. Bentley, 'Philip.')

He *will* be interested to know how the sea impressed me, though, and again I find myself wholly at a loss for words to express my feelings. It was so overwhelming in its grandeur and far-stretching expanse; so beautiful in its never-ending procession of colors; so terrible in its might, when aroused. I have seen it asleep as peacefully as one of my babies (all the hospital babies are children of my heart), and I have seen it in anger, like a brutal giant. I wish that I had not seen its latter mood, for, when it caught up the little boat that had been torn from the moorings, and hurled her again and again against the rocks until there was not a plank of her left unbroken — while the wind shrieked its horrid glee — my growing love for it was turned to fear. No, I can never care for the ocean as I do for my mountains. I cannot forget that it was the waters which stole my dearest treasures from me.

Still, the memory of that storm is nearly lost in the abounding happiness of those two weeks, and the third one which I spent with my Gertrude Merriman, who stole it from her many cases to be with me. When I set down each little incident of them in black and white, as I mean to in my letter to Don, they will appear commonplace enough, I'm afraid; but I shall tell him that their story is written on my heart in letters of gold and many colors.

He pretends to be interested in every foolish little thing that I have done, but I don't suppose that he would care to read about all the new dresses I have bought. I never realized before that a girl could get so much pleasure out of buying pretty things, and I am afraid that he would scold me if he knew how many leaves I have used out of my checkbook. Not that they have been all for clothes, little diary. I did not realize how much

I had given to war charities, and I was a little frightened this morning when I made up my balance.

But I cannot help giving for the poor French and Belgian babies. It somehow seems as though I were giving the money to Don to spend for me."

. . . .

There follow many entries, in the course of which the name of Donald appears, and many more in which that of Philip, from which one might reasonably draw the conclusion that the latter was conscientiously performing his part as *ad interim* guardian for Rose. There are also several mentions of impish, lovable Jimmy — he of the red hair, presumably — and of visits, on her afternoons off, to the cheap and somewhat squalid apartment where he lived with his thin, tired, but pitifully optimistic mother, and a stout, florid-faced father, who wore shabby, but very loud-checked, suits and was apparently a highly successful business man of big affairs, but frequently "temporarily out of funds." Indeed, it would seem as though there were times when the family — which included six other children from one to ten years old — would actually not have had enough to eat if Rose had not "loaned" the wherewithal to purchase it to the father of the household.

Under date of May 15th, 1916, appears the following.

. . . .

"*Two* black bands on the little white cap! One round table nearer the wall! Materia medica, orthopedia, medical analysis, general surgery, bacteriology, therapeutics and anæsthesia no longer mere words, whose very sound made me weak with dismay; but terms descriptive of new ways in which I can help weak and suffering babyhood. It has been hard, but soul-satisfying, work. I love it all, and have never regretted the decision made, centuries ago it seems, on the mountain. I have just been re-reading Donald's first letter to me — the one in which he frankly warned me of the hardships which would be mine to face, if I should attempt to carry out my plan. It was, I think, the only time that he was ever wrong . . . no, I had forgotten that afternoon at Judd's still. Work may be hard, and yet entail no hardship, especially when it brings the satisfaction of winning against odds. I know that he did not really mean what he said in that letter. It was written merely as a test of my resolve; to deter me, if it wasn't strong enough to carry me through. There have been times when I have myself wondered if it would, but, thanks to dear old Mr. Talmadge, and his 'sermon on the mount' I have always been able to find the help that he told us about. I wonder if Donald has, too? Surely he must have, he has been doing such wonderful work 'over there.' It is like him to say so little about it in his letters, but Dr. Roland gave us a talk about what they have been doing in Toul and Leslie, when he returned from France, and he sang Donald's praises *fortissimo*. I was so happy, and so proud.

"They all tell me that the coming year is the hardest of all with its practical training at the Massachusetts General Hospital, and in the Manhattan Maternity in New York. I have a feeling that I am not going to enjoy the former. Nursing 'grown-ups' does not appeal to me as the caring for the little flowers does. But I shall love the other. Motherhood is sacred and beautiful. . . .

"I shall have to be very economical this year, little diary, and especially careful when I get to New York. When I paid the final installment on my tuition fee, I was frightened to find how little remained of what granddaddy left me, and what I had saved, myself. Nearly thirteen hundred dollars looked like a huge fortune to me in those days, but it is nothing at all in a city, where there is so much poverty, and there are so many appeals to one's heart. I know that Donald — or Philip — would lend me a little money until the time when I get to earning it for myself, if I should ask them. But of course I cannot do that. Perhaps I can earn a little during my afternoons and evenings off duty. The girls say that I can shampoo and manicure as well as a professional. Yes, I will try to do that this year.

. . . .

January 15th, 1917.

"Thank goodness my worries about finances are almost over!

"The last few months have been simply terrible, and the hardest part of all, I think, has been my not being able to give anything to the number of splendid causes which so touch the sympathies these dark days. Perhaps I gave too much before; but I am not a bit sorry, especially now that some of the seed which I cast upon the waters is soon to bear golden fruit for me. I never believe the pessimistic people who say that those who receive charity are never really grateful, and now I *know* that they are wrong. Jimmy's father has been so appreciative of my pitifully small presents to them, that sometimes he has cried over them, and I knew that he was in earnest when he promised to repay me as soon as he possibly could. Now the chance has come. I was there yesterday and he said that he had been thinking about me just before I appeared.

"It seems that he sells stock, and has just obtained a wonderful position as agent, or whatever they call it, for a new copper mine which he says is better than the 'Calumet and Hecla.'

"He explained to me all about that one and showed me in the paper how high it was selling now — for $550 a share. He is the sole representative for all of New England, and he says that the company is at present selling its stock only to special friends in order to 'let them in on the ground floor.' The shares are only ten dollars apiece and are sure to be worth a hundred, or more, very soon, because of the war. It seems almost impossible! I told him that I had only about a hundred dollars in the world, but that, if he really felt that he wanted to do me a favor, I *might* 'invest' it (that word sounds quite impressive, doesn't it?) but that I should have to think it over, first. I remembered what Donald had told me about asking a man's advice — especially Philip's — in money matters. Perhaps it would have been wiser if I had done so before.

"I asked him this afternoon if he knew anything about the King Kopper Kompany, and he said that it was a 'get rich proposition' and that he had sunk a good deal of his own money into some just like it. I wanted to ask him more, but we were interrupted. However, I know that he is very well-to-do, so he must have made money in them and certainly I need to get rich quick. I'm going to make the investment to-morrow."

. . . .

March 11th.

"Stung! I hate slang, but sometimes nothing else is quite so expressive. I thought that I was getting to be very wise, but, oh, what a little ignoramus I have been. And to think that I thought I was following Philip's advice, and did not realize what he really meant until I read a story about a man who was called 'Get-Rich-Quick Wallingford.' Now I'd rather die than tell him that I have lost practically all of my worldly goods!"

. . . .

Finally, late in May, is an entry, longer than any of its predecessors, and the last for many a day. Rose made it seated in the soft moonlight which came through the window of her hospital room, after her roommate had fallen asleep.

"I am in a strange mood to-night, little diary, and not quite sure whether I want to laugh or cry — indeed, I think that my heart has done both to-day. I don't feel like going to sleep, but perhaps I will be able to if I get the many thoughts out of my mind and down on paper — now they are like so many little imps beating against my brain with hammers.

"Surely I *should* be happy at the thought that to-morrow is to carry me to my goal at the top of the mountain path which Donald described. In twelve hours I shall (D. V.) be a graduate nurse; but, now that the journey is almost an accomplished fact, I positively shiver when I think of the nerve of that child who was I five years ago and who, blessed with ignorance, made up her mind to become one, or 'bust' — that is the way I put it, then. Friends have sometimes told me that they didn't see how I had the courage to attempt it; but I tell them, truthfully, that it isn't courage when one tackles a thing which she — or he — doesn't know is difficult to do, and that few things are insurmountably difficult which she tackles with confidence (which is as often the result of ignorance as of faith in one's own power). So how can I take any credit for succeeding?

"It *has* been hard work, of course, and I know that I must have failed if every one had not been so good to me, and, above all, if God had not meant me to succeed. I have never forgotten that night when the 'reverend' opened my eyes to the knowledge that I am His partner in working out my life. Dear Mr. Talmadge! I am ashamed that I stopped writing to him, so long ago, yet I know that he is still my friend, although we do not see each other. That is the beauty of true friendship — it is a calm and constant star, always in its place against the time when we want to lift our eyes to seek its light. I know that it is the same with Donald.

"When I think of him to-night, and realize that he cannot be near me in my little hour of triumph to-morrow, it is hard for me to keep back the tears. Dear God, bless him and bring him happiness — with Miss Treville.

"I cannot help feeling worried about Donald, for, although his letter makes light of his illness, I have a troublesome presentiment that he is worse than he will acknowledge. He is the kind to spend every ounce of his wonderful vitality without thought of self, and the two and a half years during which he has been laboring so hard, and so effectively, must have drained even his great strength. Slight, wiry people are like the willows that bend easily, but return to normal quickly, after the stress of storm has ended; but, when big ones — like Donald — break, it is like the fall of a mighty oak.

"Still, this cloud, like all clouds, has its bright lining. *He is coming home*, just as soon as he is able to make the trip, so, although I shall miss him dreadfully to-morrow, it will not be many weeks before I shall see him again.

"But this is not all that is troubling me, diary, and if I were not quite sure that no one but I would ever look inside your covers, I would not confide it even to you.

"I have a present, a wonderful present, — and I do not

think that I ought to keep it. Help me make up my mind. When P. gave it to me this afternoon, he said that it was just a little remembrance for my graduation and that he hoped I would accept it as the gift of a semi-official guardian, just as I would if Donald himself were giving it to me. I did take it in that spirit; but, when I found a moment to steal away and open the wrapper, and beheld a beautiful morocco case containing a *gold watch* with my initials engraved on the case, my heart almost stopped beating. This was his 'little remembrance.' Of course it is something that I shall need in my work, for it has a second hand, but he must have guessed that I would be troubled by such an expensive gift, for he tried to make light of it by enclosing a foolish little rhyme, which I must copy so that I shall not forget it.

'When it is *time* to take *hour* pulse
You'll find a use for what is in it,*
(On *second* thoughts, I'd like to add
I wish you'd take mine every *minute*.)'

"Conventions are *so* puzzling, little diary, that I don't know what I ought to do. Somehow, I feel quite sure that the Superintendent wouldn't approve, for a doctor should not be making presents to a pupil nurse; yet P. has been so kind that I hate to think of hurting his feelings by giving it back. Besides, I love it . . . and it is engraved R. W. Then, too, if I should return it, he might think that I didn't credit him with having done it while acting in Donald's place as my guardian, and if it was not that thought which prompted him, why. . . . Oh, I don't know what to do!

"Worse still, Dorothy Roberts came up unexpectedly and saw the watch. Of course she wanted to know from

* Poetical license — meaning 'what is in the box.'

whom it came and I answered, on the impulse, 'From my guardian.' I'm sure that she believes that it was a present from Donald and therefore perfectly proper, for I have told her all about his relationship to me, and it hurts me to think that I have been guilty of a lie. Of course it wasn't one in actual words, perhaps; but I had the spirit to deceive, and now I can't confess without involving P. and she might think that he is in . . . Oh, I can't write it, for of course he isn't. How could he be? No, it was just a natural act of his generous heart, because he knew that I was without relatives to give me a graduation gift.

"I hope that I sleep my uncertainties away, for to-morrow must hold nothing but sunshine and smiles."

CHAPTER XXVIII

"BUT A ROSE HAS THORNS"

THE May day, the day of fulfilment for Smiles' dreams and the fruition of her work, had come. Her healthy, mountain-bred body had enabled her to keep well and strong; she had gone through the full three years with scarcely a day's illness, and she was ready to graduate with the class, some of whom would have to stay longer to make up time lost by illness.

Rose awoke early to a sense of something unusual in prospect. On the window of her room the rain was pattering merrily. All nature was one to her, and she loved the showers as much as the sunshine, but, when she began to realize what day it was, they brought a feeling of vague disappointment. Surely *this* day, which meant so much in her life, might have dawned fair! The glimpse of a leaden sky colored her thoughts for a moment, as she lay still in the drowsy relaxation of half-awakening, when dreams beckon from *dolce far niente* land, and the whispering voice of slumber mingles with the more stirring call of the brain to be up and doing. The recollection that Donald was far away, and could not be with her to witness her triumph, brought a sense of bitter disappointment to her over again. "I must write him everything that happens to-day. He will be happy in my happiness, I know," she murmured, half aloud, and her roommate awoke and answered with a sleepy, "What, dear?"

"Nothing. I guess that I must have been talking in my sleep," laughed Rose, as she now sat up energetically, fully awake. By their own request Dorothy Roberts and she still occupied one of the few double rooms reserved for third-year student nurses, who preferred to share their quarters.

The other followed, more drowsily.

"Look," called Rose, from the window. "It's going to clear. Oh, see that wonderful rainbow. I don't believe I ever saw one in the morning before."

"'Rainbow at morning, sailors take warning,'" quoted Dorothy.

"I don't believe in that, or any other *unpleasant* 'stupidstition' — as my reverend used to call them," Rose retorted, as she hastily began to dress, for the last time, in the blue striped costume which had been hers for nearly three years, but was, in a few hours, to change to one pure white, like a sombre chrysalis to a radiant butterfly. "No matter when a rainbow appears it is always an omen of fair promise. It's Mother Nature smiling through her tears."

She caught, in the mirror, a reflection of her friend's affectionate glance; her own cheek began to dimple and her lips to curve as she said, "I can tell by your expression just what you're going to say, and . . . ."

"Egoist," mocked the other. "I hadn't the slightest idea of comparing your own smile to a rainbow, so now."

"I can't help it, really." Rose spoke with unfeigned distress in her voice, and began angrily to massage the corners of her mouth downward. "There's something wrong with the muscles of my face, I think, and sometimes I get worried for fear people will think that it's affectation. I get frightfully tired of seeing a perpetually forced grin on other faces — it reminds me of Mr. William Shakespeare's remark that 'a man may smile and be a villain still.'"

"Not with your kind, dear. 'There's a painted smile on the lip that lies, when the villain plays his part; and the smile in the depths of the honest eyes — and this is the smile of the heart.'"

"Or of the cheerful idiot," supplemented Rose. "Do you really think that I'm . . . shallow? Sometimes it seems to me that the truly wise, thoughtful people, who search the deeps of life and are themselves strongly stirred, are always serious looking."

"Pooh. It's generally pose, and a much easier one to get away with. I always discount it about ninety-nine per cent."

"But, at least, others must think that I am always happy, and I'm not—sometimes I wish that I might be; but not often, for one would have to be utterly selfish and unsympathetic in order to be so, when there is so much suffering everywhere."

"I know, and feel the same way, Rose. But it

seems to me that a smile—at least one like yours—isn't so much the visible expression of joy, as it is a symbol of cheer for others . . . like a rainbow. There, I vowed that I wouldn't, and now I've 'gone and went and done it.'"

Miss Roberts spoke lightly, to cover a suspicious huskiness in her voice, for she worshipped the girl who had been so close to her for three years, and whose way and hers would necessarily diverge after that morning.

"Don't you *dare* to forget how to smile. We all love it," she added, with an assumption of a bullying tone; and then the two held each other very close and laughed and cried, both together, for a moment. They finished dressing in unusual silence, for the thoughts of each were busy with the things which the day and the future might bring forth for them.

Contrary to custom, Dorothy finished first, and preceded Rose downstairs.

When the latter reached the little assembly room, she found a small group of pupil nurses standing in the doorway. One was reading something from a page of a sensational afternoon newspaper, dated the day previous, and, as Smiles joined them, she hastily slipped it out of sight behind her. All of them appeared so self-conscious, that the new arrival stopped with a queer tightening about her heart.

"Show it to her," said Dorothy, quietly. "She's bound to hear of it sooner or later."

The sinking sensation within Rose's breast increased, and she stepped forward, saying faintly, "What is it, Dolly? Not . . . not Dr. MacDonald? Nothing has happened . . . ?"

"No, dear. That is . . . well, it concerns him; but I think that, if anything, he is to be congratulated. It is something to find out. . . . Here, read it yourself."

She took the paper from the owner, and handed it to Rose.

It was the page devoted to happenings in society, and from the top centre looked forth a two-column cut of Marion Treville's strikingly beautiful face. Beneath was a stick of text, which read:

"Back Bay society is buzzing with the rumor, which comes from an apparently unimpeachable source, that the beautiful Miss Treville of Beacon Street, who, since her début seven years ago, has been one of the leaders of Boston's smartest set, is about to announce her engagement to Stanley Everts Vandermeer, the well-known New York millionaire sportsman. Miss Treville was formerly betrothed to Dr. Donald MacDonald, the famous children's specialist of this city, who has been in France for more than two years. No previous intimation had been given that this engagement had been broken."

Rose read the brief article twice, mechanically, and almost without understanding. Then a wave of hot anger, akin to that which had possessed her on the mountain on the afternoon when her eyes had first been opened to the duplicity of human nature, swept over her. It was only by a strong effort that she refrained from crushing the sheet, and speaking aloud her denunciation of the woman whose behavior so outraged her sense of justice.

The call came for the morning prayer, and she handed the paper back without a word; but for once the simple exercises, which, on this morning, should have meant so much more than usual, wholly failed to bring their customary peace. Her lips formed the words of the prayer, and joined in the singing of the hymn, but her mind was far away in France, and her heart rebellious within her.

Her thoughts did not harbor a doubt of Donald's love for the woman, who, it was said on "apparently unimpeachable" authority, had now discarded him for another and wealthier suitor. To be sure, he had not married her, as he might have, before he went away; but this was not strange, under the conditions; indeed, she thought it to his credit, since he had left to be away so long in the performance of a hard and hazardous duty. And surely Donald had remained true! Anything else was unthinkable, and, besides, Ethel often spoke of her sister-in-law-to-be, and of the marriage which would quickly follow her brother's return. That Miss Treville had apparently remained so faithful, also, had helped to banish some of Smiles' uncertain feelings concerning her, and she had begun to hope that some day she might succeed in finding the key to the city woman's heart and enter the fold of her friendship, for she could not bear the idea that Donald's marriage might result in Donald's being estranged from her, or cause a break in their wonderful friendship. Now her thoughts railed against the woman who had been so unstable, at a time when keeping faith with those who went, perhaps to die, had become a nation's watchword. This thought completely superseded the one that had sometimes been hers — that the woman was not worthy the love of the man whom she, herself, worshipped. It was like a mother, suffering for her hurt child, and her lips quivered with suppressed hate. It passed, and left her almost frightened.

"I guess that I'm still a mountaineer at heart," she whispered, as she mechanically bowed her head with the others. "I almost feel as though I could kill her. Poor Donald! He has always been so blindly trusting where his heart was concerned. . . . Perhaps Dorothy is right, perhaps he is better off, if it is true; but if this embitters him, if it spoils his faith in womankind, I shall hate her as long as I live." Then came the reflection that the report might not be true. "I shall go and ask her, myself, this afternoon!"

Smiles arose from her knees, aged in soul.

She had looked forward to this morning with all the eager anticipation of a child; but now, as she donned the white uniform of a graduate nurse — the costume which represented the full attainment of the hard-won goal, — no smile greeted her as she looked at her own reflection in the glass.

Donald was right," she murmured. "I am just

beginning to realize that even this fulfilment of my dream is not going to bring me happiness. It is born of the heart, or not at all." And her mind travelled back to the letter which she had tearfully penned him after Big Jerry's death. "Things never happen just as we plan. When we look forward to something pleasant which we want very much to happen, we never stop to think that there may be unhappiness mixed with it." A solitary tear ran down her cheek, and made a moist spot on the front of her new uniform.

The smile, usually spontaneous, had to be forced to her lips when she went to take her place, with the score of other happy graduating nurses, in the amphitheatre of the Harvard Medical School, next door, where the exercises were to be held.

"What is the matter with my Rose?" wondered Miss Merriman, who had managed to be present. And, "What is the matter with *my* Rose?" thought Dr. Bentley. He had seen her for just a moment that morning, and, through the warm, lingering pressure of her hand, received the thanks which she could not speak.

It was, in truth, a very sober Smiles who only half-heard the words of the impressively simple exercises, during which the newly made laborers in the Lord's vineyard received the diplomas which bore the seal of the hospital — a Madonna-like nurse, holding a child. Its original, cast in bronze — the work of a famous modern sculptor — hung in the administration building of the hospital, and she had often stood before it with tender dreams. And it was a very sober Smiles upon whose dress was pinned the blue and gold cross, the emblem alike of achievement and service.

Miss Merriman spoke her thought aloud, as she took the girl into her arms, afterwards. "You looked too sweet for words, dear. But, tell me, why that woe-begone expression on this, of all days? One would think that all the worries of the world lay on your young heart."

"Perhaps they do," was the non-committal answer. And Rose pleaded a previous engagement when the older nurse begged her company for the afternoon, and Dr. Bentley for the evening.

The happy laughter, the parting words, both grave and gay, which were spoken by those who had been her companions during the long journey, fell on ears which heard, but transmitted them to her mind vaguely, and her answers were inconsequential, so much so, that more than one friend regarded her with troubled surprise and whispered to another that Rose was either not well, or was dazed with happiness. And when Dorothy ventured to hint at the latter alternative, the girl acknowledged it with a strained imitation of her usual smile, and straightway found her thoughts scourging her because of this new deception.

It seemed to her that the day, for which she had builded so long, was tumbling about its foundations, and yet, when she now and again brought her runaway thoughts up with a round turn, she could not assign any logical reason for her feeling as she did.

"After all, what is it to me?" she would ask herself, logically, one moment. And at the next her heart would reply, "Everything. He is all that you have in the world in the way of 'family,' for he *is* more than friend to you." "Yes," Rose would admit, "I am afraid for him, I could not be more so if he were really my brother. She isn't worthy of him — I've known that, somehow, since the first day that he tried to tell me about her. But that isn't the point. Love is blind, and, if her faithlessness hurts him, I will hate her always. I hate her *now*. She has spoiled my day, and I know that I have hurt Gertrude and Philip, for they can't understand what the trouble is."

The idea passed over and over through the endless labyrinth of her brain and found no escape, while she ate the noonday meal, and later changed from her white uniform to a plain blue serge walking dress, and black sailor hat. Ever with it went the accompanying thought, "I *must* see her." To what end she did not know or seriously attempt to analyze. Rose was not the first to take up cudgels in a lost cause, spurred thereto by a purpose which was incapable of receiving any logical explanation. It was the "mother spirit," fighting for its own.

. . . .

A maid opened the door on Beacon street in response to her ring, and, on entering the hall, Rose found herself face to face with Marion Treville. She was clad for the street and was at that moment in the act of buttoning a long white glove. As she recognized the visitor, a deep flush mounted quickly on the patrician face of the older woman and, for an instant, her teeth caught her lower lip.

Smiles' face was very pale, so pale that her large eyes by contrast appeared almost startling in their depth and color. There was a gossamer film of dust on her shoes and the bottom of her skirt, for she had walked all the way from the hospital, and she realized this fact with a sense of chagrin, when she saw Miss Treville's eyes travel to her feet, and mentally contrasted her own appearance with that of the perfectly appointed daughter of wealth before her.

Neither spoke for an instant. It was as though each were trying to read the thoughts of the other. Then Miss Treville said in a cool, even tone, "You may go, Louise."

The maid vanished silently, with one curious backward glance as she passed through the door at the end of the hallway.

"Miss . . . Webb, isn't it? You wished to see . . .?"

"Tell me that it isn't true," broke in Rose, her voice trembling a little in spite of her effort at self-control.

"Tell you it isn't . . . true?" echoed the other, with lifted eyebrows. "I'm afraid that I don't quite underst . . . ."

"But you *do* understand, Miss Treville, why do you say that you don't? It is in the paper."

"Perhaps I meant to say that I do not understand why you should come here to ask such a question, Miss Webb," was the icy response.

Rose was silent. What answer could she make to this pertinent question? She felt the hot tears starting to her eyes; but, even as she was on the point of turning toward the door, with a little choked sob of bitter chagrin, the other continued. Curiosity had unloosed her tongue.

"Well? May I be so bold as to inquire what interest you may have in my personal affairs, Miss Webb? Frankly, I am at a loss to understand the meaning of this unexpected, and — I might say — somewhat unusual visit."

"I . . . I don't know as I *can* explain," began Rose, hesitantly. "I . . . I felt that I had to see you, because . . . I had a letter yesterday from . . . from Dr. MacDonald. . . ."

"Ah."

"Of course he writes to me, you *know* that he is my guardian," she answered the interruption with a flash of spirit. "He said in it that he was coming home just as soon as he was able to . . . to get well and . . . be married, and then that paper. . . . Oh, Miss Treville, surely it isn't so. You wouldn't throw him over, when he is so far away, and . . . and sick?"

The other's voice was not quite as steady as before,

when she answered, "I don't see why I am called upon to explain my . . . to explain anything to you, Miss Webb."

"Then it *is* true." The sentence rang out sharply. "And he doesn't know. He thinks that you are waiting, and . . ."

"We need not discuss the matter, in fact I doubt if the doctor would appreciate your . . . shall we say 'championage'? The matter is between him and me, wholly."

"No, it is not, Miss Treville," flared Rose, with the angry color at last flooding her cheeks. "I have heard people say that, if that story is true, he is lucky to have escaped marrying you; but, just the same, those of us who *really* love him — you needn't look like that, of course I love him — don't want to have him hurt, as any man would be who was cast off like an old glove while he was far away and had no chance to speak for himself. That is why I hoped it wasn't true, and that you hadn't, perhaps, killed his faith in my kind. And that is the only reason."

Once started, her words had poured out as hot as lava which had broken from a pent-up volcano.

"So, that is the reason, the only reason, for your coming to me with your impertinent question?" Miss Treville laughed oddly. "Really! Do you know, I have always suspected that the little savage whom he brought from somewhere in the backwoods regarded him as rather more than a guardian, or a brother . . . that *was* the pretty fiction, wasn't it?" she added, with honey coating the vinegar in her speech.

Under the lash of the words Rose grew white again. Her hands clenched; but, before she could answer, Miss Treville continued:

"It really seems to me that you ought to thank me for stepping aside so obligingly."

The occupation of a high level in the civilized world, or in society, is no proof of the Christian virtue of self-control, — that has been demonstrated, in the case of a nation, all too clearly these last years; and individuals are like nations, or vice versa. The feline that lies dormant, as often in the finished product of city convention as in the breast of the primeval woman, was now thrusting out its claws from the soft paws of breeding. And Miss Marion Treville, leader of Back Bay society, was rather enjoying the sensation. She had passed not a few uncomfortable hours in company with her conscience, even while she was yielding to the glamorous flame which surrounded her new suitor. It was a real relief for her to be able to "take it out" on some one else, and a victim had offered herself for the sacrifice, most opportunely.

Rose shrank back as though she had been struck; then steadied herself and said with an effort — for her throat and lips were dry, "I think that perhaps you were right when you called me a 'little savage.' I know that I feel like one in my heart now, and I think, too, that it would be a real pleasure for me to . . . to . . ."

The other stepped hastily back, and Rose laughed, bitterly.

"Oh, please don't be frightened, I'm not going to scratch you. We wood people don't fight with your kind of animal, they're too unpleasant at close range." She paused, and then went on more steadily. "I came here . . . I didn't know just why I was coming, — perhaps to plead with you for Donald's sake. That doesn't look much as though I loved him . . . in the way you insinuate, does it? No, if I had, I should have won him away from you, long ago. It would not have been difficult, I think."

She spoke so coolly, and with such perfect confidence, that the other winced.

"There isn't anything more to be said, is there?"

Was this the simple mountain girl, whose voice was now so suave and who was smiling so icily?

There was a pause, during which Miss Treville's trembling hand sought behind her and found the servants' bell cord.

"I am really glad that I called, Miss Treville, for you have succeeded in convincing me that I have no occasion to be disturbed — on Donald's account."

"Miss Webb is going," said Miss Treville, formally, as the maid appeared.

CHAPTER XXIX

AN INTERLUDE

All things by immortal power,
Near or far,
Hiddenly.
To each other linked are
That thou canst not stir a flower
Without troubling a star.

A. QUILLER-COUCH.

LIFE is so largely a thing of intermingling currents, of interwoven threads, of reacting forces, that it is well-nigh impossible understandingly to portray the life story of one person without occasionally pausing to review, at least briefly, incidents in the lives of others with which it is closely bound up.

So it is with the story of the pilgrimage of Smiles.

While, following her graduation, she was taking a course in district nursing, giving freely of her new powers to the poor and suffering of a great city, and taking, and passing, the State examination which gave her the right to place the epigrammatic letters "R.N." after her name, something was happening more than three thousand miles away, of which she had no inkling, and yet which was closely linked with her existence.

Donald had, indeed, written in a manner to minimize his illness, which had been a prolonged and serious one; so much so that he had, greatly against his will, finally come to realize the necessity of his taking a rest from his unremitting toil, and he had agreed to return home for a vacation as soon as he should be well enough to make the long trip.

Depressed by his wholly unaccustomed weakness the doctor sat, a convalescent in his own hospital in Toul, one stifling July day. To his physical debility was added the dragging distress of mind which comes at times to those who are far away and receive no word from home. No letters had reached him for weeks. Removed from the sphere of the abnormal activity which had been his, and with nothing to do but sit and think, Donald had, for some time, been examining his own heart with an introspective gaze more searching than ever before. He felt that he had been, above the average, blessed with happy relationships, deep friendships and a highly trained ability to serve others — and he knew that he could honestly say that he had turned this to full account.

Besides, he was betrothed to a beautiful woman whom many coveted. When his mind reached Marion Treville in its consideration, it stopped to build a dream castle around her, a castle not in Spain, but in America. He had earned the right to rest beside the road awhile, and enjoy the good things of life. Marion was waiting for him at home, and whatever doubts had, at one or another time, entered his mind as to their perfect suitability, one for the other, they had long since been banished. Distance had lent its enchantment, and he had supplied her with the special virtues that he desired. His was a type of mind which held to one thought at a time, and he had always possessed a fixedness of purpose of a kind well calculated to carry through any plan which that mind conceived. Combined, these characteristics made a form of egotism, not one which caused him to overrate himself, but to plough ahead regardless of the strength of the possible opposition. When he returned to America he would marry Marion Treville immediately. No other idea had seriously entered his mind since they had plighted their troth; they had not been quite ready before, that was all, he told himself.

It was in such a frame of mind, and with a growing eagerness for the day when he might start for home to claim his reward, that he received her long-delayed letter. What it said does not matter; but one paragraph summed up her whole confession. "You cannot but agree with me that ours was never the love of a man and woman whose hearts were attuned to one another, and sang in perfect unison. We really drifted into an engagement more because of propinquity than anything else. I am a drone — the product of society at its worst — and you are one of the workers, Donald. I feel quite sure that you will always gain your truest happiness in your work. Although I know how you love children (and I don't),

I cannot think of you in the rôle of a married man, so I do not, deep in my heart, believe that this is going to hurt you very much — certainly I hope not. Indeed, I have a somewhat unpleasant suspicion that some day you are going to bless me for having given you back your freedom."

Donald read the letter through, without allowing his expression to change. Then he started to re-read it, stopped, and suddenly crumpled it up in his big fist. A low curse escaped his lips. It was heard by a passing nurse, who hurried to him with the question, "Did you call, doctor? Are you in pain?"

"No. Let me alone," was his harsh answer, and the patient girl moved away, with a little shake of her head. The great physician had not been his cheerful, kindly self for some time. Perhaps she surmised, too, that the mail which she had laid in his lap had not been all that he had anticipated.

With scarcely a move, he sat, staring in front of him, until the evening shadows had turned the landscape to a dull monotone. Then he slowly arose, and, with his mind so completely bent upon one subject that his body was a thing apart and its weakness forgotten, stepped out into the darkening city.

Time had ceased to exist for him, as he walked the almost deserted streets of Toul like a flesh-and-blood automaton. But the physical exercise brought a quota of mental relief at last, and the cool night air soothed his first burning pain and anger with its unconscious balm. At length he was able to face the truth frankly, and then he suddenly knew that all the time it was not his heart, so much as his pride, which had been hurt.

An hour earlier he would not have admitted a single doubt of his real love for Marion Treville. Now he could not but admit that the initial stab of bitterness was being healed by a real, though inexplicable, sense of relief. He could even say that she had been right. His affection for her had, indeed, been merely the outgrowth of lifelong intimacy. It was never the mating call of heart to heart; he had never felt for her the overwhelming passion of a lover for the woman in whom, for him, all earthly things are bound up.

His walk became slower; he stopped. The deep blue-black sky had, of a sudden, become the background for a softly glowing mind picture, and there seemed to appear before him the glorious misty eyes, and bewitchingly curved lips of . . . Smiles.

Her memory swept over him like a vision, and, even while he felt like a traitor to self, came the wonderful realization that in his home city, toward which his thoughts had so lately been bent, still lived the girl whom he had loved — and had held apart within a locked and closely guarded chamber of his heart — for years. It was as though scales, placed before them by his own will, had dropped from his eyes. He almost cried aloud his self-admission that he had loved her all the years from the first moment when he saw her, a barefoot mountain girl, in Big Jerry's rude cabin.

And he was *free!* Free to be honest with his own soul, free to tell his Rose of his love, and throw aside the masquerading cloak of adopted brotherhood. How strange it was! The woman whom he had thought to marry was gone from his life like a leaf torn from the binding, and the one whom he had pretended to regard as a sister would become his mate. That such would be the case he did not doubt now, even for an instant. That she had always loved him, he was certain, and, with the warmth of his wooing, he would fan that steady glow of childish affection into the flame of womanly love which should weld their hearts together forever.

. . . .

The days which followed before he was strong enough to journey to Bordeaux, there to embark for America, seemed to drag by like eternity; but Donald was Westbound at last. He was going home, home to a new life, made perfect by a great love. The deadly submarines of the world's outlaw, lurking under the sea like loathsome phantasies of an evil mind, held no terrors for him, nor could the discomforts caused by the tightly closed hatches and enshrouding burlap, which made the ship a pent-up steambox, until the danger zone was passed, depress his spirits.

The steamer crept as had the days on shore; but

there came an afternoon when she made port at last, and, spurred by a consuming eagerness, he hastened to his apartment.

He had cabled the news of his departure, and in the mail box were many letters awaiting him. Feverishly, he looked them over for one in *her* dear handwriting. To his unreasonable disappointment there was none, but there were several which required immediate reading — among them one from his sister Ethel, and one from his old friend, Philip Bentley.

The first contained disquieting news. His little niece, Muriel, had been very ill with typhoid fever and, although Dr. Bentley had pulled her through the sickness successfully, she was still far from well, and apparently not gaining at all.

He opened the other, expecting it to concern the case. But the note did not mention it. It was only a few lines and read:

"Dear old Don:

I hear that you are 'homeward bound.' Bully! As soon as you reach Boston, and can spare me a moment, I want to talk to you about an important matter.

Call me by telephone, like a good fellow, and I'll run over to your apartment at once and tell you what is on my mind.

Yours,

P. B."

CHAPTER XXX

DONALD'S HOMECOMING

"By the Lord Harry, but I'm glad to see you back again, safe and sound, you good-for-nothing old reprobate."

True to his written statement, Philip had come to Donald's apartment as fast as a taxicab could bring him, after he had heard his old friend's voice over the wire. Now the two men gripped hands, hard, and then — for just a moment — flung their arms around each other's shoulders in a rare outward display of their deep mutual affection.

Then Philip held his senior away at arms' length and said, with masculine candor but with a look of sympathy in his eyes, "Don, you poor devil, you've been killing yourself over there. Don't tell *me*. I've a mind to appoint myself your physician and order you to bed for a month."

"Good Lord, do I look as bad as that?" laughed the other. "If I do, looks are deceitful, for I feel fit as a fiddle. I need only one thing to make a complete new man of me."

"And that is . . .?"

"A secret, at present."

The two seated themselves opposite each other, and Philip continued, "I've managed to keep myself pretty well posted on the work that you've been doing, without knowing any of the details of your life — you're a rotten correspondent. Come, did you have any 'hairbreadth' 'scapes or moving accidents by field and flood?"

"Nary one. My life has been one dead, monotonous waste."

"Like . . . the deuce it has. Come, I've got just ten minutes to stay; tell me the whole detailed history of your two years and a half. Knowing your natural verbosity, I should say that it would take you just about half that time, which will leave me the balance for my own few remarks."

"Five minutes? I could tell you the whole history of my life in that time. But, before I start, I want to ask you about my little niece, Muriel? I've just been reading a letter from Ethel, which seems to indicate that they are rather worried about her; but, when I called her by long distance, she either couldn't, or wouldn't tell me anything definite."

"I don't think that there is any real occasion for being disturbed," answered Philip, quietly. "Although I'll confess frankly that things haven't been going just right, and I'm not sorry to have you back and in charge of the case. Muriel made the acquaintance of a typhus bug — the Lord knows how — and, although I succeeded in getting the best of the fever fairly quickly, thanks to the able assistance of that nurse whom you swear by . . ."

"Miss Merriman?"

"Yes, she's a wonder, isn't she? Well, as I said, we took care of the fever, all right; but the cerebral affection has been more persistent, and she hasn't convalesced as you would expect in a twelve-year-old child. She seems to be laboring under a sort of nervous depression, not so much physical as mental . . . in fact, a psychos. It's common enough in older people, of course; but hanged if I ever saw anything just like it in a perfectly normal, and naturally happy child."

"H-m-m-m. What are the symptoms?"

"Psychological, all of them. She mopes; seems to take no healthy interest in anything, and, as a result, has no appetite; bursts out crying over the most trivial things — such as the chance of you're being blown up by a submarine on the way home — and frequently for no cause at all. Of course I packed the family off to the shore, as soon as she was able to be moved, in the belief that the change of scene and the sea air would effect a cure, but it hasn't. I can't find a thing wrong with her, physically, nor could Morse. I took him down on my own hook, in consultation, one day. It's a rather unusual case of purely psychological depression, and in my opinion all she needs is . . ."

"A generous dose of Smiles," interrupted Donald.

"By thunder, you've struck it," cried Philip, as he gave the arm of his chair a resounding thump. "What an ass I've been not to have thought of that before, particularly as she has been so constantly in my thoughts. It's another case of a thing being too close to one for him to see it."

Donald stiffened suddenly. He held the match, with which he was about to light a cigar, poised in mid-air until the flame reached his fingers, and then blew it out, unused.

"In fact, it was about her, Don, that I was so anxious to see you," the other went on. His own nervousness made him unconscious of the effect which his words had produced on Donald. "Of course, she's practically of legal age now; but I know that she still regards you as her guardian and that in a sense you stand *in loco parentis* toward her. Certainly she regards your word as law. So I thought that, as she is practically alone in the world, it would be the only right and honorable thing to . . . to speak to you, first."

"To speak to me . . . *first?*" echoed Donald, a trifle unsteadily, as he struck another match and watched its flame, with unseeing eyes, until it, too, burned his fingers.

"Yes. Great Scott, can't you guess what I'm driving at? The plain fact is . . . is that I love her, Don. I . . . I want to marry her."

The words smote the older man's senses like a bolt from a clear sky, and they reeled, although he managed, somehow, to keep outwardly calm.

"You . . . you haven't told her . . . yet . . . that you love her?" he managed to say, after a moment.

"No. At least, not directly; but I guess that she knows it. I wanted, first, to be sure that you would approve . . . perhaps even sponsor my suit, for, although I mean, of course, to stand or fall on the strength of my own case, I know that she worships you, as a brother, and might be influenced by your attitude. You understand, don't you, old man?"

Donald nodded, then asked slowly, "Does . . . does Smiles love you, Phil?"

"Yes, I think that I can honestly say that I believe she does. Of course no word of love has ever passed between us, but . . . well, you know how it is."

With a mighty effort of his will, Donald conquered the trembling that had seized upon his body, and — on his third attempt — calmly lit the cigar. But his thoughts were running like a tumultuous mill-race. "Blind, egotistical, self-confident fool," they shouted. "That something like this should have happened is the most natural thing in the world, and it has been farthest from your mind."

He remained silent so long that Philip was forced to laugh, a bit uneasily.

"I know well enough that I'm not half worthy of her — no man could be — but I hope that I'm not altogether ineligible, and I'm sure that I love her more than any one else could." At his words Donald winced. "I'll do my best to make her life a happy one, if she'll have me — you know that, old fellow. Well," he laughed again, "say something, can't you? I should almost get the idea that you were jealous, if I didn't also know that that is absurd. Your engagement to Marion Treville . . . I suppose that you don't want to talk about that, but you know how deeply I feel for you."

Donald shook himself together, mentally, and made an effort to respond with convincing heartiness, although he found that his words sounded unnaturally, even to his own ears.

"Of course, you have my consent, if it's worth anything. If our little Rose does love you, I am sure that you can make her happy — you're a splendid chap, Phil, and I — and I appreciate what you have done for her while I was away. She wrote me all about it."

He stretched out his hand, and the other started from his chair, and wrung it heartily.

"Thanks, old man. You give me an added quota of courage, and I wish that I might go to her this minute; but I've been called out of town on an important case. I really shouldn't have taken the time even to stop here, but I simply had to see you to-night. Love is an awful thing, isn't it?"

"Yes," he answered, dully. "Love is always impatient . . . I know that myself. Perhaps I . . . that is, if I can get her . . . Rose, I think that I will take her down to Ethel's with me, to-night, and you can . . . can see her there. Where is she staying now?"

"With Miss Merriman's family, if she hasn't been called out on a case since morning. She's been doing district nursing, principally; but she's already had two private cases, you know."

Donald did not, and the realization of how far he had drifted away from his old, intimate association with Smiles' affairs, brought his heart an added stab of pain.

"The number is Back Bay, 4315." He glanced at his watch and then exclaimed, "Heavens, I've got to catch a train at the Trinity Place station in five minutes. Be ready to furnish bail for my chauffeur as soon as he is arrested for over-speeding. 'Night. I'll see you at Manchester in a few days . . . that is if . . ."

His words trailed off down the corridor, the front door closed and Donald was alone. No, not alone. Philip had gone, but the room was peopled with a multitude of ghosts and haunting spectres which he had left behind. The doctor had only to close his eyes in order to see them, gibbering and dancing on his hopes, which had been laid low by his friend's eager disclosure. Another loved her, another wanted to marry her, and that other could truthfully say that he believed she cared for him. No spoken words of love may have passed between them, but Donald knew well how unessential these were when heart called to heart.

This was his homecoming!

It were as though the eyes of his soul had been permitted, for a brief time, to behold a dazzling celestial light, which had suddenly failed, leaving the darkness blacker than before. The words which he had planned to utter had turned to bitter ashes in his mouth. He had to face the truth squarely. Rose was not, had never been, for him. It had been mere madness for him even to dream of such a thing. Had she not accepted him as a brother, and given him the frank affection of such relationship, which precludes love of the other sort?

His heart hurt and he felt old and weary again. Somewhere, hidden in a cabinet, was a bottle of whiskey, he remembered, and he sought it out and poured himself a generous glassful. But, when he raised it to his lips, the vision face of Smiles, as she had looked that first night on the mountain, when she told Big Jerry and Judd that "nary a drap o' thet devil's brew would ever be in house of hers," appeared before him, and, with a groan, he set it down, untasted.

Returning to his living-room, he sat a long time in mental readjustment, which was brought about with many a wrench at his heart; and when, at last, his old iron will — which had been weakened a little by illness and further softened by love — had once again been tempered in the crucible of anguish, the lines on his prematurely seamed face were deeper, and in his dark gray eyes was a new expression of pain.

. . . .

In compliance with his telephoned request, Rose had packed her suit case, and was all ready to accompany him when he arrived at the Merrimans' apartment in a taxicab, to take her with him to the North Station to catch the nine o'clock train. She was irrepressibly the child, for the time being, and in her cheeks bloomed roses so colorful that Gertrude Merriman accused her of painting, while knowing well enough that joy needs no artistry.

"I'm almost *too* happy," she cried after hearing his voice over the wire, and proceeded to dance around the room to the impromptu chant, "Donald, dear, is here, is here. Donald, dear, is here."

"Are you going to kiss him?" laughed her friend. But Rose was not to be teased, and answered, "Kiss him? I'll smother him with kisses. Isn't he my brother, and isn't he home again after being away two and a half years?"

When the apartment bell rang, it was Rose who ran to answer it, and whose sweet young voice, saying, "Oh, come up *quick*," Donald heard thrilling over the wire. His heart leaped, but his will steadied its increased pulsations. It leaped again when he reached the third floor, and the girl of his dreams threw herself upon him with laughter which was suspiciously like weeping, and with the smother of kisses, which she could not restrain nor he prevent, although each burned and seared his very soul.

She backed into the room and pulled him after her by the lapels of his coat; but, as the brighter light struck upon his face, she stopped with widening eyes, through which he could read the troubled question in her mind.

"Oh, my poor big brother. I didn't realize . . . I mean, how you must have suffered. Poor dear, you don't have to tell me how ill you have been, so far away from all of us who love you."

Her pitying words drove the last nail in his crucified hopes. Not only were they, all too obviously, merely those of a child who loved him with a sister's love, but they told him how changed, wan and aged he was; one who was, in fact, no longer fitted to mate with radiant youth.

"'Old, ain't I, and ugly?'" He imitated Dick Deadeye with a laughing voice, but the laugh was not true.

"Old and ugly?" she repeated, in horror. "Donald, how *can* you? You're tired out, that is all; and as for this —" she lightly touched the sheen of silvery gray at his temples, where the alchemy of Time and stress had made its mark — "it makes you look so . . . so distinguished that I am ashamed of my frivolously familiar manner of greeting you. But I just couldn't help it, and I promise not to embarrass you again. Yes, you *were* embarrassed. I could read it in your face."

There was but a moment for conversation with the others, and they were whirled off to catch the train for the North Shore resort.

When they were seated, face to face, in the Pullman chair car, there came a moment of silence, during which each studied the other covertly. Donald decided that, physically, the girl had not greatly changed from the picture of her which he had borne away in his heart. The passing years had merely deepened the charm of the soft, waving hair, whose rich and glinting chestnut strands swept low on her broad forehead and nestled against the nape of her neck; the slender patrician nose and wonderfully shadowed eyes; the smooth contour of cheek and rounded chin; and the tender glory which still trembled, as in the old days, on her sensitive lips. But, in her poise and speech, after the first rush of impetuous childlike eagerness had spent itself, he discovered a new maturity, and he realized that, where he had left a child, he found a woman, whose heart was no longer worn upon her sleeve. True, her gratitude and affection for him were unaltered. They showed in every word and look, and once the thought came to him that he might yet win the castle of Desire, if he should only determine to enter the lists against Philip. The primal man in him cried out against, and might have overcome, his better nature, which whispered that this would be treachery to a friend who had played fair, and was worthy, if there had not always been before his mind the consideration that the fight would be hopeless. Rose was not for him; she loved another.

And the girl? She cheered him with her smile, and loved him for the dangers he had passed as he, in the hope of in that subject finding a vent for his emotions, told her of the work he had been doing. But in her heart she was deeply disturbed. The tired, drawn look on his strong face would pass away, she felt; but the sight of the expression of pain in his eyes gave her thoughts pause. Had Marion Treville's faithlessness struck so deep? At the memory of her interview with the woman, Smiles' own eyes changed, and lost their quiet tenderness.

. . . .

Morning had come, and the sunlight danced like a myriad host of tiny sprites, clad in cloth of gold over the broad blue bosom of the Atlantic and into the windows of little Muriel's cheerful bedroom. The door opened softly, and Rose, in trim uniform and cap, with its three black bands, slipped into the room, silently motioning the man in the hall outside to keep back out of sight. The child, thin and pale on her snowy bed, turned her head listlessly and looked at the intruder.

Suddenly the suggestion of a smile touched her colorless lips, and lighted her unnaturally heavy eyes. She sat up with a glad cry of surprise and welcome, "Why, it's my own Smiles! Wherever did you come from; are you going to make us a visit? Oh, I'm so glad."

"Yes, darling. I got so tired and grumpy up in the hot city that I just had to come down here to be cheered up. Will you help do it?"

"'Course I will. Why, just *seeing* you makes me want to cheer." She quickly swung her slender legs over the bedside. "Oh, now if dear Uncle Don were only safe home again it would be perfect. I've worried and worried about his getting hit by a bomb or being blown up by a submarine. I wish . . ."

"And, presto! your wish is granted," laughed Donald, as he ran into the room and caught his small niece up in an old-time bear hug.

"Oh, oh, oh. It's better than a fairy tale. I'm so happy I could die, but instead I'm going to get well right off. I'm well *now;* where are my clothes?"

The little bare feet sought for bedroom slippers, and the light curls bobbed energetically as she enunciated, "Now that I've got you two I mean to keep you forever and ever. If you, Uncle Don, would only mar . . ."

The man made haste to clap his hand over the offending mouth; but he was too late. Rose had heard, and, with glowing cheeks, replied quickly, "But you forget that Uncle Don adopted me as a little sister, long ago."

She slipped her hand through his arm and pressed it close to her for a moment, before laughing gayly, "Run along, man. Milady is about to dress and this is no place for you."

CHAPTER XXXI

THE VALLEY OF INDECISION

EARLY evening it was, several days later, evening of a sultry, stifling day, which had escaped the bounds of longitude and invaded even the North Shore. The open ocean, itself, seemed to have forgotten its habitual unrest and yielded to the general languor. From the Thayers' summer home — a glorified bungalow, broad of veranda and shingled silvery-olive, atop a long, terraced bank — it had the appearance of a limitless mirror, reflecting the unblemished blue infinity of the sky. Only the never-ceasing series of vague white lines which ever crept up the shelving beach, to vanish like half-formed dreams, showed that, although the mighty deep slept, its bosom rose and fell as it breathed.

The sky was a hazy horizon blue, unblemished save for a few vaporous clouds far in the west; the sun, well toward the end of its journey, was hazy, too, a thing of mystery; in the far eastern distance the broad Atlantic softened to a hazy violet-gray which, in turn, blended, almost without a line of demarcation, into the still more distant heavens.

Far out, above the waters, a solitary gull circled with slow, sweeping curves, and now and again planed to the surface of the sea and struck from it a faint white spark.

On the screened-in veranda, the members of the family, which now included Rose, sat or reclined, in attitudes of indolence, the men in negligee shirts and white flannels, the women in light dresses. Rose — who had, the day before, officially declared herself "off" the case; but had stayed on, a guest, at the general solicitation — wore a white dimity faintly sprinkled with her favorite rosebuds.

Her ex-patient sat on a little stool close by her side, a book of fairy stories resting on her elevated bare knees. The companionship of her beloved Smiles had already brought the warm color of health back to her cheeks and banished the listless look from her eyes. Her mother and Mr. MacDonald, Senior, were reading. Rose, chin resting on her cupped palm, was gazing seaward with a dreamy, far-away expression in her eyes, as blue as the sea itself. Donald sat back of her, and scarcely turned his gaze from the even contour of her cheek and neck and the shimmering glory of her hair, as he pulled leisurely at his cigar.

Only little Don showed signs of activity; for, with the boundless energy of four-and-a-half years, he was skidding and rolling industriously from one end of the porch to the other on a kiddie-car — a relic of the year before, and now much too small for him. With more or less dexterity he was weaving his way in and out among the various obstacles, animate and otherwise.

After looking for many silent minutes at the girl he loved, Donald said, tritely, "A penny for your thoughts, Smiles."

"Sir, you value them too high. I was thinking about you," she laughed.

"A likely story! I know well enough that your mind was far away from the present spot — the far-off expression on your face is indication enough of that. Furthermore, I'll wager that I can guess pretty nearly where they were."

It was a random shot, but he was disquieted to observe that it brought a faint blush in her cheeks. The added color, soft and lovely in itself, was darkly reflected on his heart.

Jumping up, Smiles cried, with a mock pout, "I shan't stay here to be made the subject of a demonstration of clairvoyancy. My thoughts are my own, and I mean to keep them so, sir."

As she ran into the house Donald's eyes followed her, moodily. And if he had, indeed, possessed the power of divination which he had laid pretence to, the expression in them, and the shadow on his spirit, would have been justified.

Rose ran lightly upstairs, and, as she approached her room, drew from within her waist a letter. There was something both mysterious and childlike in the manner that she next opened one of the drawers of her dressing table and, taking out a box which held almost all of her modest treasures, started to place the letter with them.

Instead, however, she paused to lift out a neat little package containing a score or more of other epistles, tied together with a white ribbon. For a moment she hesitated, as though she were both mentally and physically weighing the objects held in either hand. A shadow of strange uncertainty came into her eyes, the outward expression of an inward uncertainty foreign to her nature. Slowly, she turned from her reflection in the mirror and dropped down on the edge of the daintily counter-paned bed. With hesitating fingers she untied the ribbon from the package and began to glance through the unbound letters, pausing at intervals to read stray paragraphs from them. Each one began and ended almost the same — "Dear little Smiles" and "Affectionately your friend, Donald."

There was the one which contained the allegory of the steep path — which now lay behind her; the one in which he told her of little Donald's advent into the world and of his own betrothal to Marion Treville, and as she read that sentence which held so much of import in the lives of both of them, she sighed, "Poor Don. He hasn't mentioned her; but her faithlessness must have struck deep, for he is, oh, so changed and more reserved." There were other letters filled with the spirit of *camaraderie*, and then the later ones, strong, simple, with their stories of others' sacrifice in the great cause of humanity.

When the last one was read and laid upon the others, she sat with them in her lap for a moment, musing. The suspicion of tears shone in her eyes as she finally shook her head, and, evening them carefully, retied them.

"No," she whispered, half aloud, "I mustn't be foolish. He's just my brother, that is the way he cares for me. It has always been like that. And I . . . I mustn't be foolish."

Almost angrily she brushed away the single tear which had started its uncertain course down her cheek.

With a gesture of resolution, she stood up and placed the package in its box. The other letter was about to follow; but, as she started to lay it down, she changed her mind, and, with the flush again mounting her cheeks, took it from the envelope, which bore a special delivery stamp, postmarked in Boston that very morning.

Opening it, she read:

"My dearest Smiles:

Will you be the bearer of a message from me to your kind hostess? As you know, she has invited me down to Manchester-by-the-Sea for the week-end, as a surprise for Donald, and I have heretofore been unable to give a definite answer. Now I have banished everything else from my mind and shall arrive about seven-thirty.

You wonder, perhaps, why I haven't written this direct to her? In answering my own question I have a confession — yes, *two* confessions to make. A poor excuse is better than none, and I have sent the message to Ethel, through you, merely as an excuse for writing you.

To my own surprise I have discovered that I have suddenly become a moral coward, and am obliged to descend to subterfuges in order to bolster up my courage. This isn't a usual thing with me, I think, but neither is the occasion. I've been wanting and planning to tell you something, face to face, for a long time; but at the crucial moment my courage has failed each time. I could not nerve myself to bear the possibility of the wrong answer.

Now I cannot put it off any longer and I am forced to tell you that 'something' in this manner. It is a simple message, dear, but it has meant more than any other to the world through all ages, and it means more to me than all the world, now. I love you, Rose, — I want to marry you.

There is not anything more that need be said; you can imagine all the rest that I would say if I were with you in person, as I shall be with you in spirit as you read those words. I suspect that even they were not necessary. You must have guessed my love, which has grown steadily during these past three years, and have understood why I could not speak it before. It was not merely that the ethics of our relation forced me to keep silent; but I have felt, since you are situated as you are, and Donald is still morally, if not legally, your guardian and protector, I should speak to him first. I have done so. My love for you was almost the first thing that he heard about, on reaching home. And Smiles, dearest, he has gladly given his consent to my suit and wished me luck.

Now that I have written the fateful message, my courage is restored, in part at least, and I want to hear the answer from your own sweet lips. I can scarcely wait to hear it, for presumptuous as it is — I cannot help hoping that it will be the one I so desire. I cannot help believing that you do care for me.

Please don't run away, dear. I want to see you, alone, as soon as I reach Manchester.

With all my heart and soul I am
Your lover, PHILIP."

Smiles slowly replaced the note, her first love letter, in its envelope, laid it in the box and locked this in the drawer. With her hands resting on the dresser she leaned forward and looked searchingly into her own eyes, as though trying to read her very heart. Her lips moved and formed the words, "He cannot help hoping that the answer will be the one he desires. He knows that I *do* care for him. Yes, he cannot help knowing it; I am too simple to hide my feelings, and he has been so sweet that I could not help . . . but . . . oh, I wish that I hadn't got to tell him . . . to-night."

Meanwhile Donald had been sitting for many minutes in the silence born of laboring thoughts. He had guessed Smiles' secret in part, but not in its entirety, and the bitter unhappiness, which had had its inception in Philip's disclosure, lay over his soul like a pall.

His father was the first to speak, and his words caused Donald to start, for they seemed to be the result of telepathic communication.

"You told us, once, that she wasn't a witch, but, by Jove, there's both witchery and healing in that smile of hers, Don. Look at Muriel now. It's nothing less than a miracle what the very presence of Rose has done for her."

"I was wrong," answered Donald, shortly, whereupon Ethel laid aside her book and joined in the conversation in a low voice, so that the absorbed Muriel might not hear.

"You love her, Don, it's perfectly obvious. What are you waiting for? Now that Marion has behaved so shamefully, it is my dearest hope that you will marry Rose. I didn't mean to speak of it; but, really, you are changing, Donald, and I don't want to think of your becoming a self-centred old bachelor."

"Ethel's right," supplemented his father. "I'm only surprised that you haven't asked her before. You've been in the same house with her for a whole week. Don't let one . . . er . . . unfortunate experience discourage you."

Donald carefully knocked the ashes from his pipe. got up, walked to the railing, and stood with his back toward them.

Then he laughed, a trifle bitterly.

"Thanks for the advice. I won't pretend that I don't . . . care for her; but I can't ask her to marry me, as you suggest — that is, not now."

"Why not, I should like to know?" demanded his sister, impatiently.

"I can't explain, either; but there is a reason. I am bound in honor. Please don't say anything more about it."

But Ethel was not to be silenced so easily.

"I don't know what you are talking about; but

it's nonsense, anyway," she answered. "Why, she worships you. Any one can see that."

"Worships me!" echoed Donald, with sarcastic inflection. "What's the sense in exaggerating like that, Ethel? I suppose that she is fond of me in a way; the way you are, but . . ."

"I never suspected you of lacking courage before," interrupted the other. "If you haven't the nerve to ask that child yourself, *I* will. I guess that I'm a better judge of feminine nature than you, Donald."

"You failed to prove it once before," he retorted, and instantly added, with a tone of unusual contrition, "I am sorry I said that. It was unnecessary and unworthy. But, really, I can't allow you to play Mrs. John Alden to my Miles Standish. There is a reason . . ."

"Oh, you men. You're all alike, when you climb on some sort of a high horse and become mysterious. I don't know what you are talking about — perhaps you are deluding yourself with an absurdly chivalrous notion about being her guardian — but I tell you this. A normal girl, who is as full of life as Rose, can't be expected to be like the wishy-washy heroines of some murky novel, remain faithful unto death to her first unrequited love, and turn into a sweetly spiritual old maid, waiting for the hero to come and claim her. ''Tain't accordin' ter huming nater,' as Captain Jim says. The mating call is too strong, and she is sure to respond to the love note of another sooner or later; — don't flatter yourself that you are the only man in Smiles' creation. She's as sweet and pure as any girl could be, but she's human, like the rest of us . . . that's what makes me love her so, and, unless 'you speak for yourself, John' . . ."

"I can't, Ethel, I . . . s-s-sh."

The girl's light footsteps on the descending stairs caused him to break off with a low note of warning, and hardly had he resumed his seat before she was sitting on the arm of the chair and rumpling his wavy hair, as naturally as a child, or a sister.

Watching him closely, Ethel saw the veins begin to swell on the back of his muscular hand, as his fingers gripped the other arm of the chair. She sighed, and then a look of wondering distress came into her face as the thought flashed unbidden through her mind, "I wonder if it is possible that he made some unfortunate, entangling alliance in France, after he heard from Marion? It isn't impossible. Men are often caught on the rebound like that."

Donald was the first to make an effort to introduce a new subject into the thoughts of all, by saying, "Doesn't the *Water Witch* look pretty in this light?" as he pointed to a trim little eighteen-foot race-about, whose highly polished mahogany sides, free from paint, reflected the water which reflected them. "I don't know as I have properly thanked you for having her put in commission for me, Ethel."

"I thought that it would please you, and I had them overhaul and rig her as soon as I learned that you were coming home."

"Please me! Well, I should say 'vraiment.' Come, Smiles, let's run away from all the world beside, and I'll show you my skill as a skipper."

Ethel sent a meaning glance in the direction of her father, but he was laughing; "'Skill as a skipper,' indeed, on such an evening as this! He would be an amateur, for certain, who couldn't steer with one arm free. Whew, there isn't a breath."

"There is going to be, and not many minutes from now. Unless I miss my guess we'll have a thunderstorm, and a west wind which will make short work of this humidity. There, feel that breeze? Ouch, you little devil, get off my foot. It may be large but it wasn't built for a kiddie-car racetrack."

The obstacle had caused an upset, and baby Don, more angry than hurt, to be sure, set up a howl and ran to Smiles' arms for comfort.

"You'll spoil that baby," growled his uncle. "Well, what do you say, are you coming?"

He stood up, and stretched his powerful frame in anticipation of the exercise that he loved.

"If you don't mind, Donald, I'd . . . I'd rather not . . . to-night," answered Rose.

"I'm afraid that you don't like the ocean; I rather thought that you wouldn't," he responded gently, for he had in mind the fact that both of her parents had met their death by drowning. The girl sat silently for a little while, with her eyes fixed upon the waters, here and there upon the surface of which had begun to appear shadowy streaks of varying tones, as though the Master Painter were deftly sweeping a mighty, invisible brush across the pictured surface. Interblending shades of soft green, gray and violet came and disappeared.

Without turning her head, she answered, pensively, "It is very, very beautiful and I love it — in a way. But I am afraid of it, too. Yes, I like the lordly mountains better, Don. To me there is always something sinister about the sea, even when it is in as peaceful a mood as this; storms come upon it so swiftly, and it has taken so many precious lives."

Donald laid an understanding hand upon her shoulder for a brief moment.

"I won't urge you," he said. "Let's go for a little walk, then."

"I . . . I can't do that, either, Donald. It was meant to be a surprise, but . . . Dr. Bentley is coming down from Boston to-night, and I promised . . . that is, he has asked me to . . . to go somewhere with him." Rose was blushing again.

"Oh, I see. I didn't know that Phil was coming, although, of course, he has a standing invitation, and knows that I'm always delighted to see him," answered Donald, in a tone which he made natural with an effort.

"I invited him especially," broke in Ethel. "And he accepted in a letter to Rose."

CHAPTER XXXII

THE STORM AND THE SACRIFICE

BABY DON put an end to the moment of strained silence which succeeded. He laid hold of two of Smiles' fingers and began to pull at her, while saying insistently, "Come down to the beach with me, Aunty Smiles, and hear the waves ro-er." This was a favorite pastime with him.

His grandfather smiled. "The waves are 'ro-ering' as gently as any sucking dove, to-night."

But the baby was not to be turned from his design, and tugged persistently until Rose was obliged to rise, laughing. Muriel also started up.

"I'll go down with you and try out the *Water Witch* alone — unless, that is, either of you want to come along," said Donald.

His father and Ethel refused, with a show of indignation over the begrudging form which the invitation had taken, and he was not sorry. Neither man nor girl could find anything to say as they walked side by side to the beach, and the former launched the dory tender. As he put off she waved him a cheery good-by, and sent her low voice across the broadening water:

"Come back to us soon. And be careful. It is beginning to get rough already."

With a note in his voice which she did not understand, he called back, "Perhaps I'll sail straight over to France. You wouldn't care."

"Foolish man. You know that I would," she cried, and then turned to join the children in their game of skipping pebbles.

Donald sent the skiff through the choppy waves with vigorous strokes and shot her around at the last moment for a perfect landing. The mainsail and jib went up with rapid jerks while the rings rattled their protest. The strenuous physical exercise brought him temporary relief; but, when he had cast off, taken the tiller and after a few moments of idle jockeying back and forth in the light puffs, squared away for the run seaward before the rising wind, his gloomy thoughts returned, to settle like a flock of phantom harpies and feast on his brain.

Out of nothing grew a vision of Judd's chalky, troubled face, and he felt a sudden rush of sympathy for the crude mountaineer, who had likewise loved and lost. "Smiles wasn't to blame then. She isn't to blame *now*. She never led either of us on," he said aloud; but his clenched teeth cut through the end of his cigar, nevertheless. With only his moody thought to bear him company, Donald steered seaward.

Starting slowly, the racing craft was momentarily given new impetus by swelling wind and following wave; but the man paid no heed to the things which should have served him as a warning — the higher heaving of the waters, now as gray and as cloudy green as a dripping cliff, and touched with flecks of milky spume; and the uneven tugging of the sail. When he did become aware of the swift change which had taken place, hardly five minutes had passed from the time he had started out, yet a quick glance behind him disclosed a new heaven and a new earth and sea; the old had passed away.

Where else is nature's stupendous power so evident as in the sinister speed with which the armies of the tempest make their swift advance, company on company, regiment on regiment, division on division?

In the moments which had passed unmarked by him in his absorption, the whole western sky had become overcast and blackened by the vaporous army of invasion, whose forecoursing streams of cavalry skirmishers were already high over his head. The earth had lost its laughing colors, and seemed to lie cowering, with its head covered with a dull mantle, and the sea had accepted the challenge of the storm clouds and was beginning to leap forward in swirling, gloomy waves.

With a strong steady pull on the tiller, Donald brought the little craft around in a sweeping curve and headed into the wind, which had suddenly become chill and moist. The boat tilted sharply, and a dash of spray leaped the bow and, changing back to water, ran down the leeward side of the cock-pit. A drop of rain splashed on his bared forearm, and then another and another. Through the dark, serried clouds came a dagger thrust of fire, to be followed by a distant detonation which bore his heart back to the shuddering fields of France.

The new picture was impressed on his mind as on the sensitized film of a camera, and simultaneously the action of distant figures were registered upon it. Toiling up the steep bank to the cottage was a marionette made recognizable as Muriel by a tiny dash of red at the waist and on the head. For an instant he wondered if Smiles and his little namesake had already reached the house. Then he caught sight of them, still on the beach. There was fully a quarter of a mile of water between him and the shore, but the distance was being cut down bravely by the race-about, whose specialty was going to windward in a blow. Steadied by her racing keel, she cut through the waves like a knife.

The child, a mere gray dot, was apparently fleeing as fast as his sturdy little legs could carry him from the pursuing girl.

In spite of his bitterness of soul, Donald's lips curved into a smile as they formed the words, "Ah, the battle is on, once more. Rose has insisted that they hurry up to the house and Don has said, 'I won't.' Jerusalem, look at him kite it!"

At that instant a tremulous curtain of light was let down from heaven, momentarily, and the two tiny figures were disclosed as clear as by day. He saw the baby dodging adroitly under Smiles' outstretched arms, and heading out onto the narrow pier, to which was attached a float for rowboats.

"He's got his 'mad' up," thought the man, as he veered off a point so as to get a better view. "He isn't afraid of thunder, lightning or of rain — or anything else, and it would be just like him to run right off the . . . Great God in heaven, he's done it!" he shouted aloud and sprang to his feet, and almost lost his grip on the straining tiller. Even as he had been thinking, the light had grown again, and he saw the child, halfway down the pier, with a rebellious jerk tear himself loose from the clutching grasp on his blouse, lose his balance, stumble and roll from the incline into the now surging water.

The *Water Witch* luffed sharply, and her sail snapped with a report like a pistol shot. Without taking his horrified gaze from the unreal picture which the ghastly lightning illumined, Donald instinctively steadied the boat, and, with his powerful body strained forward as though he were urging the craft to greater effort. "God, God, God." The words came through his clenched teeth, half prayer, half curse at the Fate which held him helpless to act — and the wind snatched them from his lips and bore them away, shrieking in malicious madness.

The darkness fell, blotting out the scene. Then the lightning flared again, and, in the brief white second that it lasted, he saw Rose climb onto a bench against the railing of the pier, and leap into the water.

"God, she can't swim a stroke," groaned the man, as he pounded his left hand against the gunwale until the blood came through the abraded skin. Plunged in darkness again, the man, whom Rose had called unimaginative, suffered all the untold agony of soul which had been hers during the moment in which she had been forced to make up her mind and carry out the act, only his anguish was the more intense, for hers was the quick action and his the forced inaction of a man bound to a stake, within full sight of a tragedy being enacted upon a loved one. The distance between the boat and shore was not so great but that he could see everything that was occurring; but, with the wind dead ahead and blowing viciously, he might as well have been in another world for aught that he could do.

The spell of darkness, doubly black after the flash, seemed like an eternity to Donald. In reality it was as brief as the others, yet, when the light came, it disclosed other forms in action. A youth, whom he had vaguely noticed working around a rowboat on the beach as he put out, was plunging into the water, and down the steeply terraced bank, with leaping strides, was running a tall, slender figure clad in light gray. Minute as it was, seen from that distance, Donald recognized it. It was Philip, and his bursting heart gave voice to a cry of welcome and hope. Philip would save Smiles!

True, he would save her for himself. He could not keep the thought out of his surge of hope; but the erstwhile bitterness was swept away. Nothing else mattered, if Rose could be saved. Measured by the ticking of a clock, the action was taking place with dramatic speed; but, to his quivering mind, it dragged woefully, and the periods when the light failed caused him to cry aloud.

Suddenly the searchlight of the sky was turned on, dazzlingly, and he saw the unknown youth wading ashore, bearing in his arms a tiny form whose animated arms and legs told the story of baby Don's timely rescue; he saw Ethel running wildly toward them, to gather her offspring into her outstretched arms; he saw Philip on the float, in the act of casting himself prone. Then the picture faded once more and he railed at the ensuing blackness as though it had been a wilful, animate thing. This time it lasted longer, and the man's deep breath came in rasping sobs before the scene was again revealed. Now there were two forms standing unsteadily on the float; two forms that were almost one, for the man in gray was holding the girl in clinging white close to him. Still, she could stand; Smiles was alive, she was saved! And the watcher's lips gave vent to a shout of relief and joy, a shout which ended in a groan. All the power of his masterful will was not enough to make him do that which he longed to — turn his tortured eyes from the picture which spelt life to Rose, and death to all his golden dreams.

Now he saw them moving slowly up the pier, the girl still leaning heavily against the man, and supported by his encircling arm. They paused, and Rose half turned, and slowly waved her hand toward the sea in a reassuring gesture, and Donald whispered, "God bless her. She knows that I have been a witness to the whole thing, and she remembers, thinks of me, even at . . . at this time. I cannot see her face, but I know that she is smiling."

The lingering effulgence from a final wave of light vanished; the two forms toiling up the shore blended into the returning shadows; the curtain of darkness fell, and the drama was ended.

"Why could it not have been I?" groaned Donald. The wind, already spent from its brief fury, chortled softly among the shrouds as though it was laughing at him, another mortal made the victim of capricious Fate. Surely it knew that he would have served as well as its agent and would only too gladly have given his very life for Smiles, but it had wilfully sent him away and sent Opportunity to Philip.

Heroes and martyrs; what are they, after all, but the creatures of that whimsical goddess? Most men and most women have within them the courage to dare all things if the occasion comes, but to a few only, chosen, it often seems, by chance, is that occasion granted. Yet, how often has the history of life, both racial and individual, been changed by such an event!

Donald knew his star had sunk below the far horizon and that Philip's had been carried to its zenith. The lover was likewise the rescuer. It were as though the play had been written and the stage set for no other purpose than to bring the romance to its culmination, and, now that this had been accomplished, the useless properties were being removed. The storm was over, ending as quickly as it had begun; the cloud-legions were hurrying eastward overhead to form the setting of another tragedy or farce somewhere else, or to return to the nothing which had given them birth. A few faint flashes and a distant rumble or two marked their passing.

Along the western edge of the world appeared a narrow streak of ruddy light, like burnished copper beneath the blackness above. Blazing forth with the glory of a conqueror, the sun appeared within it, and seemed to poise immovable for an instant 'twixt heaven and earth, while its dazzling rays turned the living waters to molten gold. Then it slowly sank from sight, and, like wraiths of the dying day, the night-shadows began to creep out from the shore, deeper and deeper, nearer and nearer, until they engulfed the little craft and its owner.

With a sudden decision, Donald played out the sheet and put the tiller over. The boat swung around into the path of the wind and fled seaward again. He could not go home, now. He must fight out the battle with self, as it is always fought, alone, and what place could be more fitting than out there in the darkness, on the face of the troubled waters?

CHAPTER XXXIII

WHAT THE CRICKET HEARD

Two hours later Donald stumbled, like a strong man physically played out, up the path to the cottage.

Ethel saw him coming, and ran part way down the steps to meet him. With her arms around his neck, she half-sobbed out the words in a choked voice, "Oh, Don. Do you know what has happened? Could you see from your boat? Little Donny? Smiles? Could you see, Don?"

He nodded, dumbly; but his sister kept on, "She couldn't swim, but yet she jumped, instantly, to save him. You see, she thought that she was alone, she didn't know about that boy. Oh, Donald, we must do something for him, something splendid. He saved my baby's life."

Ethel was crying now, and the man forgot his own misery in comforting her.

"But why didn't you come, Donald? You didn't know. . . ."

"Yes, I knew that everything . . . was all right. Rose waved to me and called. I . . . I *couldn't* come, Ethel. I can't make you understand."

With the light of understanding breaking in upon her mind, and bringing a flood of sympathy with it, his sister once more drew close and encircled his neck with her arms.

"Where . . . . where is she?" he asked, as though the words were wrung from him against his will.

"Smiles has gone for a little walk with . . . Dr. Bentley, dear," answered Ethel in a manner which she strove to make commonplace. She felt his frame quiver, and, with a motion that was almost rough, he shook off her comforting arms, and mounted the steps, holding to the rail as he did so. He went directly indoors, and to his room, with the instinct of a wounded creature to seek its cave or burrow. Save for a cold, cheerless patch of moonlight on the floor it was dark, and he felt no desire to turn on the lights. For a while he sat, silent and motionless, on the edge of the bed. But he could not stand the closed-in solitude. The place seemed filled with the fragrant presence of the girl who was not there; would never be there. He wanted to smoke, and went to the bureau to fumble blindly for a pipe which he remembered he had left on it. His hand touched something small and glazed, and he drew it sharply away. The something was the little rose jar. Smiles' first gift to him, which had travelled far since that morning on the mountain side, five years before.

The thoughts which would not be stilled repossessed his mind, and drove him out-of-doors again, — through a side door, so that he would not have to speak to his father and Ethel, whose voices he heard in low conversation on the front porch. They ceased for a moment, as though the speakers had heard the sound of his footsteps, and paused to listen. The night was still, so still that the chirp of a cricket under the piazza sounded loudly. It was a cheerful little note, and Donald hated it for its cheer, and started hastily away toward the beach.

High above, to the south, the moon was sailing through a sea of clouds, in silent majesty. Moonlit nights he had seen aplenty since that one in the Cumberlands, four summers previous, when he had climbed the mountain, impatient to see once more the strange, smiling child who had so stirred his imagination. In the old days he had loved the soft and majestic radiance. Now he hated it. Had he not lived long in war-ridden France, where every clear night illumined by that orb, which once had been the glory of those who loved, had meant merely the advent of the Hunnish fiends, whose winging visits brought death and devastation to the sleeping towns below?

He had fled from the darkness of his room, but now he craved the darkness again, for, perchance, it might blot out the memory of other nights, beautiful as golden dreams, or hideous as nightmares, when the moon had shone as it did now.

As he made a quick turn about a rocky obstruction in his rapid path, he came almost full upon two others, a man and a woman. On the yielding sand his footfalls had made no sound, and they were unaware of his sudden approach. Donald stopped, and stepped hastily back out of sight; but not before he had seen the man's arms gather the slender form of the girl in close embrace, and seen her lift her sweet young face — tear-bejeweled, but smiling with the tenderness of love — for his kiss.

With the rocks put between him and the two, Donald stood for a moment with clenched fists pressed brutally against his eyes as though to grind out the picture recorded there. Then, with blind but nervous strides, he fled from the spot which, at the one time, held such happiness and such despair.

It was close to midnight when his steps bore him instinctively back to the unlighted house; but this time the exercise and the cool night air had failed to bring relief to his heart. He could not face the idea of tossing for hours on a sleepless bed, and so passed the front door and seated himself within the dark shadows of a corner of the piazza.

"Chirr-r-p, chirr-r-p, chirr-r-p," began a pleasantly shrill little voice beneath him. Over and over it repeated the sound, until the man's feverish imagination had made it into "cheer-up," and he cursed the cricket for its silly advice. So busy was his mind with introspection that he did not hear the door open gently, and the first intimation that he was not alone was brought to him by the sound of a light footstep directly behind him. He turned his head, and saw a dim, ethereally white figure, — Rose.

"I thought that you would never come, Donald," she whispered, as she sank down close by his side on

Muriel's little stool, and laid her cool hand on his fevered one. "I have been watching from my window for an hour. I couldn't go to sleep until I had told you something."

With an effort he answered evenly, "I . . . I think that I know what it is, Rose."

"You know? But how . . . ?"

"I saw you . . . and Philip, on the beach," he replied, dully.

"You saw . . . Oh! And you heard what . . .?"

"No. I went away at once, of course. But I did not need to hear. I . . . I am glad if you are happy, Smiles."

She was silent for a long moment; then whispered with a note of joy in her low voice that wrung his heart, "Yes, I am very happy, Donald."

"Philip is a splendid fellow."

"You wanted me to . . . to marry him, Don?"

"I *wanted* you to?" He barely succeeded in checking, unspoken, the burning words on his tongue; but this time his voice betrayed him, and, if he had not been resolutely keeping his face turned away from her, he might have seen, even in that dim light, an odd change come into the expression of her lovely face, and seen a wonderfully tender and somewhat mischievous smile touch her lips. All that he did know, however, was that she gave a low, happy laugh, which was like a knife-thrust to his soul.

"Don," she said at length, "I have told no one

else of my great secret yet, for I wanted to tell you, first of all. I couldn't go to sleep without telling you, for you have been such a dear confidant and father confessor to me that it seems as though I must tell you everything. I . . . I've just got to tell you what has happened. May I?"

The man barely smothered a groan. Must he hear this girl, in her simplicity, talk on and on about the man she loved, and had promised to marry? It struck him, too, as strange that she should be willing to lay bare anything so sacred in a woman's life, but then she was her natural self, and quite different from most girls, in her attitude toward him.

But Rose was speaking quietly, and as though to herself, "Philip has been so sweet and good to me while you were away. You remember that you, yourself, told me that you meant him to take your place as my unofficial protector, and that I should go to him with my perplexities. It would have been better for me if I had followed your advice closer, but now I can laugh at spilt milk."

Rose had already confessed to Donald about her "investment" and been by him cross-examined into an admission of her little charities, which, in their aggregate, had so nearly wiped out her bank account. She could laugh about them now, for she had won to her goal, and already begun to earn a livelihood, but she had carefully hidden in her heart the story of the bitter struggle in which she had engaged to make both ends meet during the last few months of her course, when her mysterious refusals to accept any invitations from Ethel, Miss Merriman or Philip for her free afternoons and evenings, had left them wondering what on earth she was doing. No one guessed that they were spent in earning the few sadly needed dollars which her pride forbade her to borrow from any of them.

"Now I can laugh at spilt milk," Smiles' words echoed in Donald's brain, and hurt. He knew that Philip was fairly well-to-do, and, of course, Rose would want for nothing when she married him. This was the thought which brought the poignant stab.

"It was not strange that I began . . . that he became very dear to me, was it, Donald?"

The man shook his head dumbly. He could not answer her in words.

"Perhaps I should not say it; but some time ago I began to guess that . . . that he loved me. Not that he said a word, Donald, that is, not until to-day, — and then he didn't say it," she laughed a little. "He *wrote* it and he . . . he asked me to marry him. He said, besides, that he had spoken to you, first, and that you had given your brotherly consent. It was a very sweet letter, Don; the first real love letter that I ever received, think of that!"

Only by clinching his teeth and gripping the arms of the chair could the man repress a groan.

"It was after he had . . . had saved my life

that . . ." She stopped, and broke into her thought with the words, "Oh, Donald, I can never, never forget to-night, and the awful feeling that I had when little Don went into the water. You see, you were far away, and I didn't know about that brave boy on the beach, so I thought that I had got to save him if I could, and I didn't know *how* I could. And then those black, cold waves going over my head! I was quite sure that I was going to die, and I almost hoped so for . . . for I couldn't find Donny."

She leaned her head against his knee and cried a little; but, when he tried to speak, and tell her what had been in his heart, she interrupted hastily with, "Oh, please, let's not speak of it, ever again. I know how you felt, too.

"It was after that that Philip asked me for my answer. I knew what it was going to be, but . . ."

Donald could not stand it any longer. "I know. You love him, you are going to marry him, Smiles. It's all right, he is a splendid fellow, dear," he repeated mechanically.

"Yes, he is, and I do love him," she replied quietly; but she could not contain her secret any longer and added, "But a girl can't marry her *brother*, Donald."

"Her brother? Please, Rose, don't joke."

"It's true!"

"You! Philip's sister? It's impossible, unbelievable!" Yet a surge of mad, uncontrollable joy swept over him, and his heart burst into song.

"Unbelievable, yes. But it's *so*, Donald, although I can hardly credit it yet, myself."

"But how? Tell me how you found out. What happened?"

"Don't, you're hurting my hand, Donald. I'll tell you all about it as soon as I can, but please don't ask so many questions all at once, and please tell me first that you are glad, that my great secret makes you happy, as it does me."

"Happy? Oh, great heavens! But you? Are you really pleased? You said that you loved him!"

"And so I did, and do . . . dearly. But, you see, Donald, although I have cared for him for a long, long while, there was something about my affection that I could not explain, even to myself. It was . . . was different, somehow, from what . . . from what I felt it must be for the man whom I might marry. Now I know that it was the subconscious call of the blood, the love of a sister for a brother, and never anything else."

Lifted and swayed by a great happiness and reborn hope, Donald laughed aloud.

"Oh, you're a strange little girl, Smiles. I had not realized that you were fully grown up until to-night; but now I know that you are a woman, — a child no longer. My little Rose would never have tried to be so dramatic, nor would she have tried to analyze her love, and label it the call of kin, rather than that of a mate. I used to think that you were a clear crystal in which I might see reflected your very heart and soul, but now you have become a woman and therefore a mystery. Oh, woman, what do you know about love? Not the kind that Philip inspired in you; but the flame which burns unquenchable — which purifies and strengthens, or consumes the one who . . ." he stopped, surprised at his own rush of words, — and abashed.

The hand, which she had slipped unconsciously into his, trembled and thrilled him.

"Perhaps . . . I do . . . know it, Donald," came the words, barely audible.

"Smiles! It isn't possible that you . . . that I . . . Oh, my dear one, don't say anything to make me hope anew, after what I have endured to-night unless . . ."

"Do you really care, Don? In that *other* way, I mean."

He stood unsteadily up; things had become unreal and he could not speak. Smiles, still holding his hand, rose also. The top of her head came just below the level of his eyes; the moonlight across it set her wavy hair to shimmering. She could not lift her eyes to his, but with a brave, low voice, she went on, when she saw that he would not answer.

"All this past week I have been the most brazen of girls, and deliberately given you a hundred chances to tell me, if it were so. I was quite sure that it couldn't be, and besides, you told Philip . . . ."

"I know; but I thought . . . you see he told

me that he loved you, and that he was sure that you cared for him."

"I did, just as I do now. Oh, man, you have been so blind, or so noble. Have I got to *ask* you to marry me?"

For the barest instant she looked up at him, and he saw that the smile he loved was whimsical as well as madly appealing.

"No," almost shouted Donald. "I won't hear of such a thing as your being one of these 'new women.' You're a siren out of the olden days of mystic legend, and I have kept my ears stopped up against your witching song, which I was afraid to hear. But now I want to hear it, day and night, through eternity. Wait, not yet. First . . . Smiles, will you marry me?"

"Oh, what an anticlimax! Why did you have to become so practical and unromantic, after such a splendid start," she laughed happily. "No lover is supposed to ask that question with such brutal bluntness. Come, I will teach you the romance of love."

It was dark on the veranda. The moon had suddenly slipped out of sight behind one of the laggards in the retreating cloud army; but Donald needed no earthly light in order to realize that Rose was holding out her arms to him, as simply and frankly as she had five years before.

"Chir-r-r-p, chir-r-r-p, chir-r-r-p," thrilled the cricket underneath the porch.

CHAPTER XXXIV

A LOST BROTHER

How long it may have been before the man, eager as he was to hear the full explanation of the seeming miracle through which his happiness had been made possible, was ready to urge Rose to tell the story which she had promised, and what whispered words the cricket heard in the interim, concern only the three of them.

When, at last, he was able to bring his winging thoughts down from the clouds to earth, it was to discover still another unsuspected trait in the woman who had become his all; for Smiles, eager and excited, was still dwelling in a world of romance, and she insisted upon recounting what had happened, almost verbatim, and in a dramatic manner quite unlike the simplicity which naturally characterized her speech.

Nor could Donald's commonplace interruptions, during the course of which he affirmed that fact *was* stranger than fiction and that the world *was* a small place after all, check her narrative.

"I don't know whether I can make you understand why I acted as I did, when Philip asked me for my answer, dear. Indeed, I hardly know, myself," she began. "It wasn't that I didn't know what I had got to tell him, for I had made up my mind long ago — at least, it seems long ago, although it was only this morning, when I got his letter. Much as I cared for him, my heart knew that there was only one man in the world for me — even though he appeared not to want me!"

The digression caused a further and wholly natural delay.

"Perhaps it was because I hated to hurt him, and wanted desperately to postpone the evil moment; but, at any rate, I begged him to wait, and said that he didn't know all the facts about me. I told him that I wasn't sure that I ought to marry any one. And that was true, Donald. I've often worried about it, for I didn't know anything about my parents, and heredity counts for so much, doesn't it?

"Of course he replied, just as I might have expected, that he didn't know what I meant, but that nothing else could possibly matter to him, if only I . . . I cared.

"But I said that I had to explain, — I guess that I was a little panic-stricken, he seemed so deadly in earnest, — and then I told him that I wasn't Big Jerry's grandchild really, but only a little waif whom he had taken in. 'So, you see, I am a nameless girl, Philip,' I said. 'I don't mean it in a bad sense, for I know that I had a dear father and mother, whom I just barely remember, but . . .'

"I don't know exactly what I was going to add,

but he broke in with, 'What earthly difference do you think that could make to me, dear?' And then he told me that he *knew* I was . . . was good and pure, that *any one* who was acquainted with me could see that I must have come from sterling stock, even if my parents were simple mountaineers.

"'But they weren't, Phil,' I answered. 'I was a poor little city waif, who had lost her parents and didn't know where she came from, or even her name.' And then I told him the story which Big Jerry told you that first night on the mountain.

"And then, Donald, then it was my turn to be surprised, for Philip grasped my arm until he hurt me, and cried, 'I can't believe it, Rose. I *won't* believe it!'

"I didn't know what to say, and somehow I felt both hurt and a little angry that it should make any difference in his love — yes, I did, in spite of the fact that I couldn't marry him anyway. Yet, at the same time, I had an impression that it wasn't that, but something quite different, which was troubling his heart. So I said, 'What is it, Philip? I do not understand why you are acting so strangely.'

"His only reply was to ask me, in an odd voice, when it happened; how long ago.

"I told him 'eighteen years, when I was a baby about three years old.' Don, I can't tell you how I felt then, for he looked so peculiar — almost as though he were stunned. And he could not seem to say anything. I was frightened. I begged him to speak to me, and told him that he looked as though he had seen a ghost. 'I have . . . at least I have if my suspicion is true. But it can't be; oh, it is unbelievable, impossible,' he broke out.

"I didn't know what to say or do, he looked almost as though he were . . . were not in his right mind; and, when I put my hand on his arm and begged him to tell me what the trouble was, he shook it off, and began to speak . . . oh, I cannot tell you how. It sounded as though some one else were speaking, and uttering the words hesitatingly.

"'Try and remember, Smiles. Call on your memory of the long ago, if there is a single spark of it still lingering in your mind. Oh, it means so much, dear, so much that I am almost afraid to ask the question, but I have got to, I have got to!'

"He waited until I thought I should go mad, Don, and then said, in little more than a whisper, 'Did you ever, back in your babyhood, hear the name, Anna Rose Young? Think, Smiles, think hard.'

"Perhaps you will not believe it; but it seemed as though something long forgotten were actually stirring in my heart, and as though it were groping blindly in the mists of memory. I could not be sure, yet something forced me to answer, uncertainly, 'Yes, I think, I believe that I do remember that name; but I don't know where I could have heard it. What do you mean, Philip?'

"His answer surprised me as much as the first question, for he said, 'Was it in . . . Louisville?'

"'Louisville? I have never been there, Philip. And yet . . .' There was the strange stir in my memory again. Oh, it was all so puzzling.

"'Anna Rose Young,' he repeated insistently. 'They called her Rose, because . . . because her mother's name was the same.'

"'They called *her* . . . Philip, I do remember, now. It's my own name! Oh, Philip, you know who I am! But how, Phil?' I was clinging to him as though I must draw the truth from him physically; but he went on, almost mechanically, and his breath came hard, I could feel him tremble, Don."

Now her own low voice was trembling excitedly.

"'A tall, slender man, who stooped a little, Smiles,' he said. 'His face was thoughtful and kindly. He had a close-clipped, pointed beard, and wore gold-rimmed spectacles, and his eyes were very blue, as blue as your own, Rose. Tell me, does the picture mean anything to you?'

"I tried to visualize it, Don, and I could, as though it were some one far, far off whom I could see through the mist.

"'My daddy, Philip,' I whispered; I could hardly speak at all, for my throat was aching and I was crying."

She was crying, now, but did not realize it.

"'A sweet-faced woman, with wavy brown hair in which were golden glints like yours,' he went on, monotonously; but this time I could not answer at all."

Smiles stopped, and, for an instant, sobbed without restraint, with her head against Donald's arm, and he ran his hand tenderly and unsteadily over her hair.

Then she lifted her face, bathed in tears, and whispered, "You understand, don't you, Don? After all the years, to remember, ever so vaguely; but, still, to remember my former life, and to know my own name! Oh, I can't help it . . . I couldn't when he told me."

"Yes, yes. I understand, dearest."

"Philip went on, desperately, it seemed to me. 'Another picture, Smiles. Can you see a spindle-legged, mischievous boy of ten, who loved his little sister dearly; but teased her from morning until night. His name was . . .'

"'Tilly! Oh, I remember. At least, that was what baby Rose called him.'

"'Yes, she called him Tilly. She called him that because . . . because she couldn't say . . . "Philip." Oh, little Rose, don't you understand? I came to find a wife, and I have found . . . . a sister!'"

"But, his name . . ." interrupted Donald.

"I know. I will tell you. But first, Donald, my poor father and mother. I thought that perhaps I was to find them, too; but God willed otherwise. Big Jerry was right. They . . . they were both drowned."

Eager as he was to hear the rest of the story, the man could not but keep silent, in understanding sympathy, until she was ready to proceed of her own accord. It was once more as Smiles herself had written in her letter to him, after Big Jerry's death. Happiness was tinged with grief, for the night's strange disclosures had re-opened an old wound, long since closed.

Finally she went on.

"I won't try to tell you the explanation in Philip's words; but it seems that we used to live in Louisville. Philip's own father was a well-to-do physician, named, of course, Dr. Bentley. He died when Phil was a baby, and, when he was seven years old, mother married Mr. Robert Young, a mining engineer. I was born a year later — I am really his half-sister, you see."

"But," interrupted Donald, "I should think that the name Philip Bentley might have stirred a responsive chord in your memory before this — no, I don't suppose that it would have, after all, for you were so small that you didn't remember your own last name."

"Yes, and not only that, but Philip was always called 'Young' — when he was a boy, anyway. Well, it seems that, when he was ten, and I was three, he was sent all alone to visit an uncle, a brother of his own father, who lived in Richmond. It was while he was away for the summer that my dear father was sent into the Cumberland Mountains between Kentucky and Virginia, prospecting for coal on behalf of the company in the employ of which he was. He took mother and me with him for a camping vacation, and . . . and you know as much as I about the tragedy which separated us, and made such changes in our lives."

Rose paused again, a prey to memory.

"And then?" prompted Donald, gently.

"Then, Philip said, when no word came from his parents for several weeks, his uncle left no stone unturned to find them, and at length the Federal Revenue authorities located the bodies of my dear mother and father, and part of their wrecked canoe, in the swift river, almost at the foot of the mountains. Of course every one assumed that I had . . . had been drowned, too."

"Oh, thank God that you were not, my dear," breathed Donald, so softly that she could not hear him.

"Then Philip went to live permanently with his uncle, who raised and educated him as one of his own sons. Of course he took his real name again. Oh, Donald, isn't it too wonderful?"

"Yes, dear heart, wonderful, indeed." There was a long silence. Then Donald asked, softly, "And Philip? How does he feel?"

"He . . . he is happy, too," came her reply, somewhat haltingly. "Of course, just at first . . . oh, please don't ask me, Don. But now he is content, for he knows that I . . . I couldn't ever have been anything else to him, because I loved ano . . . . I loved *you*."

"He knows that? Rose, you didn't tell him?"

"Yes, I did," she answered, bravely. "And let me tell *you*, sir, that it is lucky for you that . . . that you asked me; for, if you hadn't, you would have had my big brother to deal with!"

And what the cricket heard *then*, has nothing to do with this story.

CHAPTER XXXV

THE HALLOWED MOON

THEY were to be married early in September — just a month from the day when Smiles so nearly gave her life to save another's.

During the days which must pass before she became Donald's in the full trinity of body, mind and soul, his family kept her at Manchester-by-the-Sea and each hour bound her more closely to the heart of each.

For her, Ethel planned and purchased, sewed and supervised, putting as much loving thought into the making of her simple outfit as though it was she herself who was to be wedded. The days were busy ones, the evening hours rich in love and contentment, for Donald came down from the city each night, and the two learned the way to many a secret chamber in each other's heart.

Early in the week which was to bring to a close the separate stories of the man and maid, and write the first chapter in the single history of man and wife, Donald left them to make a brief, but important, trip which, he said, could not be postponed; and oh, how empty life seemed to Smiles during those few days.

But they were ended at last, and the marriage evening came, — still and mellow, with the voices of both shore and sea tuned to soft night melodies.

Below in the hall, hidden within a bower of palms, an orchestra of Boston Symphony players drew whispering harmonies from the strings of violins, harp and cello, and, at the signal, swept into the dreamy, enchanted notes of Mendelssohn's marriage song.

Little Don, very proud and important — and somewhat frightened — picked up the train which he was to bear as page, and down the winding stairway, by the side of her new-found brother, moved Rose, gowned in traditional white, made with befitting simplicity, her shimmering hair no longer crowned with the square of a nurse cap, but by a floating, misty veil and the orange-blossom wreath of a bride. Never had her warm coloring been so delicate and changeful, her expressive eyes so deep, or the fleeting sweetness of her translucent smile so wonderful.

At the foot of the stairs stood Muriel, and three other girl companions, each with a woven sweet-grass basket — made years ago by little Smiles herself — filled with rose petals to be strewn in her path, and the bride's lowered eyes rested tenderly for a moment upon the child that she so loved. Then she started, and paused. One of them, as tall as Muriel and more slender, had hair of spun gold, and she was looking up with an eagerness which she could hardly restrain.

With a low, surprised cry, Smiles hurried downward, drawing her hand from Philip's arm and extending both her own.

"Little Lou. Can it really be you? Oh, my dear."

And, heedless of the cluster of waiting friends beyond, she caught the flushing, bashful, happy child into her arms.

"Oh, Smiles, haint hit all too wonderful. Hit's like dreamy-land, an' I'm plumb erfeered thet I'll wake up an' find hit haint real. But *yo're* real, my Smiles, an' oh, how I loves ye."

There was a suspicious moisture in more eyes than those of Rose, as she released the child and moved forward again, following the flower girls into the room where waited the man who was all in all to her.

Donald stood just to one side of a canopied altar made of white roses and interwoven ferns, and before it was a tall, slender man in the vestments of the Episcopal Church, whose thin, saintlike face was topped by hair of the purest silver-white.

Smiles felt her heart swelling almost painfully with a great new happiness; her lips parted, and she wanted to draw her hand across her eyes and brush away the sudden tears which she knew were there. For the rector was her own dear Mr. Talmadge.

Now Donald was at her side, and his strong fingers were returning the grateful, loving pressure of her own. *He* understood how full of gratitude was her heart, and was repaid.

The low, clear voice, tuned to the winds of the forest, began the words of the beautiful service. It was, indeed, all a dream, and she felt the unreality of it until the benediction had been spoken, and the hidden orchestra struck the first joyous chords of the triumphant march from Lohengrin. Then, from her husband's arms she turned to the embrace of the mountain minister, and of Philip, and little Lou, and Gertrude Merriman, and Dorothy Roberts, and of all those other friends, old and new, who were so dear to her.

No explanations were possible for many minutes to come; but at length she heard the story of the secret trip "which could not be postponed," of how "the reverend" — now well and strong at last — had gladly consented to leave his beloved mountain home, for the first time in many, many years, and come north on this sacredest of missions; of how Judd had yielded to the request that Lou accompany them, too; and finally of how her mountain lover of the old days was now himself married — to none other than the youngest daughter of the kindly agent at Fayville.

And when this news was told, Donald cried, "Why, Smiles, for shame! I actually believe that you are jealous," and she replied, "Of course I am . . . horribly." Whereupon every one laughed at her, and her husband punished her with a kiss.

It was ended at last, the lights, merry voices and laughter; and, as the two ran the ancient gantlet, the orchestra, prompted thereto by Mr. MacDonald, struck up a lively popular air, and the guests caught up the words.

They paused a moment on the path below the veranda, to quiet their hurried breathing, and look into each other's happy eyes.

"Where do we go from here?" *They* knew. There had been but one spot in all the world whose name both their hearts had spoken, when Donald first mentioned the honeymoon to be.

. . . .

Evening again — twilight on the Cumberland mountains. The moon had not yet risen; but, through the black lacework of the forest trees which stretched above Big Jerry's cabin to the mountain's summit, share the beaming radiance of the evening star.

Within the soft shadow of the doorway stood two figures, close together — one tall, broad of shoulder and heavily built, the other of medium height, slender and very graceful — and their arms were about each other's waists. A man and a woman, — as it was in the beginning.

For a long time they stood thus, without speaking, — there was no need of speech, for their thoughts were one.

"So old and well remembered; yet so new and strangely beautiful," whispered the woman, as she let her gaze travel over the broken, far-stretching skyline of the forest-clad mountain side, now fading into the sky, where a memory of the sunset's afterglow still lingered, as though loath to depart and leave the world to darkness.

"Like love: as old as the hills, yet ever new," answered the other.

"Yes. I cannot yet understand, Don, how this new life can be so strangely natural to me. We have been married only three all-too-short days, yet I can scarcely think of the other life as real. Some people speak of their honeymoon as a golden dream. To me it is the sweet reality, and all that went before the dream. Isn't it odd?"

"All of nature's laws are inexplicable, dear heart. But we should not forget that the Almighty's plan for the world did not deal with man and woman as separate entities, but man and woman as counterparts of a single unit, in which His laws should find full expression, if the two were truly mated — not merely married. You remember what Mr. Talmadge said that night."

"I know. We have found, not each other, but the other part of ourselves — ourself. Dear, when did you first realize that it was so?"

"My mind, not until it was free to face the truth; my subconscious soul the first moment that I saw you, I think."

"I know I loved you from that moment too," she answered simply, lifting her lips for his kiss.

There followed another spell of enchanted silence, broken only by the low lullaby of the night wind in the trees, and then the man spoke again.

"Smiles, are you still greatly afraid of the sea?"

"No, dear, I should not be, if you were with me. It is strange; but I lost most of the old, unreasoning fear the moment that I made up my mind to jump into it that afternoon. But, why do you ask that now, Donald?" He did not reply at once, and she continued, "I think that I know, and the same thought was in my own mind. Is it that you want to go to France again, to renew the saving work there, — and want me with you?"

He nodded slowly.

"If you hadn't suggested it, I should have, Don; for now I am doubly prepared for the work I began to long to do, so many years ago. I am not only trained for it, but I have you beside me, to comfort and strengthen me, always.

"Yes, dear," she went on softly. "Some day, God grant, we shall have little ones of our own to care for; but, until that beautiful time comes, there are no less precious babies throughout all the world — and there, especially — crying for us to help them. We must give of our best to them, for, weak, tender and helpless as they are, the hope of the world is in its babies."

Through the dark tree-tops the new-born moon appeared on the breast of night, around it a misty halo like that about the head of the Infant who came nineteen centuries ago, typifying the hope of all mankind.

"Look," said Donald. "Our honeymoon wears a halo."

"Because it is a hallowed moon," answered Rose.

The soft white radiance floated in, flooding the little porch and illuminating the wife's sweet face as she lifted it again, now touched with a smile, more meaningful and more ethereal than ever before.

For, to the smile of courage, hope and love, had been added the quality of rich, deep contentment.

THE END